Reading Development & Teaching

SAGE was founded in 1965 by Sara Miller McCune to support the dissemination of usable knowledge by publishing innovative and high-quality research and teaching content. Today, we publish more than 850 journals, including those of more than 300 learned societies, more than 800 new books per year, and a growing range of library products including archives, data, case studies, reports, and video. SAGE remains majority-owned by our founder, and after Sara's lifetime will become owned by a charitable trust that secures our continued independence.

Los Angeles | London | New Delhi | Singapore | Washington DC

Reading Development & Teaching

Morag Stuart and Rhona Stainthorp

$SAGE

Los Angeles | London | New Delhi
Singapore | Washington DC

Los Angeles | London | New Delhi
Singapore | Washington DC

SAGE Publications Ltd
1 Oliver's Yard
55 City Road
London EC1Y 1SP

SAGE Publications Inc.
2455 Teller Road
Thousand Oaks, California 91320

SAGE Publications India Pvt Ltd
B 1/I 1 Mohan Cooperative Industrial Area
Mathura Road
New Delhi 110 044

SAGE Publications Asia-Pacific Pte Ltd
3 Church Street
#10-04 Samsung Hub
Singapore 049483

Editor: Luke Block
Editorial assistant: Katie Norton
Production editor: Imogen Roome
Marketing manager: Michael Ainsley
Cover design: Wendy Scott
Typeset by: C&M Digitals (P) Ltd, Chennai, India
Printed and bound by CPI Group (UK) Ltd,
Croydon, CR0 4YY

© Morag Stuart and Rhona Stainthorp 2016

First published 2016

Apart from any fair dealing for the purposes of research or private study, or criticism or review, as permitted under the Copyright, Designs and Patents Act, 1988, this publication may be reproduced, stored or transmitted in any form, or by any means, only with the prior permission in writing of the publishers, or in the case of reprographic reproduction, in accordance with the terms of licences issued by the Copyright Licensing Agency. Enquiries concerning reproduction outside those terms should be sent to the publishers.

Library of Congress Control Number: 2015939932

British Library Cataloguing in Publication data

A catalogue record for this book is available from the British Library

ISBN 978-1-4462-4903-1
ISBN 978-1-4462-4904-8 (pbk)

At SAGE we take sustainability seriously. Most of our products are printed in the UK using FSC papers and boards. When we print overseas we ensure sustainable papers are used as measured by the PREPS grading system. We undertake an annual audit to monitor our sustainability.

This book is dedicated to a host of wonderful grandchildren

Amelia, Jake and Theo

Patrick, Alex, Charlie, Ben and Tommy; Lydia, Lucia, Olive, Indigo, Yolanda, Jude, Eden and Clemmie

The next generation.

Contents

List of tables and figures viii
Outline of contents xi
Acknowledgements xii

PART 1   TUTORIAL REVIEW 1

1 Essential knowledge about language 3
2 The Simple View of Reading: A broad conceptual framework 23

PART 2   READING THE WORDS ON THE PAGE 31

3 Visual word recognition in skilled readers 33
4 Development of visual word recognition processes 43
5 Teaching word reading skills 67

PART 3   UNDERSTANDING SPOKEN AND WRITTEN LANGUAGE 97

6 Comprehension of oral and written language 99
7 Teaching reading comprehension 128

PART 4   ASSESSMENT AND INTERVENTION 145

8 Assessing Reading: From international comparisons to individual processes 147
9 Teaching to overcome word reading difficulties (developmental dyslexia) 166
10 Teaching children with reading comprehension difficulties 180

Finale 199
References 200
Author Index 218
Subject Index 223

List of tables and figures

CHAPTER 1

Table 1.1	IPA symbols for the 24 consonant phonemes of English	4
Table 1.2	IPA symbols for the 20 vowel phonemes of English	5
Table 1.3	Subset of Turkish consonant and vowel letters and phonemes	15
Figure 1.1	Possible ways of deconstructing the syllable	11
Figure 1.2	Basic categories of writing systems	13

CHAPTER 2

Figure 2.1	The Simple View of Reading	24

CHAPTER 3

Figure 3.1a	'Words' to read aloud	33
Figure 3.1b	Words to read aloud	34
Figure 3.1c	Personal and place names to read aloud	34
Figure 3.2	Lexical processes: direct access to semantics (word meaning) and phonology (word pronunciation) from orthography (word spelling pattern)	36
Figure 3.3	Phonological recoding processes: indirect access to semantics (word meaning) from phonology (word pronunciation)	37
Figure 3.4	Specific meanings of homophonic words directly accessed from their spelling	38
Figure 3.5	'Regularization' of exception words	39

CHAPTER 4

Table 4.1	Categories of word reading error	51
Table 4.2	Findings from studies investigating the relationship of phonological awareness and word reading	56
Table 4.3	Limitations on the usefulness of an early rime analogy strategy to read unfamiliar words	58

Table 4.4	Findings from studies of orthographic learning	61
Table 4.5	Influence of pre-existing semantic and phonological representations on the formation of orthographic representations	65
Figure 4.1	Language elements that predate and underpin the establishment of word reading processes	44
Figure 4.2	Lexical processes added on to language system	45
Figure 4.3	Phonological recoding processes added on to language system	45

CHAPTER 5

Table 5.1	Grapheme-phoneme correspondences taught by the end of the EYFS in 'Letters and Sounds'	69
Table 5.2	Words to be taught by the end of the EYFS	70
Table 5.3	Factors affecting letter-sound knowledge in young children	72
Table 5.4	Activities to develop phoneme awareness or letter awareness	79
Table 5.5	Different kinds of phonics teaching	82
Table 5.6	Two further studies comparing relative effectiveness of synthetic (small-unit) and onset-rime analogy (large-unit) phonics teaching in promoting reading growth	84
Table 5.7	GPCs taught in the Shapiro and Solity (2008) programme	87
Figure 5.1	Illustration of 'progressive minimal contrasts' activity	93

CHAPTER 6

Table 6.1	The systems of language	101
Table 6.2	Results of comprehension experiment	121
Figure 6.1	The Simple View of Reading	100
Figure 6.2	Subject-Verb-Object sentence	109
Figure 6.3	Grammatical units of Subject, Verb and Object	109
Figure 6.4	Children's understanding of deixis	117
Figure 6.5	Illustration from Bransford and Johnson, 1972	122

CHAPTER 7

Figure 7.1	The components of the comprehension system	129
Figure 7.2	Examples of graphic organizer frames	141

CHAPTER 8

Table 8.1	Relationship between stanines and standard deviation scores, with the percentage of the population falling into each stanine	160

Figure 8.1	The normal distribution	149
Figure 8.2	Percentages of children achieving level 4 for reading in KS2 SATs, 1997–2013	153
Figure 8.3	Percentage of children achieving the expected level in 2012, 2013 and 2014, by ethnicity, language status and free school meals	155
Figure 8.4	Numbers of children achieving each of the different possible marks	157
Figure 8.5	The normal distribution, showing standardized scores, percentile ranks and stanines	159
Figure 8.6	The Simple View of Reading	164

CHAPTER 9

Table 9.1	Signs of dyslexia at different developmental phases	174
Figure 9.1	The Simple View of Reading	168
Figure 9.2	Most common weaknesses and strengths in the phonological dyslexic group	170
Figure 9.3	Most common weaknesses and strengths in the surface dyslexic group	172
Figure 9.4	Most common weaknesses and strengths in the mixed dyslexic group	173

CHAPTER 10

Table 10.1	Design of the study in Stothard and Hulme (1992)	184
Table 10.2	Characteristics of the two groups of participants in Oakhill (1982)	187
Figure 10.1	Modified Simple View of Reading	181

Outline of contents

The overarching aim of this book is to describe what is currently known about the processes involved in reading, the ways in which these processes develop as children learn to read, and the kinds of teaching that can foster their development.

The two chapters in Part 1 provide, in Chapter 1, a tutorial review of language concepts relevant to the development of word reading skills, with their associated linguistic terminology and, in Chapter 2, a presentation of the Simple View of Reading (SVoR), which proposes there are two interacting dimensions of reading. After the Rose report (Rose, 2006), the SVoR was adopted as the framework for considering reading in the National Literacy Strategy, and in initial teacher education. It now also forms the basis on which reading development is considered in the revised National Curriculum Programme of Study for English (Department for Education, 2014). It therefore seemed sensible to organize our book according to this conceptual framework.

Part 2 deals with visual word recognition processes, and Part 3 with comprehension of spoken and written language. Part 4 changes focus to deal with assessment, and atypical development of word reading skills and of comprehension of spoken and written language.

Acknowledgements

Both authors began teaching in London Boroughs in the 1960s. Concerns about the difficulties that some pupils experienced with reading motivated them both at different times to go to Birkbeck College, University of London, to read psychology. We owe a great debt to the Birkbeck Psychology department for opening our minds to the world of psychological research and for showing us how this can help teachers to understand the needs of their pupils.

Both authors eventually went on to do their PhDs in reading development. Our supervisors, Max Coltheart (MS) and Maggie Snowling (RS), guided us into careers researching reading development. We thank them for their academic guidance and friendship.

We eventually had the good fortune to end up working together at the Institute of Education, University of London (now the University College London, Institute of Education). This was fun and together we developed the MA in the Teaching and Learning of Reading and Writing. This course was designed to provide teachers with the evidence about the development of literacy that informs this book. The reactions of teachers on the MA have been instrumental in encouraging us to write this book. They said things like: '…Why did no one tell us about this before?' and 'So that's why XX is having such difficulty'. We are committed to enabling teachers to access the evidence about the development of reading so that they will be able to develop their own rational approaches to teaching literacy.

Research benefits from collaboration. We must acknowledge the years of intellectual support and friendship that we have received from all the members of the Forum for Research in Literacy and Language (FRiLL). One of the outcomes from the group's collaboration has been the *Diagnostic Test of Word Reading Processes* (2012) referenced in this book. We believe this test is tangible evidence of how the psychological research into reading can eventually lead to a practical, evidence-based resource to support teachers, educational psychologists and pupils who need their help.

At various times in the last 20 years we have been able to talk about our ideas and work with Sir Jim Rose. We are immensely grateful to him for all the support and encouragement that he has given us. He has paved the way for us to have opportunities to influence the curriculum for English: we hope for the better. Long may the three of us continue to put the world to rights.

It would be disingenuous of us not to admit that writing can be difficult and all-consuming. It can make one bad-tempered and self-centred. We have supported each other throughout the time of writing this book: but more importantly we have both received the selfless and unwavering support of our husbands: Bob Gray and Allan Quimby. All we can do is to thank them as graciously as possible.

PART 1
Tutorial review

1
Essential knowledge about language

Summary

In this chapter, you will learn about the phonological system of languages: the ways in which speech sounds are identified and combined to produce and understand spoken language. You will learn about the orthographic systems of languages: the ways in which written languages represent their spoken forms. This is essential knowledge for those of us involved in understanding and teaching reading. The contents of this chapter will equip you with the knowledge you need to read subsequent chapters, and will enable you to answer the question: why is learning to read words in English so much more difficult than in most other languages?

Introduction

A recent study comparing rate of development of word reading skills in children learning to read in nine European languages (Seymour, Aro & Erskine, 2003) demonstrated that learning to read words in English is more difficult than in most other alphabetic languages. For children learning to read in English, these skills developed more than twice as slowly as those of beginners learning to read in Finnish, Spanish or Greek. Of course, difficult is not synonymous with impossible. The vast majority of children in the UK (and other countries where English is the first language) learn to read words accurately and fluently in an acceptable time scale. However, the early stages of learning to read are more taxing in English, and it takes longer for children to become fluent.

The difficulty lies within the *orthography*, which Henderson (1984) defined as the conventional writing system of a language and the way this maps onto spoken language. Each language has its own pattern and rules for writing: its own *orthographic system*. Beginner readers must learn how the orthographic system relates to spoken language in a given writing system. In this chapter, we explain how writing systems work and why the English writing system is so difficult.

We need to introduce you to a number of technical terms: these help us to be precise about our meanings. We will give you some exercises to do to help you feel confident about the terms. Because you are a skilled adult reader, you have already internalized knowledge of English orthography: thus, most of the information we provide will already be part of your implicit understanding. To understand reading development and how to teach children to read, it is useful to transform this implicit understanding into accessible explicit knowledge. We hope that by the time you finish this chapter you will be convinced that, albeit difficult, English orthography can be fascinating, and good teachers can pass on their fascination to their pupils. Writing systems represent the sounds of spoken language, its phonology. Before we consider writing systems themselves, we have to make an extensive detour to describe the English phonological system, which is what English orthography represents.

Phonology: the sound system of language

The sound system of language is called *phonology*, from the Greek *phone* meaning sound and *logos* meaning speech. So the word 'phonology' literally means the sounds of speech. The phonological system is the system of language that uses sounds as its units and these sounds are combined to produce individual words.

We will first list all the speech sounds (phonemes) of English, each paired with its International Phonetic Alphabet (IPA) symbol. Each row in the tables gives you the unique IPA symbol for the phoneme and an example of that phoneme as pronounced in a real English word. Spelling of the phoneme in question is printed in bold. Table 1.1 lists IPA symbols for consonant phonemes, and Table 1.2 lists IPA symbols for vowel phonemes.

Table 1.1   IPA symbols for the 24 consonant phonemes of English

IPA symbol	Example of a word containing the sound
p	**p**at
b	**b**at
t	**t**at
d	**d**og
k	**c**at
g	**g**oat
f	**f**at
v	**v**ote
θ	**th**umb
ð	**th**ey
s	**s**at

IPA symbol	Example of a word containing the sound
z	**z**oo
ʃ	**sh**op
ʒ	trea**s**ure
tʃ	**ch**ip
dʒ	**j**ug
m	**m**at
n	**n**ot
ŋ	si**ng**
l	**l**og
r	**r**at
j	**y**ellow
w	**w**atch
h	**h**ello

Table 1.2 IPA symbols for the 20 vowel phonemes of English

IPA symbol	Example of a word containing the sound
Short monophthong vowels	
ɪ	s**i**t
ɛ	w**e**t
æ	c**a**t
ɒ	pl**o**t
ʌ	d**u**ck
ʊ	p**u**t
ə	b**a**nana
Long monophthong vowels	
i	tr**ee**
ɜ	g**ir**l
ɑː	f**a**ther
ɔ	s**aw**
u	sh**oe**
Diphthong vowels[1]	
ei	pl**ay**
əʊ	g**o**
ai	s**igh**
aʊ	n**ow**

(Continued)

Table 1.2 (Continued)

IPA symbol	Example of a word containing the sound
ɔi	b**oy**
ɪə	f**ear**
ɛə	th**ere**
ʊə	p**ure**

¹A diphthong vowel is one where the tongue moves as it is produced so that the sound appears to glide from one vowel to another.

You will see from the tables that there are 44 phonemes in English: 24 consonant and 20 vowel phonemes. These statistics alone alert us to the challenges encountered in English orthography, because English has only 26 letters to represent these 44 phonemes. This imbalance of number of phonemes and number of letters also poses a challenge when writing about the sound system of language. The International Phonetic Alphabet allows us unambiguously to represent each phoneme with a specific symbol. Throughout the book, we will be using IPA symbols when we want to specify particular phonemes.

Above, we equated 'phoneme' with 'speech sound': the box below gives a more complete definition of the phoneme.

What is a phoneme?

A **PHONEME** is the smallest unit of speech sound in a word that changes meaning.

Thus the word <BED> is composed of three phonemes /bɛd/. If we change the first phoneme /b/ to /r/ we get /rɛd/ <RED>. This is a different word with a different meaning.

[It can sometimes be very confusing to represent the sound and the look of a word in texts. In this book, where a word has been printed in brackets like so: < >, we are representing the letters. Where it is printed in slash marks like so: //, we are representing the sounds. Where the topic relates to the word *per se* and the contrast is not between the orthography and the phonology, we will just present the word in upper case letters, like so: WORD.]

There is now considerable evidence that the average adult is not explicitly aware of phonemes in words (Moats, 1994; Stainthorp, 2004). When asked, 'How many sounds are there in the word RUST?', adults are just as likely to say 'two' or 'three' as 'four'. When asked to explain their decision, one person may say that the two sounds are /r/ and /ʌst/; whereas another might say the three sounds are /r/ /ʌ/ and /st/.

The correct answer is **four phonemes**: /r/ /ʌ/ /s/ /t/. We can see how this works if we use the definition of the phoneme given above.

We start with the word /rʌst/ meaning 'iron oxide'. Changing the first phoneme from /r/ to /d/ gives us the word /dʌst/ (DUST) meaning 'tiny particles lying on a surface'. By changing one phoneme for another we end up with a word with a different meaning, so the initial phoneme and the substituted one must both be phonemes of English.

Changing the second phoneme from /ʌ/ to /ɛ/ gives us /rɛst/ (REST) meaning 'to stop work'. We can swap the final two phonemes round so instead of /rʌst/ we have /rʌts/. Again we get a different word. We can also say /rʌst/ without the /s/ phoneme and then we get yet another word /rʌt/.

You might like to try specifying the number of phonemes in this set of words:

STRAIGHT

ENOUGH

TAX

KISSED

BATTED

(Answers on the next page.)

You might also try systematically changing the phonemes in each of these five words to make new words that differ by one phoneme. By playing with the phonemes like this, you will begin to raise your level of phonemic awareness. This is important because in order to teach children their letter-sound correspondences for phonics, teachers need to be confident that they have a fluent ability to identify and manipulate the phonemes in words. Educational psychologists assessing causes of reading difficulties also need these skills. Remember to focus on the phonemes of the words and not the letters.

In the IPA table the phonemes are arranged into two primary groups: consonants and vowels, but we have not yet defined the terms consonant and vowel. These definitions are shown in the next box.

Defining consonant and vowel phonemes

CONSONANT phonemes are those sounds where there is a degree of constriction of the air as it flows out of the mouth or nose.

VOWEL phonemes are those sounds where the air flows out of the mouth without any constriction.

Counting phonemes

	Number of phonemes
STRAIGHT	5 = /s/ /t/ /r/ /ei/ /t/
ENOUGH	4 = /ɪ/ /n/ /ʌ/ /f/
TAX	4 = /t/ /æ/ /k/ /s/
KISSED	4 = /k/ /ɪ/ /s/ /t/
BATTED	5 = /b/ /æ/ /t/ /ɪ/ /d/

In everyday language, the term consonant normally refers to the 21 letters B, C, D, F, G, H, J, K, L, M, N, P, Q, R, S, T, V, W, X, Y, Z, and the term vowel refers to the five letters A, E, I, O, U. The letter Y is generally considered to be a consonant, although much of the time it is used to represent a vowel phoneme, as in BY, FLY, CRY, etc. Because this distinction between letters and sounds can cause confusion, throughout this book we will refer to *consonant letters* and *vowel letters* when considering the written form, and *consonant phonemes* and *vowel phonemes* when considering the spoken form. As already stated, in English there are not enough letters for a one-to-one match between letter and phonemes. This is particularly the case for the vowel phonemes, with only five vowel letters (plus Y) to represent the 20 vowel phonemes in English: thus, learning letter–sound correspondences for vowel phonemes poses an extra challenge for learners. As spelling has developed over the centuries and incorporated orthographic features from different languages, combinations of letters have become used to represent all the different vowel phonemes.

We have covered the smallest unit of phonology that impacts on the writing system: this is the phoneme. At the largest level there are the words themselves. These are sequences of phonemes that are blended together and that carry meaning. An additional useful technical term in the realm of meaning is *morpheme*, defined in the next box. The word comes from the Greek *morphe*, meaning form.

What is a morpheme?

A **MORPHEME** is the smallest grammatical unit of language that has meaning. Each morpheme constitutes either a word, or a meaningful part of a word.

BED is a word composed of one morpheme. It means a flat surface on which one lies to sleep (when it is used as a noun). BEDS has two morphemes, it means more than one bed.

Some morphemes are called *free morphemes*. These are words in their own right. Each word carries meaning and has its own syntactic (grammatical) status, such as noun, verb, adjective, etc. In language, words are combined together in a rule governed way to form phrases in order to convey meaning. (We cover these aspects of language more extensively in Chapter 6, when we discuss language comprehension.)

Some morphemes are called *bound morphemes*. Below the level of the word are morphemes that carry meaning, but which cannot stand on their own. Hence the term 'bound': they have to be bound to other morphemes. In the box above, the morpheme /z/ (spelled <S>), which conveys plurality, is a bound morpheme. This is because it cannot stand on its own. It has to be affixed to another morpheme. Other examples of bound morphemes include the past tense ending, -ED /ɪd/ (WANT → WANT**ED**); the present progressive tense ending – -ING /ɪŋ/ (WANT → WANT**ING**); the -ER /ə/ ending depicting an agent (FARM → FARM**ER**), or a comparative (HAPPY → HAPP**IER**); and the -EST /ɛst/ ending depicting a superlative (HAPPY →HAPP**IEST**). The new Programme of Study for English in the revised National Curriculum (Department for Education, 2014) requires most of the bound morphemes given as examples here to be taught to Year 1 pupils in England.

In between the phoneme level and the word level there are other units of phonology. One of these is the *syllable*, defined in the next box.

What is a syllable?

A **SYLLABLE** is a unit of spoken language formed of one obligatory vowel phoneme and possibly preceded by or followed by optional consonant phonemes.

BED /bɛd/ is a single syllabic word composed of the vowel phoneme /ɛ/, preceded by the consonant phoneme /b/ and followed by the consonant phoneme /d/.

BEDROOM is a bisyllabic word composed of the syllable /bɛd/ and the syllable /ru:m/.

Though most adults are not explicitly aware of phonemes, they are much more comfortable with syllables. The syllable seems to make intuitive sense to English speakers and people can happily clap to the 'beat' of language. In effect, what happens when we clap to the beat is that we clap on each syllable. When we do this, we are clapping on each vowel phoneme.

The final set of terminology about the phonological system relates to the structure of the syllable, illustrated first in 'The structure of the syllable' box below.

> ## The structure of the syllable
>
> The syllable is composed of three segments:
>
> ONSET, NUCLEUS (or PEAK) and CODA
>
> The **ONSET** is the consonant phoneme or consonant phoneme cluster at the start of the syllable. This is optional in English. The NUCLEUS is the vowel phoneme. This is compulsory. The CODA is the final consonant phoneme or consonant phoneme cluster. This is also optional in English.

Here are some examples:

> <OWE> /əʊ/ is a syllable that is a word with just the nucleus;
>
> <OWN> /əʊn/ has a nucleus + coda;
>
> <GO> / gəʊ / has an onset + nucleus;
>
> <GOES> / gəʊz / has an onset + nucleus + coda.

Try building up sets of words like this from single vowel phonemes that also happen to be words, like ARE, AIR, EAR, I, YOU. You have to focus on the phonemes and not the spelling. With a bit of perseverance, you can get up to a single syllable word that has up to three consonant phonemes in the onset and in the coda.

You are likely to find that the spelling of the word influences you too much at first. For example, you might decide not to add the phoneme /b/ to the beginning of AIR, because the spelling BAIR is not a real word in English – but the sound pattern, /bɛə/ is, and it is word sounds we are playing with here. Conversely, if you add the letter G to the word OWN you do get a real word GOWN. But the letters OW in GOWN represent the phoneme /aʊ/ not the phoneme /əʊ/, which is in the source word, OWN. So again, spelling has misled you; /gəʊn/ is not a real word in English. However, if you go on to insert the letter R to GOWN after the letter G, the nucleus reverts to the phoneme /əʊ/ as in the word GROWN or indeed GROAN. Spelling sometimes works!

It is when we begin to reflect upon how spelling and sound interact in this way that we recognize how difficult English orthography can be.

In relation to the syllable, there are just two further terms we need to define: terms that describe how the three phonemic elements (onset, nucleus and coda) can be clustered together. These terms are defined in 'The subsyllabic units of body and rime' box.

The subsyllabic units of body and rime

The **BODY** is the onset and nucleus clustered together, e.g. the BEA- of BEAT.

The **RIME** is the nucleus and coda clustered together, e.g. the -EAT of BEAT.

When two words share the same rime element, they are said to *rhyme*. Thus FOX, BOX, SOCKS all share the rime /ɒks/. They differ only in their onset phoneme. Rhyming seems to be intuitively easy for English speakers: people can happily generate strings like **BED**, **SAID**, **FED**, **HEAD** when asked to generate rhyming words. Try it yourself with CAT and TOE. Remember to ignore spelling! Playing rhyming games with young children can be fun, and helps them develop their insights into the sound structure of words.

The body seems to make less intuitive sense to English speakers. We can generate strings of words sharing the same body (e.g. **BED**, **BET**, **BECK**, **BEND**), but this seems to demand more attention and trips off the tongue less readily than rhyming strings.

The set of tree diagrams in Figure 1.1 show you the possible ways of deconstructing the syllable. SCHOOL is used as the exemplar word.

You will note that in the word <SCHOOL> /skul/, the onset has two phonemes /s/ and /k/ as an initial cluster /sk/. A *consonant cluster* is where two consonant

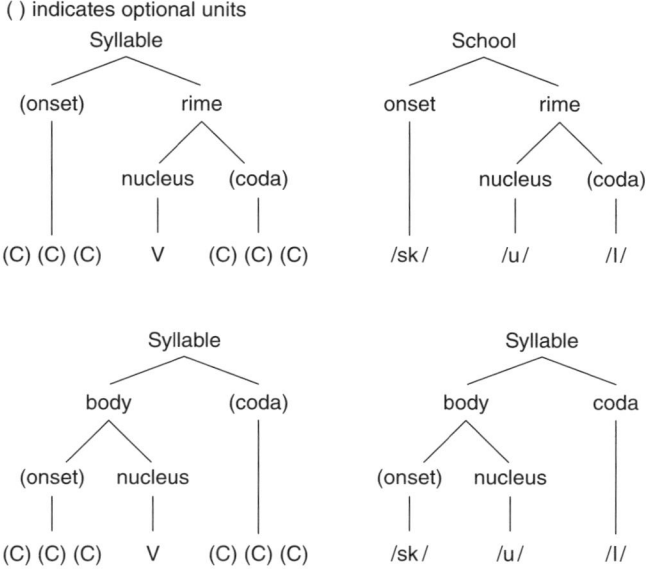

Figure 1.1 Possible ways of deconstructing the syllable

phonemes are pronounced together without any intervening vowel phoneme. Languages vary greatly in terms of the sequences of phonemes allowed in the different positions in the syllable; English permits a number of different consonant phoneme clusters in the onset position. All the consonant phonemes except /ŋ/ can occupy the onset position as single phonemes. Twenty-three different two-phoneme consonant phoneme clusters can also occupy the onset position (can you work out what they are?). English even permits three-phoneme consonant cluster onsets: <STRING> <STRETCH>. Notice that <THREE> does not have a three-phoneme consonant cluster because the letters <TH> represent the phoneme /θ/ (check the IPA list) so the three letters in the onset position represent just two phonemes: /θ/ and /r/.

Similarly, all the consonant phonemes except /j/ and /h/ can occur as the coda. Also, some consonant phoneme clusters can occur as the coda in syllables and some cannot. There is no rationale for why some consonant clusters can appear as onsets or codas in English and why some cannot. For example, the cluster /ks/ cannot appear as an onset but it can occur as a coda – e.g. <TACKS> /tæks/. It is certainly nothing to do with whether or not we can articulate them. All we can say is that some can and some cannot.

Writing systems

Having introduced you to a number of important concepts relating to the phonological aspects of language, it is now time to turn to the orthography itself.

Writing is one of the most important inventions of the human mind. Through writing, the thoughts and feelings of people long dead can speak to us down the centuries. Their voices were never recorded but, through their texts, these voices can be 'heard'. Writing systems evolved from spoken language and capture spoken language in visual form. However, whereas spoken language is a biologically determined behaviour that is common to humans as a species, writing systems are culturally determined and only found in those societies that have created and adopted them. This is what we mean by 'invention'.

Writing systems are graphic. They all have some characteristics in common. They make use of a limited set of strokes configured in different ways to represent language. They differ in terms of the stroke patterns that they use, and also in the linguistic units that are represented by the graphic units. All existing modern writing systems can be broadly categorized on the basis of the way in which the language units are mapped onto orthographic units (Gelb, 1963). The orthographic units can represent *phonemes*, *syllables* and *words*. These are all concepts with which you are now familiar. Writing systems that represent language at the level of the largest unit – the word or concept – are called *logographic* or *ideographic* orthographies. Those that represent language at the level of an intermediate size of unit – the syllable – are called *syllabaries* or *alphasyllabaries*. And finally, those that represent language at the level of the smallest unit – the phoneme – are called *alphabets*, which will be discussed later in this chapter.

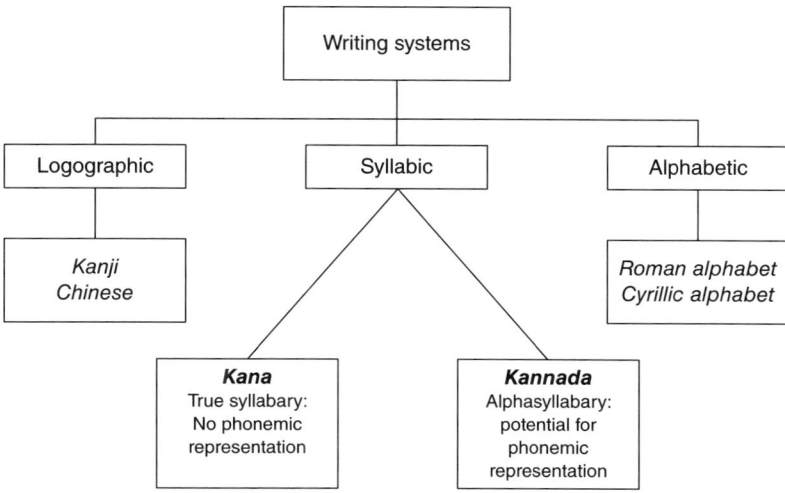

Figure 1.2 Basic categories of writing systems (from Coltheart, 1984)

Logographic writing systems

One of the most well-known examples of a logographic writing system is the hieroglyphic system used in Ancient Egypt. But we do not need to go back into the depths of history to find such a system. Contemporary Chinese and Japanese Kanji scripts are examples of logographic writing systems. Relative to English, they seem to represent language at the level of the concept or word. The graphic units are called *characters*. There are phonetic elements in some characters, which give Chinese readers insight into the sound as well as the meaning of the character. Reading in Chinese requires recognition of thousands of unique characters, with each character standing for a different concept. This poses a heavy strain on memory and, not surprisingly, it takes a long time for children to become fluent readers of Chinese and Japanese Kanji script.

Syllabic writing systems

The two Japanese Kana scripts represent language at the level of the Mora. A *mora* in Japanese is similar to a syllable in English. There are 48 different characters in each Kana script to represent the 48 different mora in the spoken language. So, to learn to read the Kana scripts, children have to learn the 48 mora-kana character correspondences in each script and then they can identify the words on the page. Most children enter school in Japan having already learned to identify the Kana characters, but they then have to learn close to 3,000 separate Kanji characters during their school years in order to be fluent word readers of everyday written Japanese.

The Kannada script, which is one of a number of different scripts used in India, is called an alphasyllabary because it represents language at the level of the syllable, but has the potential to represent phonemes as well. Children have to learn more than 400 individual characters and continue to learn these long into their primary school years (Nag & Snowling, 2012). The memory requirements are considerably more than for learning the Roman alphabet used for English, but the system is more predictable than English. Predictability is an important characteristic when learning to read.

Alphabetic writing systems

Alphabetic writing systems are the most common systems in use today. They represent language at the level of the phoneme. These writing systems largely derive from the Phoenician system, which was in use at least 3,500 years ago. The original Phoenician script just represented the consonant phonemes; the Greeks later devised letters for the vowels as well. This characteristic of representing only consonant phonemes in the written form is still found today in Hebrew and Arabic.

Modern European languages, including English, use alphabetic writing systems that represent both consonant phonemes and vowel phonemes. They do not all use the same alphabet: Russia uses the Cyrillic Alphabet, Greece has its own Greek alphabet and English uses the Latin alphabet. Across different languages, alphabets vary in the predictability with which they represent sounds. Some languages use accents (e.g. French: café, scène) or diacritic marks (e.g. Spanish: mañana, French: garçon) to modify letters: this increases the number of letters and shrinks the gap between number of letters and number of phonemes.

One of the newest writing systems is Turkish, reformed following a conference in 1929. The Latin alphabet was adopted, and a rational, consistent orthographic system was designed with one letter to represent each of the phonemes in modern Turkish. It is one of the simplest alphabetic systems in use today. The 26 letters in the Latin alphabet have to represent the 29 phonemes in modern spoken Turkish (21 consonant phonemes; 8 vowel phonemes). Some of the Latin letters were therefore augmented with accents, giving 29 letters that provide consistent one-to-one correspondences with the 29 phonemes. Thus, the Turkish language has a completely regular and consistent orthography, both when reading and spelling. Children learn to read words very quickly in Turkish (Babayigit & Stainthorp, 2007). They just have to learn the letter-sound correspondences and then by applying these consistently they have a system for identifying the phonemes in each word.

Let us play with using the Turkish alphabet for English.

Use Table 1.3 to translate each of the letters below into the phoneme that it represents.

Table 1.3 Subset of Turkish consonant and vowel letters and phonemes

Letter Upper case	Letter Lower case	IPA symbol for phoneme	Pronounced approximately as
B	b	/b/	b in *boy*
D	d	/d/	d in *dog*
E	e	/ɛ/	e in *red*
F	f	/f/	f in *far*
I	ı	/ɯ/	Roughly as *i* in *cousin*
L	l	/l/	l in *love*
O	o	/o/	o-e in *more*
Ö	ö	/ø/	ir in *bird*
P	p	/p/	p in *pin*
R	r	/r/	r in *rat*
Ü	ü	/y/	ue in *clue*
Y	y	/j/	y in *yes*

> Dü yü prıfö red o blü?

You should find that it reads as a rather mundane sentence. And, once children have learned the 29 letter-sound correspondences, it is difficult to go wrong. But think about the same sentence spelled conventionally in English orthography: Do you prefer red or blue?

The vowel phoneme is exactly the same in DO, YOU and BLUE, but the spelling is different in each case. As we have said, mapping vowel spellings onto vowel phonemes is one of the major challenges in learning to read words in English.

You may be asking yourself why we don't have a conference in the UK to reform spelling, thereby ensuring that British children could learn to read as quickly as Turkish children. The English Spelling Society has been campaigning for this since 1908, but, although it is beyond our remit to explain fully here, the losses would outweigh the gains. In the 1960s some schools introduced the Initial Teaching Alphabet (ITA) for teaching reading. The ITA alphabet consisted of 44 letters, giving a one-to-one mapping between letters and phonemes, and turning English into a regular consistent language. Downing (1967) showed that this was a very efficient system for learning to read, but it had some drawbacks. Children were surrounded by texts that were not written in ITA. The rich children's literature was not available to them to enable them to practise their developing reading skills because there were relatively few books translated into ITA script.

In the end, ITA died out as a means of teaching reading in schools, but the implicit logic of the instructional method lives on. The instructional method was phonics.

English orthography

ITA, as an artificial system, and Turkish, as a living experiment, are modern, deliberate inventions. English orthography is much older and has been influenced by many different languages and writing traditions. It has developed organically without any strategic planning, so spellings of many sounds now seem to be arbitrary. However, it is important to remember that English is an alphabetic language, and the basis of alphabetic systems is that the phonemes of the language are represented by letters. So however strange and illogical the representations might appear to be, each phoneme in a word is always given a graphic representation. The graphic representation is made up of a single letter or group of letters and is called a *grapheme*.

> ### What is a grapheme?
>
> A **GRAPHEME** is the letter or combination of letters that represents a phoneme in a word.
>
> Each word will have the same number of graphemes as phonemes but there may be more letters than phonemes.

We have used the term *regular* to describe the Turkish system. Regularity here means that the graphemes of a word all represent their most usual, frequent phonemes, so that if one knows the correspondences between graphemes and phonemes one can sound out a word. One can decode the word accurately. Examples of regular words are <DOG> <MAT> <BED> <PIN> and <RUG> which are decoded correctly as /dɒg/ /mæt/ /bɛd/ /pɪn/ and /rʌg/. There is no ambiguity about these regular words. There is one grapheme which consistently represents each phoneme. These words are therefore also said to be transparent.

As we have said, English has a complex orthography and it is difficult to make statements about the system which do not have exceptions. A case in point is the statement above. There is an exception to the rule that there is always a grapheme for each phoneme. The letter <X> generally represents two phonemes as in <BOX> /bɒks/, <FIX> /fɪks/, <EXIT> /ɛgzɪt/.

Reading vowels

There are 20 different vowel phonemes in English. The vowel phonemes in the five words <DOG> <MAT> <BED> <PIN> and <RUG> are all short vowels and, much of the time, the spelling of the short vowels is reasonably regular and consistent, as in these words. However, in the spelling of the more plentiful long vowels, regularity and consistency tend to break down. Various combinations of letters are used to represent these longer vowels.

Where two letters correspond to a single phoneme, the resulting grapheme is called a *digraph*. The words <SEED> <PAID> and <BOIL> all contain regular vowel digraphs. This means that the vowel letters <EE> <AI> and <OI> are parsed together and represent the single long vowel phonemes /i/ /ei/ and /ɔi/. The box below lists all the vowel letter digraphs (two-letter graphemes) for vowel phonemes.

> **Two-letter graphemes for long vowels composed of vowel letters**
>
> <AI>: sail   <AU>: maul
>
> <EA>: bead   <EE>: feet   <EI>: rein   <EU>: eulogy
>
> <IE>: pie
>
> <OA>: coat   <OE>: toe   <OO>: fool   <OU>: out
>
> <UE>: due   <UI>: fruit

These graphemes make a sort of sense because they are vowel letters parsed together to represent vowel phonemes. However, a further orthographic device is to create graphemes from a vowel letter and a consonant letter. In this instance <Y> is a consonant letter that has to be parsed with the preceding vowel letter. The full list is given in the next box.

> **Vowel plus consonant letter graphemes for long vowels**
>
> <AH>: rah   <AL>: calm   <AR>: car*   <AW>: saw   <AY>: play
>
> <ER>: farmer* <EY>: fey   <EW>: sew
>
> <IR>: fir*
>
> <OL>: folk   < OR>: for* <OY>: boy   <OW>: flow
>
> <UR>: fur*   <UY>: buy

Because the consonant letters are not sounded in these graphemes, they are not transparent. They are therefore said to be *opaque*. The existence of opaque graphemes is another reason why it is so difficult to learn to read English words. They are also not consistent, which adds another layer of uncertainty, but we will deal with that problem later. You will notice that we have placed an asterisk against each of the graphemes containing an <R>. This is because in some accents the <R> is sounded. In these accents, the word <CAR> is pronounced /kɑːr/ with three phonemes.

A further orthographic device for representing some long vowel phonemes is the use of the 'split vowel digraph' (or 'e-controlled vowel' in the USA). This means that the vowel is represented by two vowel letters. The first one is in the position in the word where it is sounded and the second one comes after the succeeding consonant letter. Examples of this are: <MADE>, <THESE>, <PINE>, <HOME>, <RULE>. This orthographic pattern is fairly regular but not totally transparent. Where there is the spelling <Vowel> – <Consonant> – <E> (VCE), the vowel phoneme can be reasonably reliably predicted in single syllabic words – hence it is regular, but the final letter E is not sounded – hence it is not transparent.

The VCE pattern generally stands for a long vowel phoneme rather than a short one. Though not completely reliable, there is a generality that the split vowel pattern 'makes the vowel say its name'. Indeed, digraphs and trigraphs for vowel phonemes generally code long monophthongs and diphthongs. However, this is not totally reliable. <A> in <APRON> is a single letter grapheme for the long vowel phoneme /eɪ/. And the single letter <O> codes /əʊ/ <GO>. But not always. It codes /u/ in <TO>.

The further we get into describing the orthography, the more exceptions to regularity we find. And it is this unstable predictability which makes English such a difficult language. The split vowel digraph format is a case in point.

There are two highly frequent and important words that do not have a regular pronunciation of the V-E grapheme: <HAVE> and <GIVE>. From their orthography, they should be pronounced to rhyme with <RAVE> and <FIVE>. But English orthography does not permit the letter V at the end of a word. This overrides the phonological representation of the short vowel phoneme /æ/ in <HAVE> and /ɪ/ in <GIVE>. If you are an avid Scrabble player, you might know there are twelve permitted words that all end in <V>. However, nine of these are non-English words: e.g. MAZELTOV; two are recent shortened forms: PERV and IMPROV; and one is a relatively newly coined word: SPIV. A newly coined word is called a neologism. One recent neologism ending in <V> (CHAV) has not yet made it to the Scrabble list.

Beyond the two letter digraphs, English has some graphemes that are even longer, composed of three or even four letters. The next box gives you all the remaining graphemes for vowels.

Remaining graphemes for vowels

<AIGH>: straight   <AIR>: fair   <ARE>: fare   <AUGH>: aught

<EAR>: ear   <EAU>: beau   <EER>: deer   <EIGH>: eight   <ERE>: here

<IGH>: sigh

<OUGH>: bought   <OUL>: could   <OUR>: flour

The peculiar case of <Y>

<Y> is generally classed as a consonant letter, which is rather misleading, particularly for young children learning about letters and sounds, because most of the time it represents a vowel phoneme. Whether it is a consonant letter or a vowel letter depends on its position in the word. In word-initial position, it represents the consonant phoneme /j/ as in <YELLOW> and <YES>. It also appears as a consonant letter in syllable-initial position in a few words: <ROYAL> <LOYAL>. However, as we saw above, it appears in the vowel graphemes <AY> <EY> <OY> and <UY>. It also stands for a vowel phoneme in its own right as in <BY> <MY> <FLY>, or as part of the split vowel digraph Y-E as in <TYPE> and <STYLE>. For each of these words you will notice that <Y> is representing the phoneme /ai/.

Reading consonants

We have so far focused on where vowel phonemes are spelt with at least two letters that have to be parsed together. However, this orthographic device also occurs for consonant phonemes, as can be seen in the last box. Those graphemes shown with a - before them in the next box can only be found in the coda position.

Two- and three-letter graphemes for consonant phonemes

<-CK>: deck

<-DGE>: fudge

<GH>: ghost   <GN>: gnat   <GU>: guide

<KN>: knee

<-MB>: comb   <-MN>: autumn

<-NG>: sing

<PH>: phone

<SC>: scent   <SH>: ship

<TH>: the   <-TCH>: watch

<WH>: what   <WR>: write

And finally, some consonant graphemes are *geminates*. These are double letters. The term comes from the Latin *geminus* meaning twin. The geminate consonants are: <BB> <CC> <DD> <FF> <GG> <LL> <MM> <NN> <PP> <RR> <SS> <TT>. In terms of reading, the doubling of the consonant letters is mostly redundant because they make the sound of the single letter (but they 'preserve' the sound of the preceding vowel letter when a word is affixed: e.g. <BAT> <BATTING>). However, <CC> sometimes stands for two phonemes /ks/: as in <ACCENT> and <ACCIDENT>.

The presence of digraphs and trigraphs as a characteristic of English orthography is one of the reasons that English is so difficult to learn to read. Children have to learn to recognize these orthographic patterns and also learn that they represent a single phoneme. Because consonants are used in vowel digraphs, there is a lack of transparency, so there is a lot for young children to learn.

Unpredictability

As we have said, the presence of digraphs poses challenges for reading English words because letters have to be parsed together to identify the phoneme they represent. The use of consonant letters as part of digraphs to stand for vowel phonemes is particularly challenging. But digraphs like these are not unique to English. For example, modern German has many. The ones we present here all relate to phonemes which are common to both English and German: the grapheme <EI> stands for the phoneme /ai/; <IE> stands for /i/; <EU> stands for /ɔi/; <SCH> stands for /ʃ/; and <TSCH> stands for /tʃ/. The difference between English and German is that though both languages employ multi-letter patterns for phonemes, the graphemes in German are consistent. It is easy to learn the grapheme-phoneme correspondences because they are predictable.

This is not the case with English: there is a high degree of inconsistency in grapheme-phoneme correspondences. This inconsistency is found much more in vowel phoneme spelling than in consonant spelling, but not exclusively. So we will begin with a consonant grapheme.

The grapheme <CH> usually denotes the phoneme /tʃ/. When children are learning to read they first have to be taught the grapheme phoneme correspondence <CH> = /tʃ/. However, as they expand their reading experiences they will learn that there are a considerable number of words where the grapheme <CH> stands for the phoneme /k/ (e.g. ACHE, CHEMIST, CHOIR, MONARCH, ARCHITECT, CHARACTER, TECHNICAL). You might notice that each of these words has a number of semantically related neighbours and in each of these the <CH> grapheme corresponds to the phoneme /k/ (e.g. CHOIR, CHORAL, CHORISTER). This means that there is additional learning to be done, but this is quite generative. One way of counteracting inconsistency is to learn about word families.

The examples above are of semantically related word families, but inconsistency can be countered by learning word families even when they are not semantically related – just orthographically related. The orthographic pattern <OUGH> will serve to illustrate this.

BOROUGH, BOUGH, BOUGHT, BROUGH, BROUGHT, COUGH, DOUGH, DROUGHT, ENOUGH, OUGHT, ROUGH, SOUGHT, THOROUGH, THOUGH, THOUGHT, THROUGH, TOUGH.

These words are in alphabetic order but we can sort them in other ways.

For example COUGH, ENOUGH, ROUGH, TOUGH and the place name BROUGH all have the orthographic pattern <OUGH> where the <GH> stands for the phoneme /f/. However, the <OU> grapheme stands for either /ɒ/ in COUGH or /ʌ/ in ENOUGH, ROUGH, TOUGH and BROUGH.

In the rest of the words <OUGH> is a vowel grapheme. It can be:

- /əʊ/ as in DOUGH and THOUGH
- /ɔ/ as in BOUGHT, BROUGHT, OUGHT, SOUGHT and THOUGHT
- /u/ as in THROUGH
- /ʌ/ as in BOROUGH and THOROUGH,
- /aʊ/ as in BOUGH and DROUGHT

There is no way of predicting how the <OUGH> grapheme will be pronounced. But it is possible to learn to read these words accurately. As you will see when we cover the development of reading, the way to learn to read these words accurately is to remember them as whole visual units.

<OUGH> is a very obvious inconsistent grapheme and one which is clearly opaque. However, when reading words containing this orthographic pattern, not all aspects are inconsistent or unpredictable. The onsets of all the <OUGH> words are completely regular and transparent. This means that, with a knowledge of the individual letter-sound correspondences, even if the word is not known, a first initial attempt at reading the word can give some useful information: <DR> and <B> at the beginning always represent /dr/ and /b/.

Let us consider some other types of word families. As we have already said, rhyme seems to be very salient to English speakers. Familiarity with rimes can help with developing accurate word reading skills: ATE, BATE, DATE, FATE, etc. form a completely consistent rime family. Playing with word families like this one can be very exciting for young children, and help to increase their vocabularies.

However, because English has such an inconsistent orthography, some apparent rime families are highly unpredictable and inconsistent. The <Vowel> <Consonant> <E> orthographic pattern was completely regular and consistent for the <ATE> rime, but let us consider the <OVE> family. As we said above the VCE orthographic pattern regularly codes long vowel phonemes. This means that if <OVE> were consistent it would stand for /əʊv/. It does in COVE, ROVE, STOVE and WOVE. But that leaves DOVE, GLOVE, SHOVE and LOVE where the vowel phoneme is /ʌ/; and MOVE and PROVE where the phoneme is /u/. This gives us ten base words with the same orthographic rime (-OVE) but only four of these have a regular pronunciation. This makes predicting from rime patterns both helpful but challenging at the same time.

What about the other element of the syllable: the body? Body patterns can also help with learning words. Let us take the coding of the sound /ɒ/ as in the regular word <PLOT>. What about <WHAT>? In words that have the body /wɒ/ or /swɒ/ the grapheme for /ɒ/ is more likely to be <A> than the regular <O>: WAS,

WANDER, SWAN, SWALLOW, etc. Of course you will not be surprised that there are always exceptions: WOBBLE, WOK. This makes predicting from bodies again both helpful and challenging.

Closing words

At this point we hope to have raised your awareness of the level of complexity of English orthography which makes learning to read words more difficult than in other more transparent, regular and consistent alphabetic languages. We have focused almost entirely on words and their sounds. And the examples of words have in the main been monosyllabic and mono-morphemic. You should now have the information necessary to understand about the development of word reading and how this can best be taught. In Chapter 6 we will also cover more complex aspects of words as they are encountered in phrases, sentences and texts. This will involve thinking about words with bound morphemes and complex syllabic structures. Things can only get more exciting. We hope that all professionals working with young children will find English orthography a source of enjoyment and intellectual entertainment as well as a source of frustration. But remember – you have been able to read this chapter – so you cracked the code. It is not impossible.

2
The Simple View of Reading: a broad conceptual framework

Summary

In this chapter, you will learn about the Simple View of Reading: how it was developed, and some of the evidence that suggests it provides a broad but accurate and useful conceptual framework for considering reading. You will understand that it does not, however, provide a full description or explanation of reading.

What is reading?

Reading is one of the most complex activities human beings engage in, and one of the most difficult to understand. Gates (1949: 3) defined reading as:

> ... a complex organisation of patterns of higher mental processes ... [that] ... can and should embrace all types of thinking, evaluating, judging, imagining, reasoning, and problem-solving.

This seems quite a comprehensive definition. Yet, as Fries (1963: 118) points out, all these 'higher mental processes' can, and have been, developed by persons who cannot read: they are not therefore uniquely involved in reading, but in oral language use too. What is unique to reading is the requirement to process language presented in visual rather than acoustic form, i.e. as written text, rather than as heard speech.

The Simple View of Reading (SVoR) proposes there are two interacting dimensions of reading, which we will call *visual word recognition processes* and *language comprehension processes*. Readers' abilities vary continuously along each dimension, from having very poor to excellent visual word recognition processes, and from having very poor to excellent language comprehension processes.

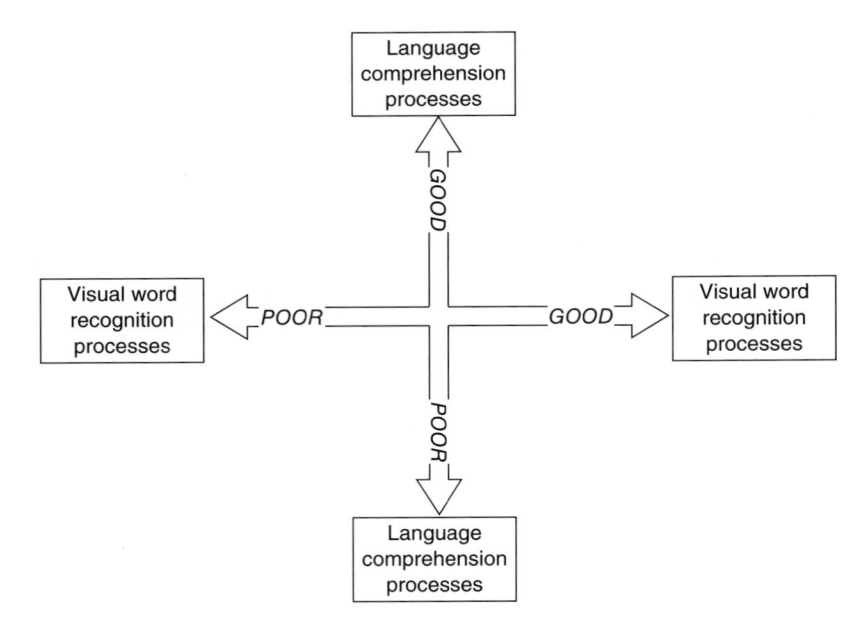

Figure 2.1 The Simple View of Reading (SVoR) (Crown copyright)

By *visual word recognition processes*, we mean the ability to recognize, understand and (if required) pronounce the words on the page, whether these are presented in isolation or within a sentence or text. That is, *visual word recognition* means the ability to process language presented in visual form. This is an essential prerequisite to, but not sufficient for, comprehension of written sentences and texts.

Understanding spoken and written language *both* require word recognition processes and language comprehension processes. To understand spoken language we must recognize and understand the words we *hear*; to understand written language we must recognize and understand the words we *see*. As words we hear or see are recognized and understood, they pass into the language comprehension system, which enables us to understand both spoken and written language. The language comprehension system comprises our tacit knowledge of vocabulary and of grammar (morphological knowledge and knowledge of sentence structure). The language comprehension system arises from, and remains intimately connected to, our knowledge of the world.

The Simple View of Reading was first proposed almost three decades ago, in 1986, by two psychologists, Gough and Tunmer, who specialized in studying reading development. They published a brief paper called 'Decoding, reading and reading disability' (Gough & Tunmer, 1986). Publication of this paper possibly arose from concern that, throughout the 1980s, the importance of teaching children how to read the words on the page was being neglected in the teaching of reading in many English-speaking countries. They proposed that the exceptionally complex activity that is reading could be encapsulated in a simple equation: **R**eading = **D**ecoding × **C**omprehension. The claim here is that every act of reading (**R**) involves recognizing and understanding written words (**D**, decoding) combined with understanding the sentences and texts the written words comprise (**C**, linguistic comprehension).

Given that reading is such a complex act, this reduction to a simple equation with only three elements (R, D and C), together with the very label 'the *Simple View of Reading*', aroused (and continues in some quarters to arouse) a rather hostile reaction. However, at no time did Gough and Tunmer make the mistake of suggesting that reading itself is a simple process. Far from it: they point out that reading is the result of the output from two sets of very complex, separable but linked processes (decoding, linguistic comprehension) which we consider in detail in Parts 2 and 3 of this book.

Part of the hostility might also be down to Gough and Tunmer's use of the term *decoding* to describe the act of reading the words on the page. This term continues in some quarters to be identified solely with using phonic rules to translate the written word to sound, with word meaning retrieved from the sound pattern of the word. However, Hoover and Gough (1990) go to some lengths to clarify this is not what they mean by *decoding* in the Simple View of Reading. They define decoding thus:

> Skilled decoding is simply efficient word recognition: the ability to rapidly derive a representation from printed input that allows access to the appropriate entry in the mental lexicon,[1] and thus, the retrieval of semantic information at the word level. (Hoover & Gough, 1990: 130)

As we shall see in Chapter 3, it is now recognized that 'efficient word recognition' in reading results from a combination of two sets of processes. One set of processes does involve using phonic rules to translate printed words to their sound patterns, from which word meaning can be accessed. The other set of processes involves accessing a previously stored 'sight vocabulary' representation of the spelling pattern of a word, which is linked directly to its meaning(s) and its phonology. *Decoding*, as defined by Hoover and Gough (1990), includes both these sets of processes.

In fact, it is precisely because of the complexity of reading that researchers investigating reading have chosen first to identify and seek to understand separate components of the reading system. Coltheart (2006: 5) justifies this approach by proposing that, in investigating reading:

> It does not seem likely that much progress would be made if we started off by investigating 'real reading', seeking for example to discover how readers, as they read *The Brothers Karamazov*, develop an understanding of what life might have been like in Imperial Russia. No one has any idea about how to carry out such an investigation; so more tractable reading situations have to be studied first. This is done by breaking up 'real reading' into simpler

---

[1] The 'mental lexicon' is conceived as a kind of dictionary in the mind, which contains information about the spelling pattern, meaning and pronunciation of all written words known to the reader.

component parts that are more immediately amenable to investigation, with the hope that as more and more of these component parts come to be understood we will get closer and closer to a full understanding of 'real reading'.

Coltheart identifies visual word recognition as one of the component parts of reading, and gives a clear account of the processes involved in this. *Decoding*, as defined by Hoover and Gough (1990) (and thus as in the SVoR), equates exactly to *visual word recognition* as conceived by Coltheart (2006). Throughout this book, we have used the term *visual word recognition processes* rather than *decoding*, as a more accurate summary of the complex processes involved in this dimension of reading.

Hoover and Gough also provide a clear definition of the second component, *linguistic comprehension*, which is 'the ability to take lexical information (i.e. semantic information at the word level) and derive sentence and discourse interpretations. Reading comprehension involves the same ability, but one that relies on graphic-based information arriving through the eye' (Hoover & Gough, 1990: 131). Throughout this book, and in our diagram of the Simple View of Reading (Figure 2.1), we use the term *language comprehension* rather than *linguistic comprehension*, as a way of emphasizing that the same, single, language system underpins understanding of both written and spoken language.

The SVoR predicts the existence of four different reading profiles. Skilled readers are those who have well-developed abilities on both dimensions, who read words fluently and accurately and show appropriate understanding of what is read. The remaining three profiles all describe readers whose abilities along one or other or both dimensions are not sufficiently well developed to ensure fluent, accurate reading with appropriate understanding of what is read. Poor language comprehension will jeopardize reading comprehension, even if word recognition processes are well developed; intervention should aim to develop language comprehension abilities. Inaccurate and dysfluent word recognition will also jeopardize reading comprehension; intervention here should aim to develop word recognition processes. The most severely compromised children are those who have underdeveloped abilities on both dimensions, whose reading is slow and inaccurate and whose language comprehension ability does not allow comprehension of what has been so laboriously deciphered. These children require consistent and systematic teaching designed to improve both their word recognition processes and their language comprehension.

The SVoR framework serves as a constant reminder that both language comprehension processes and visual word recognition processes are essential to understanding written texts, at all levels of reading development. Presentation of the two dimensions in the form of a cross is intended to emphasize that visual word recognition and language comprehension processes interact continuously with each other in every act of reading and throughout the course of reading development.

The Rose Review into the Teaching of Early Reading (Rose, 2006) recommended that the Simple View of Reading should be adopted as a valid conceptual framework (but not as a complete description or explanation of reading) which:

- encourages teachers not necessarily to expect that the children they teach will show equal performance or progress in each dimension
- offers the possibility of separately assessing performance and progress in each dimension, to identify learning needs and guide further teaching
- makes explicit to teachers that different kinds of teaching are needed to develop word recognition skills from those that are needed to foster the comprehension of written and spoken language
- emphasises the need for teachers to be taught about and to understand the cognitive processes involved in the development of both accurate word recognition skills and of language comprehension

(Rose, 2006: 77–78)

Is the Simple View of Reading a valid conceptual framework?

A conceptual framework is valid to the extent that it provides a well-founded account of the concept it seeks to explain: the concept in this case being reading comprehension. So the question becomes, how well founded is the claim that reading comprehension can be explained by visual word recognition and language comprehension abilities? If this claim is well founded, the following broad statements should be true.

First, factor analysis of reading data should reveal two factors, one representing the visual word recognition dimension, and one representing the language comprehension dimension. Several studies have now measured a variety of different abilities known to be involved in reading. Nation and Snowling (1997) assessed Key Stage 2 children's word reading accuracy (with and without context), non-word reading, narrative listening comprehension, and reading comprehension at text and sentence level. Factor analysis revealed two factors. The three visual word recognition measures (word reading accuracy, with and without context, nonword reading) loaded heavily on one factor, while the two text comprehension measures (narrative listening, text reading) loaded heavily on to a second factor. Kendeou, Savage and van den Broek (2009) also identified two factors underlying reading comprehension in studies with US and Canadian children, as did Protopapas, Simos, Sideris and Mouzaki (2012) in studies of Greek children.

Second, if the two dimensions are separable, it should be possible to show that different underlying skills and abilities contribute to the successful development of each. Several studies have now shown this. Muter, Hulme, Snowling and Stevenson (2004) studied 90 children for two years from school entry as 'rising fives'. They showed that later visual word recognition skills were predictable from earlier measures of letter knowledge and phoneme sensitivity, but not from earlier measures of oral vocabulary, rhyme skills or grammatical skills. In contrast, later reading comprehension was predictable from earlier visual word recognition skills, vocabulary knowledge, and grammatical skills. Similarly, Oakhill, Cain and Bryant (2003) showed that the abilities that facilitate development of visual word recognition skills are quite distinct from those that facilitate text comprehension.

Third, there should be children whose word reading ability (good) is discrepant with their reading comprehension (poor): such profiles are evident in studies by Aaron, Joshi and Williams (1999), Catts, Adlof and Weismer (2006), and Nation, Clarke, Marshall and Durand (2004). Conversely, there should be children who show a discrepancy between listening comprehension (good) and reading comprehension (poor), a discrepancy which can be attributed to their poor visual word recognition skills: such profiles are evident in a study by Spooner, Baddeley and Gathercole (2004).

Fourth, we know that children differ in their reading comprehension ability. If it is true that visual word recognition processes and language comprehension processes underlie reading comprehension ability, then scores on measures of visual word recognition skills and language comprehension abilities should account for these differences in reading comprehension. Many studies have now demonstrated that, to a large extent, they do (e.g. Adlof, Catts & Little, 2006; Johnston & Kirby, 2006; Savage & Wolforth, 2007; Tilstra et al., 2009), with studies showing that from 45% to 85% of the differences in reading comprehension can be accounted for by measures of visual word recognition skills and language comprehension processes (Conners, 2009), depending on the measures used and the nature of the study (e.g. longitudinal or concurrent data collection).

Thus, it seems safe to conclude that the SVoR is a valid conceptual framework 'for understanding the broad landscape of reading' (Kirby & Savage, 2008). However, that is not to say that it provides a detailed description or complete explanation of reading.

Is the Simple View of Reading a complete description or explanation of reading?

If **R**eading = **D**ecoding × **C**omprehension – that is, if reading comprehension is the product of visual word recognition skills and language comprehension ability – then measures of visual word recognition ability and language comprehension ability should predict most, if not all, of the differences in reading comprehension. But, as shown above, they don't account for all of these differences, so there must be other things that matter.

Several recent studies have tried adding further measures over and above visual word recognition and language comprehension, to see whether adding additional measures will account for more of the differences in reading comprehension. To date, some additional measures have been shown slightly to improve accountability, but results from different studies are conflicting. For example, Adlof, Catts and Little (2006), working in the USA with children from second, fourth and eighth grade (aged 7, 9 and 13), added a measure of word reading fluency to measures of word reading accuracy and listening comprehension. They found that word reading fluency did not further explain differences in reading comprehension. However, other studies (Aaron, Joshi & Williams, 1999; Cutting & Scarborough, 2006; Tilstra et al., 2009) have shown that adding a measure of reading fluency does slightly improve the prediction of reading comprehension, particularly in older children. This suggests it might be wise to specify that the visual word recognition dimension of the SVoR needs to take account of both accuracy and speed of word reading. We have always interpreted the term 'well developed visual word recognition processes' to mean word reading that is accurate, fluent and automatic, but clearly others do not share our interpretation.

In other studies, discrete measures of oral vocabulary have been added to measures of visual word recognition processes and language comprehension, with large improvements reported in some cases to the amount of differences in reading comprehension accounted for. For example, Ouellette and Beers (2010), working with children in Grade 1 and Grade 6, found that an additional measure of oral vocabulary improved the prediction of reading comprehension in Grade 6, but not in Grade 1. This is interesting: we have always considered oral vocabulary knowledge to be part of the language processing system, and yet adding measures of oral vocabulary increases the predictive power of the SVoR, when the contributions of visual word recognition and language comprehension have been taken into account. This might suggest the measures frequently used to assess language comprehension in research studies do not cover all aspects of language processing. As in the case of visual word recognition processes, it might be wise to provide a more complete specification of what is involved in language comprehension, and to reflect this in the measures used to assess it.

Pressley et al. (2008) have argued that the SVoR cannot provide a complete picture of the development of reading because it ignores important aspects such as fluency and speed, vocabulary, inference, background knowledge, working memory capacity, and the need for 'active' reading. As shown above, researchers have begun to address some of these supposedly ignored aspects. We would argue that many of the 'ignored' aspects are in fact subsumed within the language comprehension system (hence the need better to specify just what is involved in language comprehension). For example, vocabulary, inference and working memory are clearly involved in oral as well as written language comprehension, and might therefore be considered part of the language comprehension system.

Earlier in this chapter we stated, 'The language comprehension system arises from, and remains intimately connected to, our knowledge of the world'. As our first understanding of language is based in our growing knowledge of the world, it seems sensible to assume that knowledge of the world (background knowledge) continues to contribute to both oral and written language comprehension. That is, background knowledge is constantly available to the actively engaged listener and reader. And here we acknowledge Pressley et al. (2008) are right to argue that the SVoR takes no account of the degree to which the reader is actively engaged in reading. This engagement, which has recently been recast as a 'drive for coherence' on the part of the reader – a determined and active motivation to make sense of what is being read – underpins deployment of the comprehension strategies discussed in Chapters 7 and 10.

Closing words

Each of the two dimensions of the SVoR summarizes a host of complex processes involved in each. Chapters 3 and 4 provide a detailed description of the processes involved in recognizing and understanding the words on the page, and the ways in which these processes develop in children. Chapter 6 describes processes involved in oral and written language comprehension, and Chapter 7 concentrates on reading (written language) comprehension. To begin to be able to teach all children to read beyond the risk of failure, we need to know and understand the complexity that underlies each dimension.

PART 2
Reading the words on the page

3
Visual word recognition in skilled readers

Summary

In this chapter, you will learn about the two sets of processes that underlie skilled word reading. Understanding what is involved in skilled word reading will enable you to answer the question: How do we, as skilled readers, read words? But, as skilled word reading is the endpoint of development, this chapter will also help you understand what it is that children need to do to develop their word reading skills.

Different processes to read words

As skilled readers, we effortlessly absorb the meanings of the words on the page without conscious awareness of the complex processes that enable us to do this. The following exercise is designed to make you aware that there's more than one way to read a word.

A demonstration of the processes involved in skilled word reading

Try reading aloud the 'words' in Figure 3.1a

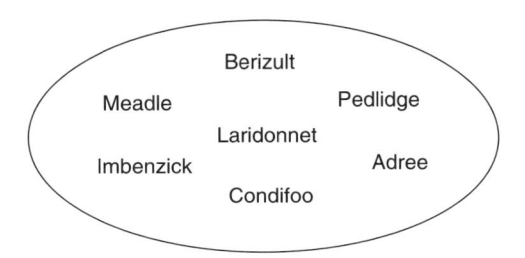

Berizult
Meadle   Pedlidge
     Laridonnet
Imbenzick   Adree
     Condifoo

Figure 3.1a   'Words' to read aloud

We know you've never seen them before because we just made them up, they are pronounceable nonwords. But you could read them, and you probably assigned stress patterns correctly too. So, as skilled readers we have processes allowing us to read words that are unknown to us in their written form (although we might understand them if we heard them spoken). These processes allow us to translate written segments into spoken segments, and produce a pronunciation. Now try the words in Figure 3.1b.

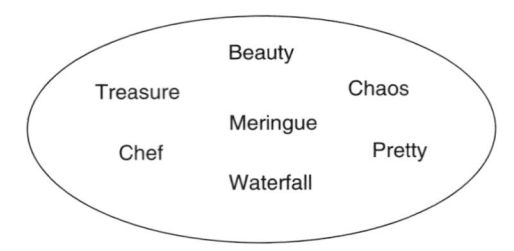

```
         Beauty
Treasure         Chaos
       Meringue
  Chef           Pretty
       Waterfall
```

Figure 3.1b   Words to read aloud

There are some odd looking words here, but it is unlikely you mispronounced any of them: you've read them and heard them spoken many times before. But how did you do it? We need to stress the system a bit more to show you that this ability to pronounce such odd looking words correctly is indicative of a second set of processes. What about the words in Figure 3.1c?

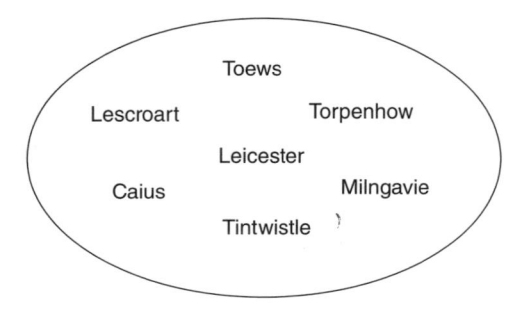

```
         Toews
Lescroart         Torpenhow
       Leicester
  Caius           Milngavie
       Tintwistle
```

Figure 3.1c   Personal and place names to read aloud

These are all real words: either place names or personal names. We are pretty sure that you mispronounced at least some of them. We think, if you are an English speaker based in the UK, you probably pronounced Leicester accurately (Lester), and maybe also Caius (Keys). But, unless you live in the locality, you probably pronounced Torpenhow, Tintwistle and Milngavie just as they are spelt, although they are actually Trepenna, Tinsel and Mulguy. And who would have thought that Mr Toews is actually Mr Taves, or Ms Lescroart, Ms Lezkwar?

What these three exercises demonstrate is that skilled readers can read unfamiliar words and nonwords they have never seen before, and they do it fluently and fast, without any obvious signs of 'sounding out' the letters. Skilled readers can also read words that can't be 'sounded out' accurately, as long as they have seen them before and learned how to pronounce them. In this chapter, we describe the processes involved in each of these feats of word reading. We do this because, to enable children to become skilled word readers who absorb the meanings of the words on the page with the speed and effortlessness that characterize skilled reading, it is useful to be aware of the processes that are involved. We need to understand what it is we are trying to teach.

What do we mean by 'visual word recognition'?

We mean the ability to look at a written word, whether presented in or out of context, and recover the word's meaning and pronunciation from the sequence of letters that compose it. Visual word recognition depends on three kinds of linked representations: orthographic, semantic and phonological. An *orthographic representation* is the *stored spelling pattern* of a word. A *semantic representation* is the *stored meaning(s)* of a word. A *phonological representation* is the *stored sound pattern* of a word. Spelling patterns and sound patterns of words can each be represented at two levels: at the level of the whole word, and at the level of segmented, subword level units (e.g. graphemes and phonemes).

As we have just demonstrated, a model of word reading must include two different sets of processes – it must be a dual-route model. All contemporary models of reading are dual-route models. Different models disagree in the details of each set of processes and how they operate, but all agree there are two sets. One set works very well for unfamiliar words and nonwords, but cannot provide an accurate pronunciation for the odd-looking words and names, some of which we are sure you mispronounced when doing the exercise we set you. So another set of processes is required for these 'irregular' or 'exception' words that don't obey standard spelling-sound correspondences.

In the interests of clarity of exposition, we will choose just one from the set of dual-route models, and describe the two sets of processes as they are implemented in the Dual-Route Cascaded (DRC) model (Coltheart, Rastle, Perry, Langdon & Ziegler, 2001).

Two sets of processes underlying skilled visual word recognition

As shown in Figure 3.2, one set of processes (akin to 'sight vocabulary') accesses word meaning directly from the orthographic representation of the word. This is how you are able to understand exception words like CHAOS, PRETTY and MERINGUE. Orthographic representations also link directly to their phonological representations in the phonological lexicon, as well as indirectly to these through word meaning. This is how you are able to pronounce exception words like CHAOS, PRETTY and MERINGUE correctly. We use the term *lexical processes* to refer to all these processes because they link word spellings directly to word meanings, and also to word pronunciations. The term lexical comes from the Greek word *lexis*, meaning word.

```
        lemon      meringue
           │          │
           ▼          ▼
    ┌─────────────────────┐
    │ Abstract letter units│
    └─────────────────────┘
              ▲
              ▼
    ┌─────────────────────┐
    │ Orthographic lexicon │◄──┐
    │ (store of orthographic│   │
    │   representations)   │   │
    └─────────────────────┘   │
              ▲                │
              ▼                │
      ╭─────────────╮          │
     (  Semantic lexicon )     │
     (  (store of word   )     │
     (    meanings)      )     │
      ╰─────────────╯          │
              ▲                │
              ▼                │
    ┌─────────────────────┐   │
    │ Phonological lexicon │◄──┘
    │ (store of phonological│
    │   representations)   │
    └─────────────────────┘
              ▲
              ▼
    ┌─────────────────────┐
    │   Phoneme system    │
    └─────────────────────┘
           │          │
           ▼          ▼
         lemon      merang
```

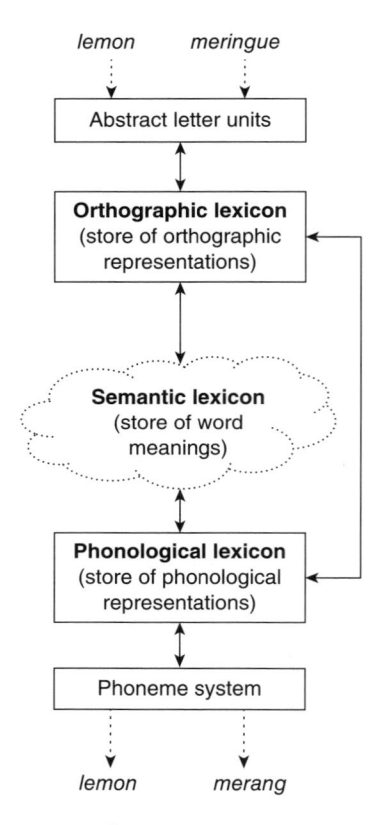

Figure 3.2 Lexical processes: direct access to semantics (word meaning) and phonology (word pronunciation) from orthography (word spelling pattern)

A further set of processes (shown in Figure 3.3), akin to use of phonic rules, links written segments of words (e.g. graphemes) to their corresponding sound segments (e.g. phonemes), which are blended into a pronunciation of the whole word. Word meaning is accessed from this blended pronunciation. Thus, in this set of processes, written segments must be recoded into sound segments before the word can be understood. We use the term 'phonological recoding processes' to refer to these processes.

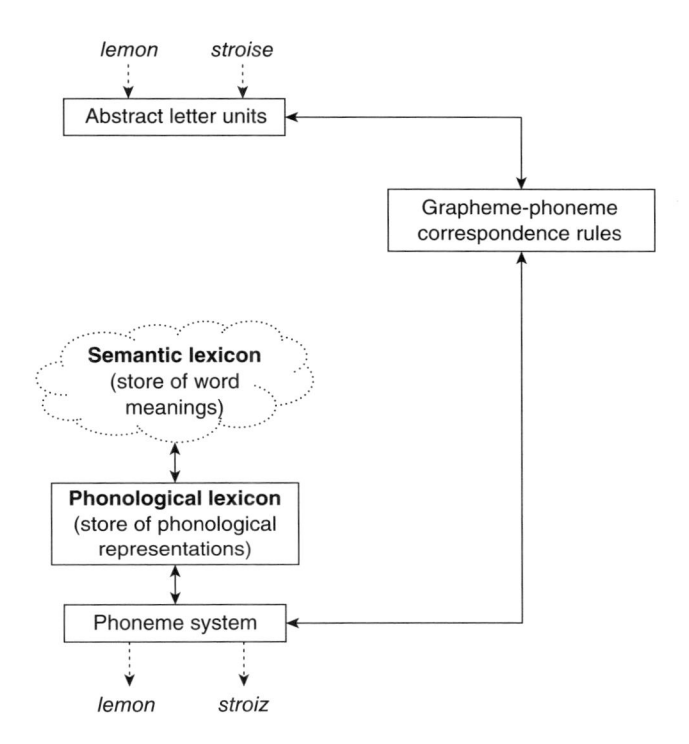

Figure 3.3 Phonological recoding processes: indirect access to semantics (word meaning) from phonology (word pronunciation)

More on lexical processes

Lexical processes allow the reader to read, accurately and fluently, any word they have seen before and stored. The existence of direct links from the spelling pattern of each word to its meaning explains how readers can understand homophonic words (words that have the same phonology but different meanings: e.g. feat, feet; medal, meddle; pair, pear) even when these are seen in isolation with no disambiguating context. This is illustrated in Figure 3.4.

More on phonological recoding processes

Phonological recoding processes allow us to derive pronunciations for *all* words, whether or not their written forms are familiar to us: no previously stored representation of the word is needed. However, as shown in Figure 3.5, only 'regular' words (words which obey the major spelling-sound rules of the language) and/or 'consistent' words (words whose rime unit is always pronounced in the same way in all words in which that unit is found) are pronounced *correctly* by these processes. Exception words (which violate the major spelling-sound rules of the language) are mispronounced because they are regularized – treated as though they

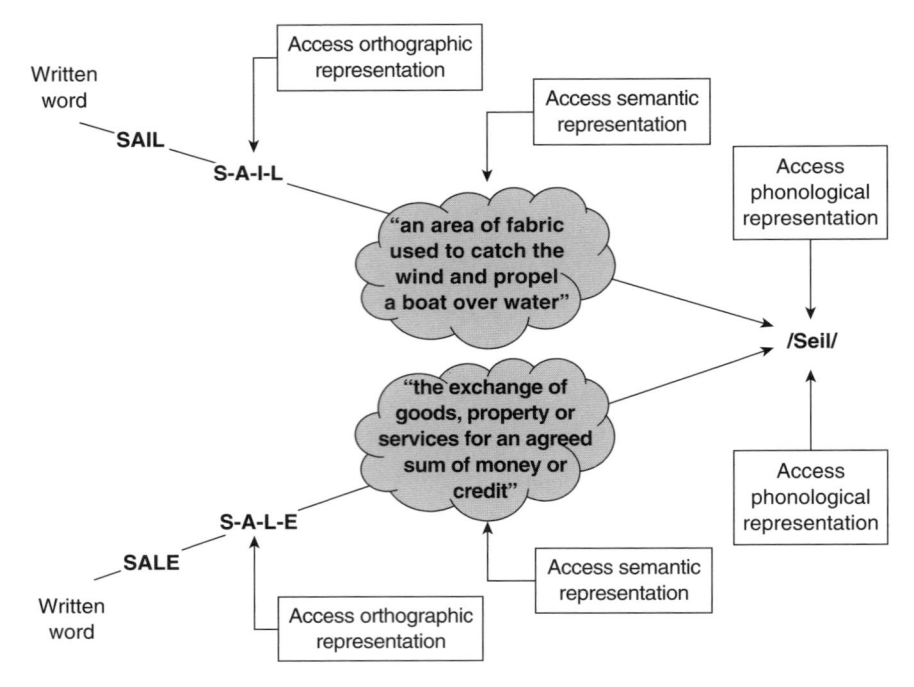

Figure 3.4 Specific meanings of homophonic words directly accessed from their spelling

did obey the rules. And, as meaning is retrieved from the blended sound pattern of the word, words that are mispronounced may also be misunderstood because the wrong meaning is accessed.

Phonological recoding processes are essential for reading new words the reader has never seen before. Even we as skilled readers occasionally come across such words, but young children are constantly coming across them. Once the phonology of a word never before seen in print has been derived, as long as the spoken form of the word is familiar to the reader, its meaning will be accessed, because the phonology of each known word is already linked to its meaning. However, readers who rely exclusively on phonological recoding processes to read words may access incorrect meanings for exception words. In the example of 'gauge' shown in Figure 3.5, 'gauge' is regularized to 'gorge', and therefore understood to mean 'a deep valley'. Of course, not all regularizations result in a real word. In some cases, it may not be possible to access any meaning at all: for example, the regularized pronunciation of 'yacht' is /jætʃt/ to rhyme with patched. /jætʃt/ is not a real word in English, and therefore cannot be understood.

Fortunately, skilled readers do not rely exclusively on phonological recoding processes: if they did, they would frequently access the wrong meanings of words. Nor do skilled readers rely exclusively on lexical processes: if they did, they

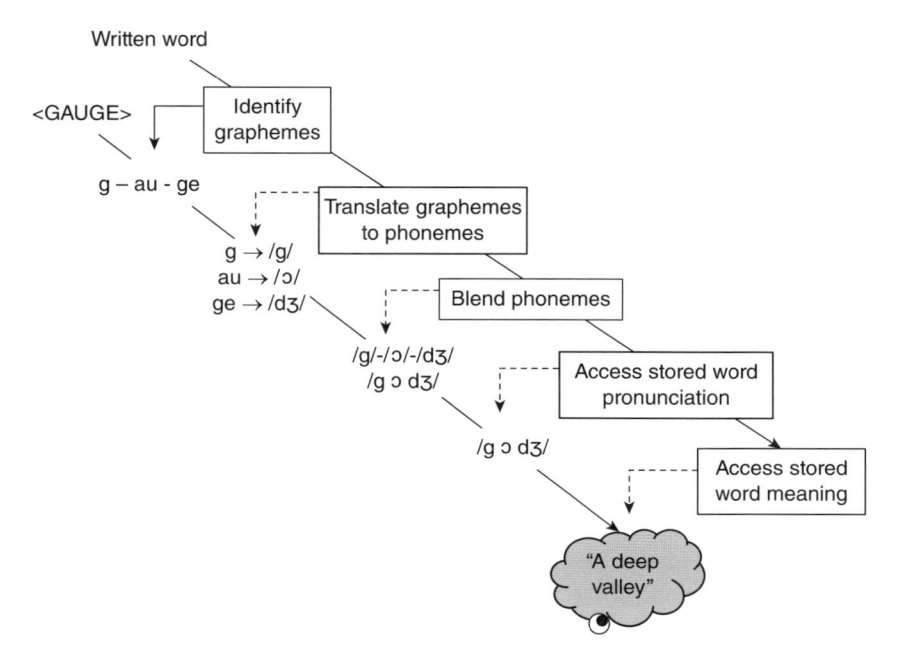

Figure 3.5 'Regularization' of exception words

would be unable to read any previously unseen words – readers cannot have stored orthographic representations of words they have never seen before. Lexical and phonological recoding processes operate in tandem in skilled reading, with lexical processes usually operating faster than phonological recoding. The two sets of processes ensure that skilled readers with intact word reading systems invariably access the correct meanings of words, even in the absence of any context, while also being able to work out pronunciations for (and thus access the phonological representation of) unfamiliar written words.

Summary so far

Models of processes involved in word reading broadly agree that skilled readers use a combination of lexical and phonological recoding processes to recognize, understand and pronounce written words. Skilled readers have a store of 'sight vocabulary' – words that they have seen frequently before and stored for future instant recognition and understanding. Skilled readers also have good stored knowledge of the phonic rules of their language, which are applied automatically and unconsciously as they read words, and which are essential to read words that even the skilled reader has never seen before, and therefore has not stored in their sight vocabulary. As these are the processes known to be used by skilled readers, it follows that children learning to read need to develop these two sets of processes.

Evidence that skilled readers use two sets of processes in visual word recognition

Psychologists interested in word reading have carried out hundreds of experiments exploring factors that influence the speed and accuracy of word reading in skilled readers, and in formerly skilled readers who, following brain damage, have lost some of their word reading skills. Two main tasks are used in this research: *reading aloud* tasks and *lexical decision* tasks.

In *reading aloud* tasks, participants see words and/or pronounceable nonwords presented singly on a computer screen and are instructed to read each item aloud. The experimenter notes the accuracy of the response; the computer times the speed of the response. In *lexical decision* tasks, participants see words and pronounceable nonwords presented singly on a computer screen and are instructed to press a 'yes' key if the item is a real word, and a 'no' key if the item is not a real word. The computer measures both the accuracy and speed of responses.

The weight of evidence supports the view that two sets of processes operating together provide the best explanation of known facts about word reading. For example, skilled readers read words faster than they read pronounceable nonwords, an effect first demonstrated by Baron and Strawson (1976). Words are read faster because they are stored in sight vocabulary and access to sight vocabulary is faster than application of phonic rules. Conversely, pronounceable nonwords are read more slowly because they are not stored in sight vocabulary and so have to be read by applying phonic rules. In lexical decision tasks, skilled readers also respond 'yes' to words faster than 'no' to pronounceable nonwords. This again is because skilled readers have already stored representations of the spelling patterns of familiar words, and if words are highly familiar to the reader, a 'yes' decision is typically made on the basis of fast access to this orthographic information alone.

Skilled readers also read words that are highly frequent in written texts faster than words of low written text frequency. This is because the more often a reader has seen a word in print, the stronger its memory trace is in the reader's sight vocabulary. In lexical decision tasks also, skilled readers respond 'yes' faster to high frequency than to low frequency words.

And readers read regular words faster than exception words (Baron & Strawson, 1976; Seidenberg, Waters, Barnes & Tanenhaus, 1984). This is because lexical and phonological recoding processes operate in tandem during reading. For regular words, the two sets of processes converge on a single pronunciation. But for exception words, two pronunciations are obtained: the correct pronunciation, through lexical processing (e.g. /jɒt/ for 'yacht'), and a 'regularized' pronunciation, through phonological recoding processes which apply grapheme-phoneme correspondence rules that exception words do not obey (e.g. /jætʃt/ for 'yacht') and there is a time cost to choosing which is the correct reading.

Regularity and frequency interact with each other. If we compare the speed of skilled readers when reading words that are both highly frequent and regular with their speed when reading words that are highly frequent but exceptions, we find no difference. That is, skilled readers show no speed advantage in pronouncing high frequency regular over high frequency exception words (Seidenberg & McClelland, 1989; Seidenberg et al., 1984; Waters & Seidenberg, 1985). This is because access to stored sight vocabulary representations of high frequency words is so rapid that no regularized pronunciation of high frequency exception words is available from phonological recoding processes before the word is pronounced.

In some lexical decision tasks, participants are presented with pseudo-homophones. These are pronounceable nonwords that sound like real words. For example, GOTE sounds like GOAT and WOCH sounds like WATCH. When pseudo-homophones are used in lexical decision tasks, skilled readers respond 'no' more slowly to pseudo-homophones than to non-homophonic pronounceable nonwords. This is because phonological recoding processes access the pronunciation of the real word equivalent of the pseudo-homophone, making it harder to reject, despite the absence of a stored spelling pattern in the orthographic lexicon.

As we have seen, as well as being categorized as regular or exception, words can be categorized as 'consistent' or 'inconsistent'. This categorization depends on rime rather than phonemic segments. A word is consistent if the rime is pronounced in the same way across all words containing that rime: thus, COAT is a consistent word, because all monosyllabic words ending in -OAT are pronounced to rhyme with COAT, and no words with the -OAT rime are pronounced differently from COAT. A word is inconsistent if the rime is pronounced differently in different words containing that rime: thus, words with the rime -OVE are inconsistent because the rime is pronounced differently in words like DOVE, MOVE and COVE. In reading aloud tasks, skilled readers read consistent words faster than inconsistent words (Cortese & Simpson, 2000; Jared, 1997, 2002; Jared, McRae & Seidenberg, 1990). To accommodate consistency effects, phonological recoding processes must include rime as well as grapheme-phoneme correspondences. Until recently, the phonological recoding route of the dual-route cascaded model was set up simply to translate graphemes to phonemes through applying a set of grapheme-phoneme correspondence rules (as we have shown it in Figure 3.3). However, a new version of the DRC model (DRC2.0) has been developed, incorporating rime as well as grapheme-phoneme correspondences. Preliminary results suggest it succeeds in explaining the consistency effects which the original DRC model could not explain (Coltheart, personal communication, 2015).

Closing words

We have presented here just a small part of the simplest kinds of evidence that suggest more than a single set of processes is involved in skilled word reading. There is a massive, extremely complex literature on this subject, which is not relevant to our purposes in writing this book. We hope the glimpse of relevant evidence provided here is sufficient to convince you that two sets of processes are necessary for skilled visual word recognition.

We have presented the two sets of processes in some detail because of the implications for teaching children to read. If children are to become skilled word readers, they need to develop both sets of processes. They need to set up a store of spelling patterns of words that are linked directly to their meanings and pronunciations – a set of lexical processes, dependent on stored sight vocabulary. These processes are fast acting and essential to the correct pronunciation of exception words. Children also need to acquire knowledge of the grapheme-phoneme and rime correspondences in their language, and the ability to blend sound segments into whole word pronunciations – a set of phonological recoding processes, an ability to apply phonic rules. These processes, although slower, are essential to the pronunciation of previously unseen written words.

Throughout this book, we describe the details of the ways in which both sets of processes operate in accordance with their description in the DRC model. One reason for this choice is that the DRC provides fairly accessible explanations which accord with everyday concepts of word reading processes (the development of sight vocabulary and the use of phonic rules).

4

Development of visual word recognition processes

Summary

In this chapter, you will learn how the two sets of word reading processes available to skilled readers develop as children learn to read. In Chapter 3, we argued that to become skilled readers, children must develop the word reading processes available to skilled readers: phonological recoding processes, which rely on the use of relations between letters and sounds, and lexical processes, which rely on direct access to meaning and pronunciation from stored sight vocabulary. Understanding what is involved in developing these processes will allow you to answer the question, how do children learn to read written words? It will also enable you to tailor your teaching to maximize children's learning.

The oral language basis of word reading skills

Some elements of the skilled word reading system exist before children begin to learn or be taught to read. Pre-reading children understand words they hear, and can find words to express their thoughts and feelings. This means they have already established a semantic lexicon, an internal dictionary containing the meanings of all the words they know, and a phonological lexicon containing the pronunciations of all the words they know. They have also set up links between word meanings and pronunciations: they can pronounce words to convey their intended meaning, and retrieve the meaning of words they hear. Word reading processes, like reading comprehension processes, are built on the pre-existing foundations of oral language shown in Figure 4.1.

As time goes on, oral vocabulary continues to develop: more word meanings are stored in the semantic lexicon; more word pronunciations are stored in the

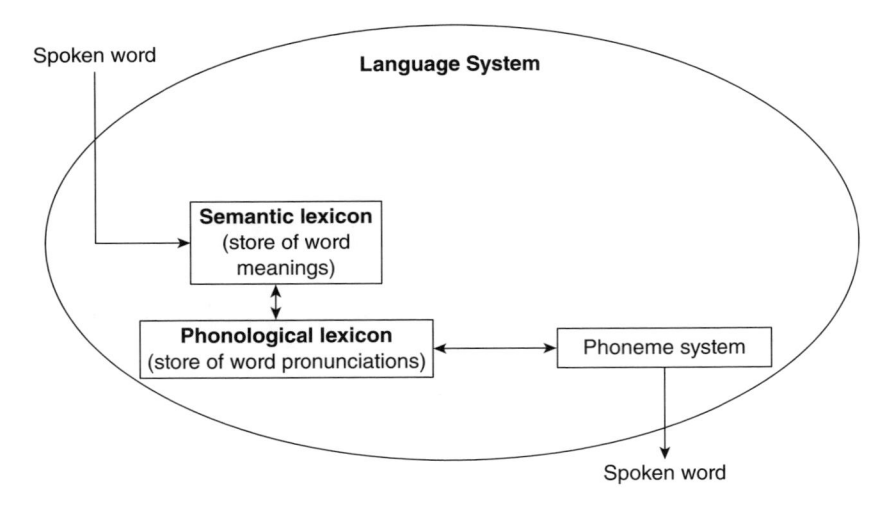

Figure 4.1 Language elements that predate and underpin the establishment of word reading processes

phonological lexicon; and links are formed between these new word meanings and their pronunciations. What needs to be grafted on to these pre-existing elements to enable children to become readers as well as speaker-listeners of words? First, they need to construct ways of getting into the semantic lexicon from visual (i.e. written) as well as spoken input. This involves several developments. For the lexical processing of written words to be possible, children must learn to recognize the letters that compose written words. They must devise ways of remembering and storing orthographic representations of each written word they see. And they must form links between these orthographic representations and the meanings and pronunciations of the words they represent. Accomplishing these developments results in the formation of lexical processes, as shown in Figure 4.2.

Establishment of phonological recoding processes also requires several developments. Children need to learn the correspondences between graphemes and phonemes. They need to learn to convert graphemes into phonemes, and blend phonemes into whole word pronunciations. Accomplishing this learning results in the establishment of phonological recoding processes, as shown in Figure 4.3.

Figure 4.3 shows that a system for identifying letters is common to both lexical and phonological recoding processes. Unique to lexical processing is the establishment of an orthographic lexicon, containing representations of the spelling patterns of words, with input from letters identified in the words seen, and links to each word's meaning and pronunciation. Unique to phonological processing is the establishment of grapheme-phoneme conversion procedures, with input from letters identified in the word seen, and links to the phoneme system, where phoneme blending takes place.

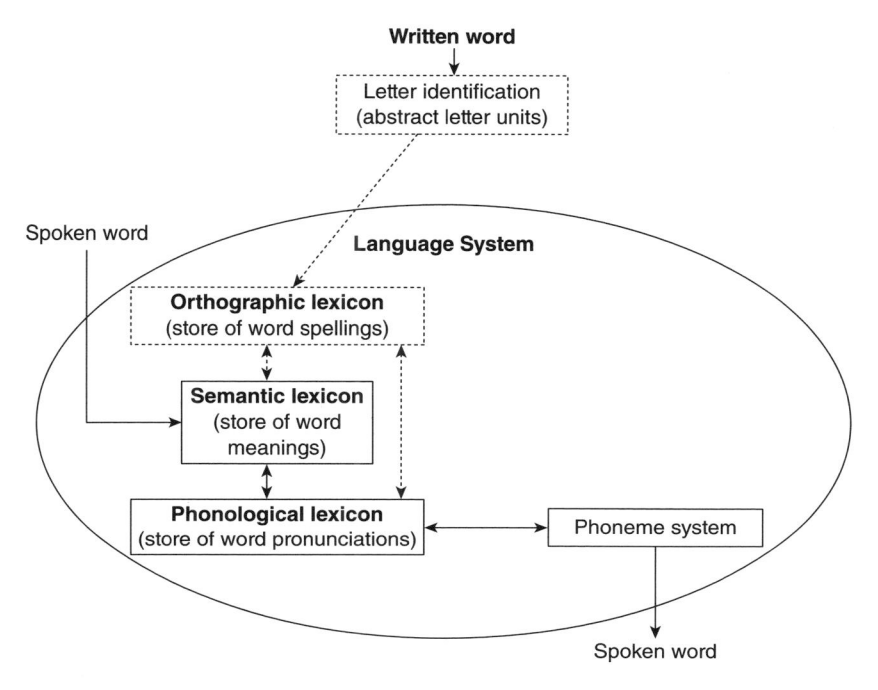

Figure 4.2 Lexical processes (dashed lines) added on to language system

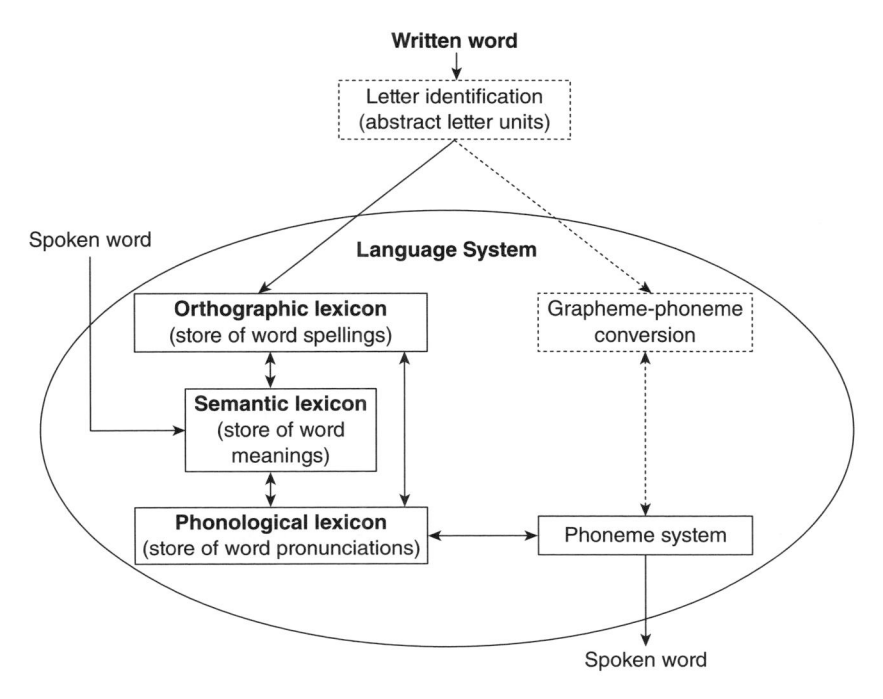

Figure 4.3 Phonological recoding processes (dashed lines) added on to language system

There is good evidence that skilled word recognition depends on processing each of the letters that compose each word (Pelli, Farell & Moore, 2003). And, as shown in Figures 4.2 and 4.3, letter identification is the entry point to the word reading system. Therefore, it is important that children learn to identify letters. What is known about how this learning is accomplished?

Learning about letters

The category of 'letter' and learning letter shapes

Some children enter school with little knowledge of letters. Stuart (1986) showed that, on school entry, some 5-year-olds confused letters and numbers, giving '2' as the name for S and Z; '9' for P; '4' for A; '7' for L. They also gave verbal descriptions: X named as 'like a cross' or O as 'round'. These responses indicate some confusion of the categories of letters, numbers and geometric shapes, and the need to isolate the concept of a letter. Five-year-olds tended to confuse visually similar letters (e.g. PBR, IJL, MW in upper case; bdpq, un, ft, mw, zx in lower case), indicating a need also for perceptual learning if children were to reliably identify and name letters. In Chapter 5 we suggest activities that might help such children distinguish letters from numbers, and pay close attention to letter features to develop finer discrimination of visually similar letters.

Letter names

Many children do have some knowledge of letters before they enter school and are taught to read. They tend to know more letter names than sounds (Arrow, 2007; Mason, 1980; McBride-Chang, 1999; Stuart, 1986), and can name more upper than lower case letters (Evans, Bell, Shaw, Moretti & Page, 2006; Stuart, 1986; Worden & Boettcher, 1990). Interestingly, Ellefson, Treiman and Kessler (2009), comparing letter knowledge of children in the USA and England, found the English children had better knowledge of the sounds than the names of letters, perhaps because of the renewed emphasis on phonics teaching for beginner readers in England. The Ellefson et al. study took place in only one English school, and thus may not reflect general practice in England, but it provides a stark contrast to the earlier findings of Stuart (1986). Children apparently learn what they are taught, which should both encourage us and urge us to caution – we must ensure we teach the things children need to know, in ways that do not distort their understanding of the bigger picture.

Letter-name knowledge on school entry is a powerful predictor of reading skills by the end of the first year in school (Bond & Dykstra, 1967; Share, Jorm, Maclean & Matthews, 1984; Walsh, Price & Gillingham, 1988). Some argue this relationship is causal, that children can use letter-name knowledge to read unfamiliar words (Treiman & Rodriguez, 1999; Treiman, Tincoff & Richmond-Welty, 1996), although simply training children to name letters does not improve early word reading skills (Jenkins, Bausell & Jenkins, 1972; Silberberg, Silberberg & Iverson, 1972), possibly because of the decontextualized nature of the training given (Wasik, 2001). Others argue letter-name knowledge predicts reading because it is an indicator of the richness of the home literacy environment (Share, Jorm, Maclean, Matthews & Waterman, 1983; Venezky, 1975), which does influence reading development (Burgess, Hecht & Lonigan, 2002).

Letter sounds

Why is letter-sound knowledge generally poorer than letter-name knowledge on school entry? Both parent and teacher practices may be responsible for this: parents and US kindergarten teachers tend to name letters for children rather than give their sounds; parents and kindergarten teachers teach children the alphabet song which names letters and use alphabet books where illustrations do not always represent the letter's sound (e.g. 'X' illustrated with a picture of a xylophone). So how do children acquire knowledge of letter sounds? There are three ways in which this learning is accomplished: children learn when they are explicitly taught letter-sound correspondences in school; children develop processes for working out the sounds of letters from their names; and children infer letter-sound correspondences from their repeated experience of reading words. As explained below, these last two ways of learning depend on children's phoneme awareness.

The role of phoneme awareness in letter-sound learning

We defined the phoneme in Chapter 1 – refer back to this if need be. Children who can tell you the first sound of a word (e.g. <CAT> begins with /k/) have achieved some degree of phoneme awareness, of understanding that spoken words contain phonemes. Children are said to be fully aware of phonemes when they can recite the sequence of all the phonemes in a word (e.g. <CAT> is /k/ /æ/ /t/).

Pre-school children are typically not aware of phonemes in words, but are more likely to be aware of the subsyllabic units of onset and rime (defined in Chapter 1). Rime awareness is likely achieved through early experience of nursery rhymes, and rhyming jingles, stories and games: Bryant, Bradley, MacLean and Crossland (1989) showed that 3-year-old children's knowledge of six common nursery rhymes was strongly related to their sensitivity to rhyme two years later. Experience of playing with rhyme might help induce some degree of phoneme awareness: to produce a rhyming word, you change the onset, the phoneme(s) that precede the rime. For example, /kæt/ rhymes with /hæt/ and /fæt/ and /flæt/. Pre-school children tend to treat onsets as a single unit: so, /flæt/ begins with /fl/, and /spæt/ with /sp/. But sometimes the onset is a single phoneme, providing an opportunity for children to learn to isolate and identify initial phonemes (/fæt/ begins with /f/, and /sæt/ with /s/). Untaught children first become able to identify initial phonemes, then final phonemes (Stanovich, Cunningham & Cramer, 1984; Stuart, 1990). Phonemes in the middle of the syllable or word, inevitably vowels, are the most difficult for young children to isolate. It is their position within the syllable rather than the fact that they are vowels that makes these phonemes difficult to isolate: vowel phonemes at the beginning (e.g. /æ/ in <AT>) or end (e.g. /eI/ in <SAY>) of syllables provide no such difficulty.

For letter names to serve as cues to letter sounds, children must be able to segment and identify the phonemes in the letter name: they must have some degree of phoneme awareness. Treiman, Tincoff, Rodriguez, Mouzaki and Francis (1998) showed children are more likely to be able to give the sound for a letter if the sound is heard in the letter name, especially if it is the first sound of the letter name (e.g. /b/ in B). Letter-name cues are less helpful where the sound is the final sound of the letter name, with some non-phonics taught children giving /ɛ/ as the sound of all those letters of the alphabet (F, L, M, N, S, X) whose names begin with /ɛ/ (Stuart, 1986). Letter names can mislead in other ways: children in Stuart's study gave /d/ as the sound for W, /w/ for Y, /eI/ for H, and /J/ for U. Early explicit teaching of letter sounds can forestall these problems.

Similarly, phoneme awareness is necessary for children to be able to infer letter-sound correspondences from their experience of reading words: we return to this later when we examine how children begin to set up an orthographic lexicon containing mental representations of the spelling patterns of words.

Clearly, there are initial inequalities in children's letter knowledge when they start being taught to read. As letter identification is essential to word reading, it is important that pre-school settings decrease these initial inequalities by introducing children to the shapes, names and sounds of letters. As phoneme awareness has been shown both to facilitate letter-sound learning and to reliably predict the successful development of word reading skills, it is also important that pre-school settings develop phonological and phoneme awareness by engaging children in suitable activities and games. In Chapter 5, we suggest some developmentally appropriate activities and games relevant to learning about letters and developing rhyme and phoneme awareness.

Forming abstract letter units

The letter identification system used by skilled readers has developed beyond a simple ability to recognize, name or give the sound for the visual forms of letters that we try to induce in beginner readers. Skilled readers have developed abstract letter units (ALUs) that enable the identification of each letter regardless of font (g *g* g **g** g g; G G *G* **G**) or case (g G). Thus, for efficient word recognition, children must also develop abstract letter units. There are currently two hypotheses of how these abstractions away from visual forms of letters are constructed. Jackson and Colheart (2001: 103) propose that knowing the names of both upper and lower case versions of the same letter allows children to abstract across letter case – the 'common letter name' hypothesis – but this does not explain how they also become able to abstract across different fonts, and nor do these authors provide any empirical evidence to support their view. Thompson and Johnston (2007) produced results inconsistent with the common letter-name hypothesis: children who were 100% accurate in naming both members of upper and lower case pairs of visually dissimilar letters (e.g. aA, bB, gG, eE, hH, rR, dD, nN) still read words containing those letters more accurately in lower case than upper case. This should not have been so if their letter-name knowledge had allowed them to form ALUs for those letters. Polk, Lacey, Nelson et al. (2009) offer a different hypothesis: children see different visual forms of the same letter written in the same words but different formats (e.g. giant Giant *Giant giant* Giant giant) and this repetition of different visual forms within similar contexts facilitates the formation of ALUs. This hypothesis has the advantage of enabling abstraction across both letter case and font, and Polk et al. (2009) also provide some supporting evidence. It is more plausible as a developmental account: the 'common letter name' hypothesis assumes that on school entry and before being taught to read children can already name all the upper and lower case letters. The evidence does not support this assumption: 5-year-olds can typically name 85%–90% of upper case and 65%–75% of lower case letters (Evans et al., 2006; Worden & Boettcher, 1990).

Polk et al.'s (2009) proposals have implications for teaching: if children are to develop ALUs, their reading should not be limited to experience of a single font or case. To develop an ALU for each of the letters 'g' and 'a', children would need experience of both of the most frequent printed versions of these letters ('g' as well as 'g', 'a' as well as 'a') and of their upper case equivalents (G and A). These implications could (and should) be investigated empirically.

Setting up an orthographic lexicon containing spelling patterns of known words

Learning to recognize words generally takes place alongside learning to identify letters. This raises the question, how can children set up a store of word spellings if they cannot identify letters? Ehri (1999, 2005) describes these children as 'pre-alphabetic'. She proposes they store 'selected visual attributes of words', which are not necessarily letters. Stuart (1986) asked 5-year-old beginning readers to read single words they were reading in school. One child, shown the word 'driver', read it as 'television'. On being asked how he knew it was 'television' he replied, 'Oh, that's easy. It's got a dot. Actually, television's got two dots, but I don't care'.

A study by Gough, Juel and Griffith (1992) further illustrates this lack of attention to letters. They taught pre-school children to read four words, presented singly on cards. One of the word cards had a large thumbprint in one corner. This was the first word the children mastered. When children's ability to read each word was later assessed, if this card was shown without the thumbprint, fewer than half the children could read the accompanying word. Yet if the card was shown with just the thumbprint and no word, nearly all children pronounced the word that had been taught on that card. The thumbprint was the most powerful cue to memory for the word!

And Masonheimer, Drum and Ehri (1984) demonstrated that children in the pre-alphabetic phase who appeared able to read 'environmental print' – signs that reappear often in the environment – were in fact paying no attention to the print.

They were 'reading' the environment – relying on contextual cues. Shown a picture of a McDonald's restaurant complete with name sign and familiar golden arches logo, children readily responded 'McDonald's'. When shown just the name sign complete with golden arches logo, many children still were able to respond 'McDonald's'. But, when shown the name sign without the golden arches logo, only six of over 200 children were able to respond 'McDonald's'. The other children were relying on the golden arches logo and paying no attention to the print. Only the six children who did respond 'McDonald's' when just shown the print had some knowledge of letter names. Perhaps some knowledge about letters is the impetus that causes children to begin to pay attention to print rather than to contextual cues in the environment in which the print is embedded.

It is clear from these examples that without attention to and storage of letters, no generalizable learning is taking place. Storing a dot or a thumbprint does not provide any reliable means of identifying a word on subsequent experience of it (think how many words have a dot or two! and how few can be identified by a thumbprint or a golden arch logo!). This again emphasizes the importance of letter knowledge.

The importance of letters and phoneme awareness in establishing entries in the orthographic lexicon

Once children can recognize letters, these are the elements of words that begin to be stored in the orthographic lexicon. Stuart and Coltheart (1988) report a longitudinal study of beginner readers in six Inner London primary schools, examining the growth of children's word reading skills over their first 18 months in school. The study took place in the early 1980s, when there was no systematic phonics teaching in any of the schools the children attended: at best, children were introduced to one letter and its sound each week.

Children were first assessed in their last term in nursery classes (aged 4–5 years) with further assessments at roughly two-month intervals throughout their first 18 months in school. The first assessment comprised a set of six phonological awareness tasks probing rhyme and phoneme awareness; these six tasks were repeated at the end of the children's first year in school.

Once children entered school, their reading records were regularly consulted to prepare lists of words appearing frequently in the books they had read, and which they might perhaps be expected to have learned and stored. Children were asked to read their sets of words presented singly on cards, on seven occasions over the course of the study, and on each occasion the children's error responses were recorded. In total, 3,836 different single word reading errors were recorded.

At the beginning of the second term in school, children's knowledge of names and sounds of upper and lower case letters was separately assessed; assessments were repeated on six subsequent occasions, at roughly two-month intervals. Finally, the children's word reading skills were assessed four times using the British Abilities Scale Single Word Reading Test (Elliott, Murray & Pearson, 1983).

Children's word reading errors were classified into groups, as shown in Table 4.1.

Table 4.1 Categories of word reading error

Error group	Identifying characteristic	e.g. target	e.g. error
1	partial/irrelevant information used	lorry play look rat-tat	a paper shop sister baby ice-cream
2	some shared letters, regardless of position or sequence	m*il*k *p*lay *s*aw *ma*de	*i*l*ke he*l*p *was* *a*m
3	shared beginning letter or letters	*c*at *post*card *y*ellow *w*ait	*c*ar *post*man *y*ou *w*hite
4	shared final letter or letters	ha*t* birth*day* read*ing* lorr*y*	ca*t* Sun*day* driv*ing* bo*y*
5	shared beginning and final letter or letters	*b*ir*d* *go*a*t* *bo*ot*s* *b*el*l*	*b*a*d* *go*t *bo*at*s* *b*al*l*

Stuart and Coltheart (1988) assumed children would bring to bear whatever relevant knowledge and skills they had on the problem of storing orthographic representations of written words, and their analyses of children's errors tend to support this view. Children who could give the name or sound of a few or no letters made large proportions of Group 1 errors with little or no overlap in shared letters between target and error. After a whole year in school they remained unable to demonstrate phoneme awareness and, after four terms in school, knew fewer than 13 letter sounds. They might have relied on dots, hyphens, golden arches and thumbprints to remember words, but letters? – No. These children consistently had the lowest word reading ages of children in the study, and when followed up at age 11 they were still poor readers (Stuart & Masterson, 1991).

In contrast, children who already knew the names and sounds of at least half the letters of the alphabet and had some degree of phoneme awareness made few Group 1 errors from the start, with the proportion of such errors falling close to zero as phoneme awareness and letter-sound knowledge improved.

All other error categories included letters shared between the target and the child's error response. Over time, both Group 2 and Group 4 errors became negatively correlated with reading age: the lower a child's reading age, the higher the proportion of these errors. So, storing letters haphazardly with no reference to their order or position within the word does not seem a fruitful strategy to ensure future recognition of the word, and nor does storing letters that appear only at the end of the word.

Group 3 and Group 5 errors that preserved initial letters or both initial and final letters were positively correlated with reading age: the higher a child's reading age, the higher the proportion of these errors. This suggests that children making good progress in developing word reading skills during the first 18 months in school are able to make this good progress, at least in part, by storing orthographic representations of words that include their boundary letters. But what enabled children to do this? Stuart and Coltheart (1988) proposed that a combination of phoneme awareness and letter-sound knowledge facilitated formation of this kind of representation.

In this view, beginner readers who are aware of the initial and final phonemes in spoken words (CAT begins with /k/ and ends with /t/) and who know the letters that correspond to those phonemes are able to inject a little logic into the essentially arbitrary links between written words and their meanings. That is, including boundary letters into their orthographic representations of words partially links these orthographic representations to their pronunciations stored in the phonological lexicon, as well as to their meanings stored in the semantic lexicon. And these logical links allow faster learning and storage of new written words, because learning is no longer completely arbitrary.

This is similar to Ehri's proposal (Ehri, 2005, 2014) of a phase of 'partial alphabetic' reading, during which beginners form connections between some of the letters in written words and some of the corresponding sounds in spoken words. However, Stuart and Coltheart's (1988) data cannot be used to support the existence of a partial alphabetic 'phase' in reading development. This is because they only analysed children's reading *errors*: the children also read many words with complete accuracy, and thus may be assumed to have formed complete rather than partial representations of such words. For example, reading <BEAT> as <BOAT> might indicate a partial representation B - - T for <BOAT>. <BEAT> would map equally as well as <BOAT> on to this partial representation, because it has the same boundary letters as exist in the already stored partial representation of <BOAT>. Children with a complete representation of all the letters in <BOAT> would be less likely to make this error.

The important similarity is that both Ehri and Stuart and Coltheart propose that phoneme awareness and letter-sound knowledge underpin the development of representations in the orthographic lexicon. This extends the role of phonological analysis and letter-sound knowledge beyond their universally accepted role in developing phonological recoding processes to a role also in the development of lexical processes.

Evidence that phoneme awareness and letter-sound knowledge underpin children's earliest orthographic representations

Stuart, Masterson and Dixon (2000) worked with absolute beginners (5-year-olds in their first term in Reception) to test whether phoneme awareness and letter-sound knowledge led to faster acquisition of new print vocabulary. They should, if phoneme awareness and knowledge of letter-sound correspondences underpin the development of orthographic representations.

Children were put into two groups: those who could identify the first phoneme in spoken words and point correctly to the letter that represented that phoneme (Group 1), and those who could not (Group 2). Pairs of children then repeatedly read two specially prepared books with the researcher, who did not know which group any child belonged to. The books contained 16 words printed in red, which none of the children could read at pre-test, and which they were told they should try to remember. Each word appeared four times in every book reading session. After nine sessions children had been exposed 36 times to the 16 target words. After 12, 24 and 36 exposures, children were asked to read the words presented singly on flashcards.

As predicted, children in Group 1 read significantly more words correctly than children in Group 2 on all three assessment occasions: their phoneme awareness and letter-sound knowledge had facilitated the learning of new print vocabulary. But, even after 36 exposures to each word, no child could read all 16 words: learning was much slower than anticipated, based on previous reports of rapid acquisition of new print vocabulary after as few as four exposures. In a second experiment, Stuart et al. (2000) showed that teaching 5-year-olds single words on flashcards was more efficient than teaching words through repeated reading in story context, with twice as many words learned in the flashcard condition, in half the time taken by the story condition. Better learning by phonemically aware children with some knowledge of letter sounds was also found in this second experiment.

More recently, Landi, Perfetti, Bolger et al. (2006) also conducted a study comparing children's learning of new print vocabulary when words are presented in context or in isolation. Working with 6- and 7-year-old children, Landi et al. also found better word learning when words were presented in isolation rather than context, extending the finding beyond the absolute beginner readers in Stuart et al.'s (2000) study.

There are lessons here for teaching. After 24 repetitions, children in Stuart et al.'s (2000) *faster* learning group could on average read 3/16 words accurately. Very few words were repeated as frequently as this in the books children read in school: between 0 and 14 words appeared more than 20 times in any individual child's word pool, with on average only three words repeated as often as this. When asked to read the most highly frequent words from their individual word pool, most children could read only one or two accurately. Therefore, in the first year of reading tuition, it is wise to ensure the books children are given to read introduce new print vocabulary gradually, and provide lots of repetition of this vocabulary. After all, children in this first year are not just learning to read: they are also learning what is involved in learning to read. If the books we expect them to read introduce large numbers of new words with no opportunity to consolidate learning, children may well conclude that learning words is not part of learning to read. But, as we have seen, it is!

In a further training study with 5-year-olds, Dixon, Stuart and Masterson (2002) investigated whether children's earliest orthographic representations would include the letters corresponding to the initial and final phonemes they could isolate in the spoken word. Three groups were formed: one group could identify both word initial and word final phonemes, the second could identify word initial but not word final phonemes, and the third group could not identify phonemes. The first two groups had equal knowledge of letter-sound correspondences, both knowing more than the third group.

All children were taught to read ten two-syllable words presented singly on flashcards, with four presentations of each word in each of nine teaching sessions (36 presentations of each word). All words were six letters long, and written in upper case, to abolish word length or word shape cues, and force attention on to the letters. So that children needed to attend to more than just the initial letter of each word, two words started with each of the five letters used in initial letter position. The prediction was that children who could identify both initial and final phonemes would learn the most words, and their orthographic representations would include the initial and final letters. Children who could identify only initial phonemes would learn fewer words, and their orthographic representations would contain only the initial letter, causing them to confuse words that began with the same initial letter. Children who were unable to identify phonemes and who also knew fewer letter-sound correspondences would find the learning task almost impossible.

As predicted, children who could identify phonemes in both word initial and word final positions learned the words more quickly than children in both of the other groups, learning all ten reliably after 24 presentations. Children who could not identify phonemes showed less learning than both other groups. But did the fast learners include initial and final letters in their orthographic representations, as predicted, with children who could only identify initial phonemes including only the initial letter?

Three post-tests examined this. First, children were asked to write each word, receiving one point for each correct initial and final letter. As predicted, children who could identify both initial and final phonemes were significantly more likely to include the initial and final letters in their spellings, with initial letters present in 91% of spellings, and final letters in 54%. Children who could identify only initial phonemes were equally likely to include the initial letter (85% of spellings), but were significantly less likely to include the final letter (8% of spellings). Children who could not identify phonemes in either position were significantly less likely than both of the other groups to include either initial or final letters (initial letters,

32% of spellings; final letters, 2%). Thus, children's orthographic representations tended to include the letters that represented phonemes in positions where the children could identify phonemes.

Next, children were presented with eight written versions of each word: one correct plus seven incorrect, formed by substituting or transposing initial, final or medial consonant letters. For example, children were shown the taught word SANDAL and its seven incorrect versions **P**ANDAL, SANDA**N**, SA**R**DAL, SAN**C**AL (letter substitutions), **N**A**S**DAL, SAN**L**A**D** and SA**DN**AL (letter transpositions). Children were asked, 'Which one of these do you think looks most like the word we've been learning?' The child picked one of the words, which was removed from the array, and they were asked if any of the other words could be 'SANDAL'. If they selected further words, each choice was noted and each word successively removed. This process continued until a child said, no, none of the remaining words was 'SANDAL', when the next word and its seven alternatives were presented.

Children who could identify both initial and final phonemes selected on average three items, including the correct word, significantly fewer than children in the other two groups, and, as predicted, were least likely to choose alternatives where word initial and final letters had been changed. Children in the other two groups selected on average five to six items, and their performance did not differ. Their comments suggested that they found the task very difficult: 'I know which ones say ROCKET, nearly all of them!' and 'But all of them look like TURNIP to me!' In both these groups, it was only a change of initial letter that prevented an item from being chosen, with children who could identify initial phonemes being less likely to choose items with the initial letter changed than children who could not identify phonemes.

Finally, children were presented with seven correct spellings of each word, and one version of each incorrect alternative, and asked to post each word they had been learning into a post box. Only children who could identify both initial and final phonemes performed non-randomly on this task. They were most likely to reject items where the initial letter had been changed, then items where the final letter had been changed, with letter changes in the middle of the word being hardest to reject, again supporting the hypothesis that for these children, initial and final letters were likely to be included in their orthographic representations.

So far, we have dealt with the earliest stages of development of orthographic representations, which link directly to their meaning(s) in the semantic lexicon, and whose development is facilitated by the ability to form partial links between boundary letters in the written word and boundary phonemes in the spoken word, i.e. direct partial links between entries in the orthographic lexicon and entries in the phonological lexicon. Both phoneme awareness and letter knowledge contribute to this earliest development. But how do these partial representations of words become filled out into complete representations that uniquely distinguish each written word the child knows? Current explanations of how this development occurs propose that it depends on the establishment of phonological recoding processes; we therefore first turn our attention to the development of phonological recoding processes, with a promise to return to the further development of orthographic representations later.

Development of phonological recoding processes

As we saw in Figure 4.3, the unique processing element that needs to be developed to enable phonological recoding is knowledge of the rules linking letters in written words to their corresponding sound segments in spoken words.

In Chapter 1, we saw that alphabetic languages use graphemes (letters and letter groups) to represent the phonemes in the spoken language. We saw how complex and inconsistent the grapheme-phoneme rule system for English is, making it harder to learn to read in English than in other languages with more regular and 'transparent' orthographies. However, as we show later, there is more regularity in English than is often assumed, and most children do eventually master the complexities of the rule system. What enables them to do this?

Phonological awareness, letter-sound knowledge and the development of phonological recoding processes

From the early 1970s, many research studies have investigated the relationship between phonological awareness and the successful development of word reading skills. Table 4.2 lists the major findings from this body of work.

Table 4.2 Findings from studies investigating the relationship of phonological awareness and word reading

Finding	Studies
Syllable awareness precedes phoneme awareness	Liberman, Shankweiler, Fischer & Carter (1974)
Rime awareness precedes phoneme awareness	Kirtley, Bryant, MacLean & Bradley (1989)
Phonological awareness instruction facilitates the development of word reading skills – but...	National Reading Panel Report (NICH & HD, 2000)
Phonological awareness instruction is significantly more effective when combined with phonic reading instruction	Ball & Blachman (1991) Bradley & Bryant (1983) Byrne & Fielding-Barnsley (1989) Cunningham (1990) Hatcher, Hulme & Ellis (1994) Iverson & Tunmer (1993)

Finding	Studies
Phoneme awareness is a better predictor of development of word reading skills than is rime awareness	Duncan, Seymour & Hill (1997) Hoien, Lundberg, Stanovich & Bjaalid (1995) Hulme, Hatcher, Nation, Brown, Adams & Stuart (2002) Muter, Hulme, Snowling & Taylor (1998)
Teaching phoneme segmentation and blending has the strongest effect on development of word reading skills	National Reading Panel Report (NICH & HD, 2000)
Phoneme awareness instruction at the start of phonic reading tuition is selectively beneficial for children at risk of reading delay	Hatcher, Hulme & Snowling (2004)

As shown in Table 4.2, studies carried out following the initial excitement at the finding that phonological awareness was related to the development of word reading skills have gradually refined its role. It is now generally accepted that *phoneme* awareness is responsible for this relationship, with phoneme segmentation and phoneme blending skills of prime importance. This is likely because, as shown earlier in this chapter, ability to segment phonemes in word initial and word final positions influences which letters are likely to be stored in children's early orthographic representations. And, phoneme blending is an essential component of phonological recoding: in skilled readers, this happens automatically within the phoneme system; however, beginner readers need to give conscious attention to blending.

In sum, the findings from this huge body of research suggest that explicit, systematic and structured phonics teaching needs to include three elements: teaching grapheme-phoneme correspondences, phoneme segmentation, and phoneme blending. However, beginners who are at risk of reading delay have been shown to benefit from additional phonological awareness instruction. How might such a risk be identified early on? Hatcher, Hulme, Miles et al. (2006) identified Year 1 children as at risk on the basis of an initial screening test in which children were asked to spell six words (ball, hut, star, fork, ten, jam, vest and crown). In Chapter 5 we suggest that close monitoring of children's earliest progress is essential to identify those at risk of reading delay.

What kind of phonics teaching best facilitates development of phonological recoding processes?

This continues to be a source of controversy in England, with some proposing children should first be taught rime correspondences (e.g. <-ANE> = - /eɪn/;< -IGHT> = -/aɪt/) rather than grapheme-phoneme correspondences (GPCs). Here, we outline two arguments that form the basis for this proposal. We return to studies comparing the relative effectiveness of large (onset-rime) versus small (GPC) unit phonics teaching in Chapter 5.

The first argument stems from the claim that vowel pronunciations in English monosyllables are to some extent determined by the final consonant (Treiman, Mullennix, Bijeljac-Babic & Richmond-Welty, 1995). Therefore, rime pronunciations are more consistent than grapheme pronunciations. For example, the vowel grapheme <EA> can be pronounced in several different ways (e.g. /i/ in <B**EA**D>; /ɛ/ in <H**EA**D>; /eɪ/ in< GR**EA**T>), but when <EA> is followed by a final <P> or <M>, it is always pronounced /i/ (try it!). Both children and adults are sensitive to consistency of rime pronunciation. Laxon, Masterson and Moran (1994) showed that 9- but not 7-year-olds were more likely to read words accurately if their rimes were consistently pronounced in the same way; and Bowey and Hansen (1994) showed that above-average first grade readers tested towards the end of first grade also showed this effect.

Second, children become aware of rimes earlier than they become aware of phonemes. Therefore, they might find it easier to learn to read words if teaching emphasized the onset-rime segments they are already aware of in spoken language (e.g. /m--eɪn/ for <MANE>; /s--aɪt/ for <SIGHT>). One of the earliest proponents of this view was Goswami (1986), who used a 'clue word' task to investigate children's ability to use analogy with the rime unit of the clue word to read unfamiliar target words. In this first experiment, she showed a 'clue' word such as 'BEAK' to children between the ages of 5 and 7 years. With the clue word in view, children attempted to read target words sharing a letter string which represented either the rime unit <-EAK> (e.g. <**PEAK**>), the body unit <BEA-> (e.g. <**BEAN**>), or had some letters in common with the clue word (e.g. <**BASK**>). Children were better able to read target words that shared a rime unit than words that shared a body unit with the clue word.

Subsequent investigations of children's ability to use rime units to read unfamiliar words by analogy have produced conflicting results that set some limits on the usefulness of this as a strategy for *beginning* readers. These limits are outlined in Table 4.3.

Table 4.3 Limitations on the usefulness of an early rime analogy strategy to read unfamiliar words

Limitation	Described by
When the clue word is no longer present, the advantage for targets sharing a rime unit with the clue word falls off sharply, casting doubt on beginner readers' ability to use this strategy *spontaneously* in their reading (clue words are not present in children's reading materials)	Muter, Snowling & Taylor (1994) Savage (1997) Savage & Stuart (1998)

Limitation	Described by
Use of GPCs to read unfamiliar words is apparent earlier than use of rime correspondences	Bowey & Hansen (1994) Bowey & Underwood (1996) Duncan, Seymour & Hill (2000)
Equivalent use of rime analogy is apparent when the clue word rime has a different spelling from the target (e.g. clue 'B**ONE**' → target '**M**OAN' is as effective as clue word 'B**ONE**' → target '**C**ONE'), and just hearing a clue word is as effective as seeing and hearing a clue word; both findings cast doubt on use of the *written rime* unit and suggest phonological priming of the target word	Bowey, Vaughn & Hansen (1998) Nation, Allen & Hulme (2001)
Equivalent advantage for clue words sharing medial vowel digraph with target words as for those sharing rime units (e.g. clue words BARK, DARK, PARK lead to equal likelihood of correct readings of H**AR**P (which shares vowel digraph) and L**ARK** (which shares rime))	Savage & Stuart (1998)

Two early studies (Bruck & Treiman, 1992; Wise, Olson & Treiman, 1990) investigating the effectiveness of teaching that emphasized rime correspondences found children did learn words more quickly when they were taught in this way, but they also forgot them more quickly: the effect was ephemeral, and had vanished a day later. However, later studies have produced more promising results, with Levy and Lysynchuk (1997) arguing that 'overlearning' (i.e. practice until complete mastery is achieved by all children) is more important than type of units taught.

What is certain is that children would have to be taught a large number of rime correspondences if reading words by rime analogy is to become a fruitful strategy for deciphering unfamiliar words. Ziegler and Goswami (2005) estimated that a child would need to learn approximately 600 rime correspondences to read the 3,000 most frequent monosyllables. Masterson, Stuart, Dixon and Lovejoy (2010) counted 87 different rime correspondences in the 300 most frequent monosyllabic CVC words in the Children's Printed Word Database, which contains words found in reading materials used in school by 5- to 9-year-olds. Fifty-five of these rime correspondences appeared only once in the 300 most frequent words. Thus it appears that using a rime analogy strategy in early reading relies upon learning a large number of orthographic patterns that may not be heavily represented in early reading materials.

Further support for this view comes from analyses of 3,066 monosyllabic words from an earlier word frequency list of children's early reading vocabulary (Stuart, Dixon, Masterson & Gray, 2003). Vousden, Ellefson, Solity and Chater (2011) showed that while knowledge of 237 grapheme-phoneme mappings would allow children to read the full set of 3,066 monosyllabic words, knowledge of almost five times as many onset and rime mappings (1,141) would be required to achieve a comparable degree of success.[1]

Vousden et al. (2011) exhaustively analysed this set of monosyllables to attempt to identify what kind of teaching strategy would most efficiently result in children having the necessary knowledge to read all 3,066 accurately. They concluded that, for children at the start of reading tuition (defined as children who have a reading vocabulary of up to 50 words) teaching whole words is the most efficient strategy – because neither grapheme-phoneme nor rime mappings are repeated sufficiently often in such a small set of words for there to be gains in efficiency from teaching these. As soon as reading vocabulary exceeds 50 words, teaching grapheme-phoneme correspondences offers the most efficient route to word reading. Knowledge of larger rime units is useful as this helps to resolve ambiguities of inconsistent vowel grapheme pronunciations.

But, is it necessary to teach children as many as the 237 grapheme-phoneme correspondences required to read the set of 3,066 monosyllables described above? Probably not: Vousden et al. (2011) estimated that knowledge of 118 GPCs would allow children to read 73% of these monosyllables. In an earlier paper, Shapiro and Solity (2008) taught children to read the 100 most frequent words as whole words: teaching (at least some of) the highest frequency words as whole words makes sense, as many of these are exception words that cannot be pronounced accurately by the application of grapheme-phoneme correspondence rules. Alongside this they taught children a relatively small subset of 64 grapheme-phoneme correspondence rules, teaching only the most frequent pronunciation of each grapheme. This combined approach was sufficient to bootstrap the acquisition of word reading skills in most children. From this starting point, most children are able to infer further rules from their reading experience. However, there is likely to be a small subset of children who cannot engage in inferential learning from reading experience, and who will continue to require systematic phonics teaching for much longer. We return to this in Chapter 9.

How phonological recoding processes contribute to acquisition of orthographic representations

We promised we would return to consider how the beginning reader's earliest partial orthographic representations become completed, so that each word is uniquely and fully represented in the orthographic lexicon. The currently most influential account of the development of orthographic representations is David Share's self-teaching hypothesis (Share, 1995). Share argued that development of phonological recoding

---

[1] The discrepancy between knowledge of 600 rime units estimated by Ziegler and Goswami (2005) to be necessary to reading their 3,000 most frequent monosyllables, and the estimate here of knowledge of 1,141 onset and rime units is due to the fact that Ziegler and Goswami did not take any account of the fact that children would also need knowledge of onset units.

processes allows children to work out the pronunciations of unfamiliar written words. In the early period of reading development, children's spoken vocabulary is much more extensive than their reading vocabulary. Therefore, it is likely that these pronunciations are already stored in the phonological lexicon, with links to their meanings: so, words successfully sounded and blended are likely to be understood as well as pronounced. Importantly, phonological recoding forces attention sequentially to each grapheme in the unfamiliar written word, and, according to Share's hypothesis, this close attention is what allows the complete orthographic representation of the word to be stored for future 'on sight' recognition.

The self-teaching hypothesis has been tested in a number of studies investigating orthographic learning. Children are asked to read short passages containing a few target nonwords, used as names for places, people and things. All nonword targets are pseudo-homophones, where a different spelling of the nonword would result in the same pronunciation (e.g. <FERB> could equally plausibly be spelt <FURB>; <WOAT> could equally plausibly be spelt <WOTE>). Studies differ in age of participating children (from first to fifth grade); whether reading is silent or aloud; whether children are trained to spell or to repeatedly read the targets; in the number of times the target nonword is read or spelled (from one to eight repetitions); and in time interval between training and post-testing (from one to 30 days delay). Three post-tests are usually implemented: children are asked to read aloud the target items embedded in lists that include non-target items, presented on computer; children are asked to spell the target items; and children are asked to select the target item from four items, which always include the nonword experienced in training as well as its pseudo-homophone counterpart (not experienced in training), and two control items having some orthographic overlap with targets. For example, if a child has experienced <FERB> during training, they might be asked to choose between <FERB> (target), <FURB< (pseudo-homophone), <FRUB> (transposed letter control) and <FELB> (letter substitution control).

Table 4.4 Findings from studies of orthographic learning

Findings	Studies
Orthographic learning has been demonstrated in children from grade 2 through grade 5, and is evident across different languages. *One study of first grade children found no evidence of orthographic learning in these young beginner readers (Share, 2004a)*	Bowey & Muller (2005) Cunningham (2006) Cunningham, Perry, Stanovich & Share (2002) de Jong, Bitter, van Setten & Marinus (2009) Kyte & Johnson (2006) Nation, Angell & Castles (2007) Ouellette & Fraser (2009) Ouellette & Tims (2014) Ricketts, Bishop, Pimperton & Nation (2011) Shahar-Yames & Share (2008) Share (1999, 2004a) Wang, Castles, Nickels & Nation (2011) Wang, Nickels, Nation & Castles (2013)

(Continued)

Table 4.4 (Continued)

Findings	Studies	
Orthographic learning is evident after silent reading as well as reading aloud	Bowey & Muller (2005) de Jong et al. (2009)	
Orthographic learning is evident after spelling practice as well as after repeated reading of targets	Shahar-Yames & Share (2008)	
Consistent finding across studies that orthographic learning increases as number of training exposures increases	Orthographic learning evident after a single exposure	Kyte & Johnson (2006) Share (1999, experiment 2)
	More learning evident with 8 than with 4 exposures	Bowey & Muller (2005)
	More learning evident with 4 than with 2 than with a single exposure, but some learning after single exposure	Nation et al. (2007)
	More learning evident with 6 than with 3 exposures	de Jong et al. (2009)
	More learning evident with 4 than 3 than 2 than 1 exposure	Wang et al. (2011)
Retention of orthographic learning over time: the most frequent finding is that, while there is evidence of orthographic learning up to delays of 30 days, more learning is evident at immediate than delayed post-test	More retention on immediate than 6 day delayed post-test	Bowey & Muller (2005)
	More retention on 1 day than 7 day delayed post-test	Nation et al. (2007)
	More retention on 1 day than 10 day delayed post-test	Wang et al. (2007)
	Equal retention after 1 day and 7 day delayed post-test	*Ouellette & Tims (2014)*
	Equal retention after 3, 7 and 30 day delayed post-tests	*Share (2004a)*

Overall findings about orthographic learning from these studies are shown in Table 4.4.

Thus, there is much evidence broadly supporting Share's self-teaching hypothesis. However, the strong version of this hypothesis predicts children should only be able to form orthographic representations of unfamiliar words *that they have succeeded in decoding using phonic rules*. Findings from studies examining individual children's performance on items that were or were not successfully decoded during training provide only weak and inconsistent evidence for the strong version.

Cunningham, Perry, Stanovich and Share (2002) found a significant (0.52) correlation between correct decoding and orthographic learning. Wang, Nickels, Nation and Castles (2013) found that formation of orthographic representations only depended on successful decoding of the target item during training for items with irregular spellings. In contrast, Nation, Angell and Castles (2007) found no item-by-item effect of successful decoding on orthographic learning. As with so much else, more research is needed before definitive conclusions can be drawn.

Savage and Stuart (2006) provide an alternative account of how children's early partial orthographic representations might become completed. Stuart and Coltheart (1988) had demonstrated that errors of children with good word reading skills at the end of the first year in school mostly preserved the boundary letters of the target word. The existence of 'boundary letter' partial orthographic representations has also been shown by Savage, Stuart and Hill (2001): 6- and 7-year-olds who scored highest on tests of single word reading tended to make errors that included the letters representing the boundary phonemes of the target word (e.g. <B**O**AT> for <B**E**AT>). Savage et al. (2001) called these errors 'scaffolding errors'. On re-assessing the children's word reading skills two years later, Savage et al. found that, with word reading ability at age 6 controlled, 'scaffolding errors' at age 6 were significantly and positively associated with word reading ability at age 8. So, partially specified representations are a good thing, but how do they become completed? In children's partially specified, boundary-letter orthographic representations, it is letters representing the vowel that remain unrepresented. Savage and Stuart (1998) used the clue word task to show that children were equally well able to read targets sharing the medial vowel digraph spelling with the clue word as those that shared the rime spelling (e.g. the <**AR**> in the clue word <H**AR**K> enabled reading of the target <F**AR**M> as effectively as the <**ARK**> in the clue word <H**ARK**> enabled reading of the target <L**ARK**>). Children's ability to use vowel digraph information from clue words was associated both with the degree to which they made scaffolding errors in single word reading and with their later word reading ability.

Savage and Stuart (2006) therefore proposed that, since children can develop partially specified orthographic representations containing boundary letters, *and* can use 'clue word' information about vowel digraph pronunciations to read unfamiliar target words, they might also be able to use information about vowel digraph pronunciations available in the words they are exposed to in the texts they read to fill out their partially specified ('scaffolded') orthographic representations. Stuart, Masterson, Dixon and Quinlan (1999) had already shown that 6- and 7-year-old children not taught any grapheme-phoneme correspondences for vowel digraphs were able accurately to read nonwords containing vowel digraphs they had experienced frequently in the books they read at school. This confirms children can learn pronunciations for vowel digraphs from their experience of reading.

In essence, this theory proposes that early ability to identify phonemes in spoken words, combined with knowledge of some letter-sound correspondences, allows children to form partial representations of words in the orthographic lexicon;

representations that include boundary letters. As these orthographic representations are based in the child's awareness of boundary phonemes, the words <BOAT>, <BEAT>, <BAT>, and <BOOT> will all have the same orthographic representation, <B_T>. Exposure to each word in reading material at an appropriate level of difficulty will enable the child to fill in the relevant orthography for the vowel digraph: context provides sufficient information for the child to select the relevant word from multiple candidates activated in the orthographic lexicon. So, for example, repeated exposure to <BOAT> in contexts that bias towards one of the words associated with the <B_T> orthographic representation ('I can sail my b..t'; 'The b..t went out to sea') will eventually allow incorporation of the appropriate vowel digraph spelling to complete the representation of <BOAT> and thus distinguish it from <BEAT>, <BAT>, <BOOT>, etc.

But the child will also anticipate that other words with these same boundary phonemes (e.g. /bait/) should map on to this <B_T> orthographic representation – but they don't necessarily (e.g. <BITE>). Thus, seeing and reading <BITE> in a suitably disambiguating context will strike a discordant note ('Oh, that's not what I expected, there should be a <T> at the end'), and noticing such discrepancies will motivate the child to revise their pre-existing orthographic representation.

We like this alternative view of ways in which partial orthographic representations become fully specified in the orthographic lexicon (naturally, because we were involved in its development!), but it remains at present a speculative account. Further experimental work is required to test whether the theory can ever be more than speculation.

Influences of oral vocabulary on the development of orthographic representations

Recent research suggests that children's pre-existing oral vocabulary also influences the development of orthographic representations: children with better oral vocabularies tend to be more proficient word readers (Nation & Snowling, 2004; Ouellette & Fraser, 2009; Ricketts, Nation & Bishop, 2007). This is not surprising, given that words in the orthographic lexicon have to be linked to their meanings in the semantic lexicon as well as to their pronunciations in the phonological lexicon. It should be easier to learn words unfamiliar in their printed form if these are already in a child's oral vocabulary, because the meaning and pronunciation are already there to be linked to: the child does not have to learn an unfamiliar printed form together with a new meaning and a new pronunciation, but merely to link the unfamiliar printed form to its existing meaning and pronunciation.

Knowing the meanings and pronunciations of words should contribute most to reading exception words: as we saw in Chapter 3, exception words (which do not conform to grapheme-phoneme correspondence rules) can only be read accurately by lexical processes, and so depend on the existence of a stored representation in the orthographic lexicon. There is some evidence that this is the case, at least in older children. Bowey and Rutherford (2007, working with 13-year-olds) and Goff, Pratt and Ong (2005, working with 10-year-olds) found that oral vocabulary was most strongly linked to exception word reading proficiency.

Recent studies have begun to investigate the influence of semantic knowledge on orthographic learning. All such studies to date have used the orthographic learning paradigm described above, in which children read brief passages containing target nonwords. However, in studies of the influence of vocabulary knowledge on orthographic learning, children are provided with short verbal descriptions and sometimes pictures of the people and objects represented by each target nonword, to encourage them to store meanings. In some studies, children are also told how each nonword is pronounced; in others they are left to work out the pronunciation for themselves (as they are in studies investigating the influences of phonological recoding on orthographic learning). These two manipulations ensure children have some semantic knowledge for each target nonword, as well as phonological knowledge about their pronunciations, either given or self-generated.

Overall findings from studies exploring the relative contributions of knowing the phonology of a target nonword and being given a meaning for the target nonword on the likelihood of the child forming a complete orthographic representation of the target are shown in Table 4.5. It can be seen that, to date, there is little evidence of a semantic influence on the storage of orthographic representations; knowing the phonological form of a word, however, does influence the ease with which its orthographic form is learned.

Table 4.5 Influence of pre-existing semantic and phonological representations on the formation of orthographic representations

Findings	Studies
Equal orthographic learning whether targets are presented in context or singly with no context: suggesting that the semantic information provided by the context does not facilitate learning	Nation, Angell & Castles (2007)
No additional benefit to orthographic learning from knowledge of semantics once knowledge of phonology is taken into account	Nation & Cocksey (2009)
No additional benefit to orthographic learning from being taught either specific or general meanings for nonwords (but provision of specific meaning → better learning of word *meaning* than provision of general meaning)	Ricketts, Bishop, Pimperton & Nation (2011)

(Continued)

Table 4.5 (Continued)

Findings	Studies
No additional benefit to orthographic learning from being taught meanings for nonwords over being taught phonology of nonwords	Duff & Hulme (2012), Experiment 2 McKague, Pratt & Johnston (2001)
Providing 9-year-olds with definitions and illustrated verbal descriptions for target nonwords led to improved orthographic learning, but only when learning was tested through a recognition task rather than a spelling task	Ouellette & Fraser (2009)
Better learning of imageable than non-imageable words after 3–6 learning trials, and performance on defining the words was significantly related to orthographic learning. However, this benefit from a semantic factor did not selectively favour exception word reading	Duff & Hulme (2012), Experiment 1

Closing words

We have come to the end of our attempt to convey some of the complexities involved in learning to read written words, and to outline recent research studies that contribute to understanding how these complex processes develop. If nothing else, this chapter illustrates just how complex the Simple View of Reading is. The two interacting dimensions of word reading skills and language comprehension processes can be portrayed simply in the form of a cross, and this serves well to remind us that there can be no comprehension of written text without the ability to read the words on the page, but that being able to read the words on the page does not guarantee the ability to comprehend the written text.

Unfortunately, it is not so easy to portray the development of skill in each dimension with such simplicity, and it is the complexity of processes involved in each dimension that those of us involved in teaching children to read need to know about and understand. We hope very much that this chapter has contributed to your knowledge and understanding of the complex processes involved in visual word recognition – in learning to read the words on the page.

5
Teaching word reading skills

Summary

In Chapter 4, we looked at the processes children need to develop to become fluent and accurate word readers, and at some of the factors intrinsic to word reading that are thought to facilitate the development of these processes. In this chapter, you will learn about research evidence relevant to teaching children to read words, as a guide towards what might currently be considered best practice in teaching word reading skills. Understanding the evidence will enable you to adapt your teaching to give children the best chance of acquiring fluent and accurate word reading skills as quickly and easily as possible.

Preamble

In teaching, things are never simple. That's why we have already devoted four clearly structured chapters to presenting reliable current knowledge about four things: writing systems and ways in which they represent spoken words; the place of word reading within the framework of reading for meaning; the processes known to be involved in word reading, and the ways in which these processes develop.

In providing a clear structure for each of these chapters, we have separated processes that are never separate in the act of reading, to consider in isolation what is known of each process. Teachers do not have the luxury of teaching children one aspect of reading in isolation from all the others: nor should they, because different kinds of knowledge and understanding develop in tandem and influence each other. But a major motivation for writing this book is our firm belief that if teachers have a clear idea of what is involved in each of the reading processes children need to develop, this will improve their ability to teach children efficiently and effectively – because they will feel more confident that they know what to teach, and *why they need to teach it*. Thus it is important, while reading this present chapter, to keep in mind the knowledge about reading and its development set out in previous chapters.

It is obviously not enough simply to know the kinds of teaching practices shown to be effective in teaching children to read the words on the page. We also need to know the circumstances in which these practices have been effective. So, we will need to weave in matters of practical implementation: what is the place of whole class, small group and individual teaching? To what extent and in what circumstances can teaching be delivered effectively by teaching assistants? To what extent can and should ongoing assessment of children's progress be embedded within and continually inform teaching?

We start by presenting the kinds of activities and teaching that research studies have shown help develop the twin foundations of word reading skills (phoneme awareness and alphabet knowledge) and then continue with the kinds of activities and teaching that research studies have shown foster development of the fluent and accurate word reading ability necessary (but not sufficient) for reading comprehension.

Establishing solid foundations for the development of word reading processes: the Early Years Foundation Stage

The Early Years Foundation Stage (EYFS) in England 'sets the statutory standards that all early years providers must meet'. It extends from birth to age 5. We are interested here in the EYFS as it applies to 4- and 5-year-olds and, in particular, in the Early Learning Goal for Reading at the end of the EYFS (which coincides with the end of the Reception year).

This Early Learning Goal for reading states:

> Children read and understand simple sentences. They use phonic knowledge to decode regular words and read them aloud accurately. They also read some common irregular words. They demonstrate an understanding when talking with others about what they have read. (Early Years Foundation Stage Profile Handbook, 2014: 24)[1]

At the end of the EYFS, children are aged between 5 and 6 years. They should be able to use phonics to read regular words accurately, and to read 'on sight' some common irregular words that cannot be read accurately by applying phonic rules. This implies that they will have begun to develop both the phonological recoding processes and the lexical processes employed by skilled readers. However, the definition of these beginnings is vague: should 5-year-olds be able to use phonic rules to read long regular words like LEMONADE or CONTINENT? Or will reading

---

[1]There are similarities between suggested word reading outcomes for the end of the EYFS and those described for the end of kindergarten (= end of Year 1 in England) by the US Common Core Standards. For example, by the end of kindergarten, children should 'Know and apply grade-level phonics and word analysis skills in decoding words' and 'Read common high frequency words by sight (e.g., the, of, to you, she, my, is, are, does)'.

short regular words like CAT and DOG suffice? What does 'common' mean in the phrase 'common irregular words'? We interpret 'common' to mean words children come across frequently in their reading, but which words are these, and how many times must a child see a word before it can be deemed to be a 'common' word?

These are non-trivial questions: the way we answer them has the power to radically change the nature of the goal, and thus affect what we need to teach children of this age in order to achieve the goal. Fortunately, the goal is specified in more detail in the 'Letters and Sounds' phonics programme, published in 2007 by the erstwhile Department for Children, Schools and Families (DCSF) in response to the Rose Review (Rose, 2006). We chose this programme to further specify the nature of the EYFS reading goal, as it is freely downloadable – currently from www.gov.uk/government/publications/**letters-and-sounds**.

Table 5.1 Grapheme-phoneme correspondences taught by the end of the EYFS in 'Letters and Sounds'

grapheme	phoneme	pronounced as in:	grapheme	phoneme	pronounced as in:
s	/s/	sit	w	/w/	win
a	/æ/	apple	x	/ks/	fox
t	/t/	tin	y	/j/	yes
p	/p/	pig	z	/z/	zip
i	/ɪ/	ill	zz	/z/	buzz
n	/n/	net	qu	/kw/	queen
m	/m/	mud	ch	/tʃ/	chip
d	/d/	dog	sh	/ʃ/	shop
g	/g/	got	th	/θ/	thin
o	/ɒ/	orange	th	/ð/	then
c	/k/	cat	ng	/ŋ/	ring
k	/k/	king	ai	/eɪ/	rain
ck	/k/	back	ee	/i/	feet
e	/ɛ/	egg	igh	/aɪ/	night
u	/ʌ/	up	oa	/əʊ/	boat
r	/r/	rat	oo	/ʊ/	look
h	/h/	house	oo	/u/	boot
b	/b/	bat	ar	/ɑː/	farm
f	/f/	fat	or	/ɔ/	corn
ff	/f/	puff	ur	/ɜ/	hurt
l	/l/	love	ow	/aʊ/	cow
ll	/l/	ball	oi	/ɔɪ/	coin
ss	/s/	class	ear	/iə/	hear
j	/dʒ/	jam	air	/ɛə/	fair
v	/v/	vet	er	/ɜ/	her

Table 5.2 Words to be taught by the end of the EYFS (containing irregular GPCs or GPCs not yet taught)

the	me	are	there
to	be	said	little
go	was	so	one
no	my	have	do
I	you	like	when
he	they	some	out
she	her	come	what
we	all	were	

It states that by the end of the EYFS, children should have been taught:

- the grapheme-phoneme correspondences shown in Table 5.1
- to blend and segment VC, CVC, CCVC and CVCC words and nonwords
- to read on sight the words shown in Table 5.2

We might therefore interpret the word-reading goal for children taught using the Letters and Sounds materials as:

> Children should be able to use phonological recoding processes to read any VC, CVC, CCVC or CVCC word or nonword containing any of the 50 grapheme-phoneme correspondences they have been taught. Children should have stored orthographic representations of the 31 words they have been taught to read on sight.

This can be modified for any group of EYFS children by considering what they have been taught in the school's chosen phonics programme: major phonics programmes currently used in UK schools differ but slightly in the order in which grapheme-phoneme correspondences are taught.

What kinds of knowledge and skill do we need to teach to ensure children meet these word-reading goals? What are the best ways of teaching this knowledge and these skills? A recent meta-analysis in the USA (National Early Literacy Panel (NELP), 2008) reviewed pre-school and kindergarten studies. Most focused on developing children's knowledge and understanding of the alphabetic principle – the idea that spoken words are composed of sequences of speech sounds, and those sequences of speech sounds are represented in written words by sequences of letters. Almost all were carried out with small groups of children or on a one-to-one basis, and included some kind of phonological awareness training. These 'code-focused' interventions had moderate to large effects on reading, spelling, phonological awareness and alphabet knowledge. Intervention was equally effective for younger (pre-school) and older (kindergarten) children. Teaching was equally effective in improving phonological awareness regardless of children's starting levels of phonological awareness, but the impact on alphabet knowledge was greater for children with lower levels of knowledge at the start – there is a limited set of 26 letters to learn about, so children with initial low levels of knowledge have more scope to show improvement.

Comparison of children's learning across different interventions mainly provided further evidence that children learn what they are taught. The most important finding (also reported for school-age children in Chapter 4) was that only interventions including *both* phonological awareness *and* print knowledge, either as alphabet activities or as phonics teaching, had a significant effect on subsequent word reading ability.

These studies were all published before 2003. We report below on findings from studies, mostly published since then, that provide more detailed guidelines to content and activities most likely to be effective in promoting development of the twin foundations of word reading skills: alphabet knowledge and phoneme awareness. We introduce this as a series of questions. A word of caution: almost all these studies were carried out in the USA, where teaching practices differ from those in the UK. It is usual practice in the USA to teach upper case letters and to teach letter names first, whereas in the UK it is usual practice to teach lower case letters and, increasingly, to teach letter sounds first. Nonetheless, most findings can be applied to UK as well as US teaching practice. Where research studies include details of the content of effective activities and ways in which children were engaged in them, we describe these activities in detail.

When should we start to introduce activities to develop letter knowledge?

The results of the NELP meta-analysis show that 3 years old is not too young to start playing with letters: in many cases parents begin to do this before the age of 3. For example, Robins, Treiman and Rosales (2014) report on parent–child conversations about letters. Before the age of 3, parents talked about the colour, size, shape or material of letters. After age 3, both parents and children were more likely to talk about the shape of the letters. These conversations occurred incidentally during everyday interactions as well as during picture book sharing. Where incidental learning about letters is not fostered at home, suitably playful activities to promote learning about letters need to be explicitly provided in early years settings. A recent study (Duncan, Castro, Defior et al., 2013) comparing development of alphabet knowledge and phonological awareness in children from six European countries and languages found that, on school entry, English children were among the highest scorers on tasks assessing letter knowledge, despite being one year younger than children from the other countries. Their earlier start had not adversely affected the development of their letter knowledge.

Are some letters easier to learn than others – and, what makes a letter easy to learn?

Some letters are indeed easier to learn than others. Huang, Tortorelli and Invernizzi (2014) examined factors associated with letter-sound knowledge at the start of kindergarten (equivalent of Year 1 in England) in a sample of 1,197 5-year-old children from disadvantaged backgrounds. They predicted that several factors would affect the likelihood of a child knowing a particular letter sound. These factors, and studies showing their effect on letter-sound learning, are shown in Table 5.3.

Table 5.3 Factors affecting letter-sound knowledge in young children

Factor	Description	Studies finding an effect on letter-sound learning
Letter is first letter of child's first name	This is known as the 'Own name advantage': children are more likely to know the name of the first letter of their own first name than any other letter	Justice, Pence, Bowles & Wiggins (2006) Treiman & Kessler (2003)
Child's letter-name knowledge	Letter names may help children learn letter sounds by giving them a stable referent for an abstract concept that includes many parts (name, sound, upper and lower case, different fonts). Knowing the letter's name allows children to store all these pieces of information together under a single label	Evans, Bell, Shaw, Moretti & Page (2006) McBride-Chang (1999) Share (2004b) Treiman & Broderick (1998)
Position of letter in the alphabet	Sounds of letters that occur early in the alphabet are more likely to be known	McBride-Chang (1999)
Frequency of occurrence of letter	Sounds of letters that occur frequently are more likely to be known	Treiman, Kessler & Pollo (2006)
Letter-name structure	Letter sounds are more likely to be known if the name of the letter contains its sound, especially as its first sound (e.g. B /b/, D /d/, P /p/, T /t/, etc.)	Evans et al. (2006) Kim, Petscher, Foorman & Zhou (2010) McBride-Chang (1999) Piasta & Wagner (2010) Share (2004b) Treiman & Broderick (1998)
Letter-sound ambiguity	Letters that can represent more than one sound at the beginning of a word (cat and circle; apple and ape), or that share beginning sounds with other letters (C and K for /k/) are less likely to be known	Scanlon, Anderson & Sweeney (2010)
Phonological awareness	Phonological awareness may contribute to letter-sound knowledge by making letter sounds more salient for children and thus easier to remember and to associate with letter forms	Evans et al. (2006) Foy & Mann (2006)

All factors contributed to the likelihood of children knowing a letter sound as they start kindergarten. The guidelines for effective teaching practice are not entirely clear from this overview, and several different orders of the relative difficulty of learning letter names have been published. For example, Phillips, Piasta, Anthony, Lonigan and Francis (2012) asked a sample of 1,333 under-6-year-olds in Florida and Texas to name upper case letters. O was the letter most likely to be named correctly (86% of children), followed by B (81%) and A (80%), then (in descending order) C, S, P, E, T, H, R, K, M, X, D, L, F, Z, Y, J, G, N, I, Q, W (58%), U (54%) and V (49%). Teaching implications again are not clear, with some advocating starting with easier letters, and others advocating starting with harder letters, on the grounds these will require more teaching time.

Nevertheless, a few tentative suggestions may be warranted. It seems sensible first to introduce young children to letters through activities connected to letters in their own name and the names of other children in the group, which is probably already part of best practice in early years settings. It would also be sensible to be aware that prior letter-name knowledge can influence letter-sound knowledge, particularly where letter names contain their sounds, and especially where the letter name begins with its sound. However, as we saw in Chapter 4, letter-name knowledge is not always beneficial to the acquisition of *accurate* letter-sound knowledge: some children infer that the first sound of the letter name is *always* the letter-sound correspondence for that letter, and consequently wrongly give /ɛ/ as the sound for F, L, M, N, and S, /w/ for Y, and /d/ for W. We suggested that early teaching of letter-sound correspondences, as currently practised in England, could forestall these tendencies to overgeneralize.

We also outlined the different types of learning involved in developing knowledge of all the different aspects of letters: the category they belong to (letters or numbers?), their form in upper and lower case and in different fonts, their names, the sounds they represent, how they are written. This learning culminates eventually (but we know not how!) in the establishment of *abstract letter units* involved in both lexical and phonological recoding processes, in both routes to word reading. What do we know about the best ways of teaching children all these different aspects of letters? There is now some research evidence from well-designed studies to help answer these questions.

How can we help children distinguish letters from numbers?

The difficulty some young children demonstrate in understanding which symbols belong to the category of letters and which to the category of numbers has not been explored in the research literature. The only reference we found to any kind of difficulty in this area was in a paper by Castles, Coltheart, Wilson, Valpied and Wedgwood (2009). They tested children's letter awareness, using a letter/non-letter discrimination task. They originally intended to use numbers as the non-letters, but had to abandon this as the 3- to 5-year-olds in their study found it too confusing. Instead, Castles et al. (2009) formed a non-letter category using other typewriter symbols (£, %, &, @, etc.). The suggestions we make in the activity below are not solidly based in research evidence, but probably worth trying.

Activities to help children distinguish letters from numbers

Make letter cards for each letter of the alphabet, in upper and lower case forms (or use magnetic letters – see focusonphonics.co.uk for suitable resources).

Start with letters that begin the first names of children in your class, in upper and lower case. Show them one by one to the class. For upper case letters, ask 'Whose name starts with this letter? Who knows what this letter is?' For lower case letters, ask 'Who has this letter in their name? Who knows what this letter is?'

Go through the letters two or three times, for a few minutes two or three times in the week. Notice which children respond to more than their own first name letter.

Gradually increase the letters until you have shown all 26 letters, repeating the letter activities outlined above. When no child lays claim to a letter, suggest names beginning with/containing that letter and ask if the children know anybody with that name.

Show the children each upper case letter and ask them to find the matching lower case letter, and vice versa.

Make a mixed set of letters and numbers. Show each in turn and ask the children, 'Is this a letter?' If it is and they say 'Yes', agree: 'Yes, this is one of the letters we've been learning – who can tell me what this letter is?' If it isn't and they say it is, say, 'Oh, I don't remember learning this one – I think this one is a number, not a letter. It's number (8).'

Notice which children are secure in rejecting the numbers.

For children who are not secure, repeat the letter-learning activities in small groups. Make a letter grid, and ask the children in the group to match letters to the same letter on the letter grid. If you have some number cards in the pile, they will not be able to find a match. When no match can be found, explain 'We can't find a letter for that one, because it's a number, not a letter. It's number (7).'

Mix up letters and numbers and ask the children to sort them into numbers and letters. For error-free learning, prepare two large cards, one with the numbers written on it, and the other with the letters written on it. Children place their letter or number beside the appropriate card.

Et cetera! We're sure you are considerably more creative in inventing enjoyable activities than we are …

Which should we teach first: upper or lower case letters?

Studies investigating children's alphabet knowledge tend to concentrate on upper case letters, probably because (a) children entering kindergarten know more upper than lower case letters, so teaching upper case builds more on what they already know; (b) children are most likely to recognize the first letter of their own name, which is always written in upper case; (c) children in US kindergartens are taught to both name and write letters, and upper case letters are easier to write, partly because they are all the same size; (d) upper case letters are less confusable than lower case letters (Ehri & Roberts, 2006; Popp, 1964). Sebastian Wren, who co-ordinates a centre at the University of Texas at Austin which provides high-quality reading interventions, suggests the letter sorting activity shown below for children who cannot quickly and accurately identify all of the letters of the alphabet in both upper and lower case.

Activities to help children discriminate visually similar letters

Put letter tiles or letter cutouts in a pile and ask the children to sort them by some salient feature (e.g. put all of the letters with straight lines in one pile and all the ones with curves in another).

Then ask them to sort by another salient feature (e.g. diagonal lines versus lines that go up and down).

Then by another and another feature, until the children are looking at small sets of two to four letters with similar, confusable features, but which differ in important ways (e.g. O and Q or b, d, p and q).

When the children can see confusing letters side by side, they can focus on the salient features that make those confusing letters distinct.

It is also likely that teaching children to form letters correctly will help them to discriminate between similar letters, especially if you encourage them to talk through the letter formation as they write. The letter d then becomes associated with the jingle, 'round in a circle up and down', while the letter b becomes associated with, 'down halfway up and around.'

Eventually, children must learn to recognize and name letters in both cases, which is one step towards developing the abstract letter units on which skilled word reading depends. We have found no evidence that teaching both upper and lower case forms simultaneously, or that teaching upper before lower case (or vice versa) adversely impacts on children's learning. It is usual practice to use lower case letters when teaching children letter sounds, and it is likely helpful for children to be familiar with lower case letter forms for this purpose. However, if we follow advice to start teaching with the letter children are most likely to be familiar with, the first letter of their own first name, this is inevitably an upper case letter.

What should we teach first: names or sounds?

Young children tend to know more letter names than letter sounds. This probably links to practices at home and in early years settings that encourage children to learn to sing the alphabet song, which names letters. However, young children with good letter-name knowledge are more able to give the sounds of letters too (Burgess & Lonigan, 1998; Worden & Boettcher, 1990), indicating that learning both letter names and letter sounds does not confuse children, as is sometimes suggested (McGuiness, 2004). We have presented evidence that letter-name knowledge facilitates the development of letter-sound knowledge, particularly for sounds whose corresponding letter starts with the sound it represents (e.g. B /b/, D /d/, etc.). There is perhaps a growing consensus that teaching letter names and letter sounds simultaneously has more positive than negative effects on children's acquisition of letter knowledge. Piasta, Purpura and Wagner (2010) found that teaching the name and sound of letters simultaneously tended to be more effective in promoting learning. They recommend that early childhood educators should teach both together. Piasta and Wagner (2010) give detailed examples of the content and delivery of this kind of training; one such example is shown next.

Activities to introduce letter names and sounds together

Give each child an illustrated alphabet card. Place piles of magnetic letters in front of the children. Show them 'B' and put this on the magnetic board. 'This is letter B. It makes the sound /b/. Everyone find a letter B from the pile. Show me your letter. What is it called?'

'Everyone put your finger on letter B on your alphabet card. Watch me trace my letter B.' Trace the letter B on the flashcard. 'Use your finger to trace the letter B on your card.'

'The letter B says /b/. Let me hear you say /b/. What picture is above the letter B on your cards [bear]? That's right, bear' [or 'That's a bear']. Place the word Bear on the magnetic board. 'Bear starts with the /b/ sound. B–ear [emphasize /b/ sound]. Bear starts with the letter B, see?' Point to B at the beginning of the word. 'Let me hear you say /b/ for bear.'

Take out stack of B picture cards [butterfly, balloons, banana, baby, basket, ball, bells, books]. 'Let's play a game. What is this?' Help the children to name each picture as you place it in front of them. Say to each child individually: 'Show me one that starts with the /b/ sound. That's right, _____ starts with the /b/ sound because it starts with the letter B. Let me hear you say /b/ for _____.' Put the written word on the magnetic board. 'Show me the letter B in the word _____. Let me hear you say B. Put your B on the B in the word _____.' Help the child to cover the letter in the written word with his or her magnetic letter. Repeat the picture card game for each child in the group.

After each child has had a turn, hold each of the remaining B picture cards one at a time. 'This is _____. Does it start with the /b/ sound? Yes it does.' Put the written word on the magnetic board.

'What letter does _____ start with?' Point to the letter B at the beginning of the word. '_____ starts with the /b/ sound because it starts with the letter B. Let me hear you say /b/ for _____.'

'Nice job today! You can all have a sticker for working so hard.' Say to each child individually: 'Come find the letter we learned about today.' Let the child find the B sticker on the sheet. 'What do we call this letter? What sound does it make?' Repeat this with the other children while lining them up.

What letter(s) should we start with?

Justice, Pence, Bowles and Wiggins (2006) found that children are *eleven times* more likely to know the first letter of their first name than any other letter. If you start with the first letters of children's first names, every child in your group will likely know at least one letter, which can be a very motivating experience. However, in England, you will be using a structured phonics programme with your older EYFS children (those in the Reception year), which will dictate the order in which you teach letter sounds. We suggest there may be added value in engaging children in a few activities based on letters in their names, to stimulate interest in and excitement about letters before you start implementing your chosen phonics programme. The activities we describe are all appropriate for 4-year-olds, as preparation for the more structured programme they will be following in the Reception year. You need a stock of plastic or wooden letters, or cards with letters printed on them, to implement the kinds of activity suggested next.

Activities focusing on letters in children's names

Make sure your set of letters includes both upper and lower case versions of each letter – upper case is necessary for names. Talk about the fact that we use letters to write our names. Can children find the letter that starts their name? Does anyone else's name start with that letter? Can they find another letter that's in their name?

Arrange letters to spell the name of one of the children in the group: Whose name is this? Let's read this name together. Do this for each child in turn, and emphasize that we can read the name. Whenever you do this activity, finish by saying that we use letters to read and write words, like our own names. Can any of the children use the letters to write their own name? Can any of the children read someone else's name?

Write a letter from a child's name on the white board, and talk about its shape (e.g. M is like two mountains, m has two humps, s is like a snake, O is round, x is a cross). As you name and talk about each letter, trace its shape on the white board with your finger, and invite each child to do this too. Talk through the motor movements as you model tracing

(Continued)

> *(Continued)*
>
> a letter: for example, for lower case h the patter would be something like 'start at the top, straight down, halfway up again and over and down'.
>
> As you read with children, draw their attention to letters they know in the text, and ask them to find another instance of that letter on the page.
>
> If you have an alphabet frieze on the wall, make sure it is at child height. Ask children to touch and trace with their finger the letter that starts their name, their brother's or sister's name, their mum's name, their friend's name, etc.

When should we start to introduce phonological awareness activities?

Some children appreciate rhyme from an early age: 3-year-olds can perform above chance levels when asked to say whether or not words rhyme (Maclean, Bryant & Bradley, 1987). It would seem sensible with 3- and 4-year-olds to start with activities that promote rhyme awareness: there are nice examples of these in Phase 1 of the Letters and Sounds phonics programme mentioned earlier. However, a word of warning: Martin and Byrne (2002) show that rhyme awareness does not *automatically* develop into awareness of phonemes. Our advocacy of providing rhyme activities for younger children rests largely on the enjoyment children get from these activities, and in their power to give children an 'Aha!' moment when they first become aware that words do not just represent meanings, but are themselves objects with properties of their own, are patterns of sounds. This awareness is an essential step towards understanding the alphabetic principle.

What kinds of phonological awareness should we develop?

As we have seen, phoneme awareness is more strongly related than rhyme awareness to the successful development of word reading skills. Only two phoneme awareness abilities are directly involved in reading and spelling: phoneme blending is essential to reading unfamiliar words once these have been sounded out; phoneme segmentation is essential to producing phonologically plausible (but not necessarily conventionally correct) spellings. The obvious implication is that teachers should concentrate on teaching phoneme blending and segmentation skills.

Castles, Coltheart, Wilson, Valpied and Wedgwood (2009) describe several activities that proved successful in developing phoneme awareness in 3- to 5-year-old children. Presented in Table 5.4, these can be adapted to develop either phoneme or letter awareness.

Examining the ways in which phoneme awareness has been assessed in research studies is another useful starting point for designing development activities.

Table 5.4 Activities to develop phoneme awareness or letter awareness

Activity	Develops awareness of	Description
Card match	phonemes	Match picture cards beginning with the same phoneme
	letters	Match cards with the same letter
Dominoes	phonemes	Connect dominoes with pictures starting with the same phoneme
	letters	Connect dominoes with the same letter
Bingo	phonemes	Put tokens on pictures starting with presented phonemes
	letters	Put tokens on letters matching those displayed by the trainer
I Spy	phonemes	Look at a picture book and find objects starting with a given phoneme
	letters	Look at a picture book and find hidden letters
Snap	phonemes	Take turns with the trainer to place down cards and say 'snap' when two sequential pictures begin with the same sound
	letters	Take turns with the trainer to place down cards and say 'snap' when two sequential letters are the same
Memory	phonemes	Turn over pairs of face-down cards to find two pictures beginning with the same phoneme
	letters	Turn over pairs of face-down cards to find two with the same letter

Assessment often involves using dolls or puppets who come from another planet, or speak like robots. To assess phoneme blending ability, children are asked to work out what the alien doll or puppet is trying to say when it utters /f/ /æ/ /t/ (<FAT>). Turn this into a game where children take turns in pronouncing the doll's or puppet's intended word. To assess phoneme segmentation ability, 'talking like a robot' is modelled for the children and then they are told a word (<FAT>) and asked to say it like a robot (/f/ /æ/ /t/). This too can be turned into a game.

A general conclusion from training studies investigating the effects of phoneme awareness in young children on word reading (e.g. Hatcher, Hulme & Ellis, 1994) is that phoneme awareness has the strongest effect on word reading skills when it is combined with teaching children about the letters which represent phonemes, and providing opportunities for children to use their new-found letter knowledge and phoneme blending and segmentation skills in reading and writing. This is clearly teaching phonics, and we will therefore consider this later, when we discuss phonics teaching.

Which are more beneficial to learning: whole-class, small group, or one-to-one activities?

Almost without exception, research interventions designed to promote phonological awareness and alphabet knowledge with pre-school, kindergarten and EYFS children implement teaching activities with small groups of from three to five children. Occasionally children are engaged in pairs, or one-to-one. Large group and whole-class teaching are virtually never used with the very young children enrolled in these studies. The National Reading Panel Report published by the National Institute of Child Health and Human Development (NICH & HD, 2000) showed the effects of teaching to promote phoneme awareness were twice as large for small-group as for whole-class or individual teaching. As our prime interest is in ensuring that *all* the children in our class gain complete mastery of what we are teaching them, we suggest implementing activities with small groups of from three to five children under adult supervision. This allows us more easily to notice and record which children in the group are showing confusion, and which children already have a secure grasp of the concept or knowledge the activity is designed to promote. These children no longer need this kind of activity, allowing time and attention to be concentrated on the children who do. Frequent informal assessment of children's learning is essential to ensure teaching consistently addresses children's current learning needs. Children whose learning is slower really do benefit from additional opportunities to practise, in the context of encouraging feedback and support.

It can be difficult to implement this kind of focused small-group activity regularly in an EYFS setting. To do so successfully requires a considerable degree of careful planning. We can illustrate this from our own experience. In a study designed to promote oral language development in pre-school children (Dockrell, Stuart & King, 2011), we worked in settings where most activities were child-initiated, and many children chose to spend most of their time in outdoor play. Our intervention required staff to make changes to the normal structure of the day, and ensured children participated in certain adult-initiated and adult-led small-group activities regularly over a period of ten weeks. The ideas we agreed with staff to help them organize these changes are shown below.

Organizing regular small-group teaching sessions in the EYFS

Staff grouped the children into groups of no more than five, and gave each group a name (e.g. Lions, Tigers, Elephants, Crocodiles and Rabbits).

A chart with the illustrated name of each group and the children in it was displayed on the classroom wall, for quick reference by both staff and children.

> Staff helped children make animal badges to display their group membership. The children loved wearing their badges and quickly learned which group they were in. They enjoyed being summoned to take part in a group activity – in fact groups were sometimes disappointed when it wasn't their turn.
>
> To save time finding the children in each group, who could be indoors or outdoors at any time, group activities were timetabled to take place immediately after the children were all together in one large group, for example, after snack time or lunchtime.
>
> A timetable was prepared in collaboration with staff who were going to lead group activities. Displayed on the classroom wall, this showed which groups were taking part in which group activity with which staff member, at which time, and on which days in the week.

This is likely to be the minimum degree of organization necessary to implement regular adult-led small-group activities in EYFS settings. Staff in the settings where we worked found it quite hard to accomplish, but agreed the effort was very worthwhile, as they saw the growth in children's ability to understand and express ideas.

How frequent and how long should a teaching session be?

Most teaching sessions in intervention studies with young children last from 10 to 20 minutes, and take place from two to five times per week. McGinty, Fan, Breit Smith, Justice and Kaderavek (2011) examined the effects of intensity of instruction on print knowledge development in pre-school children. They explored two kinds of intensity: number and frequency of sessions, and 'amount of exposure to instructional targets' within a session: i.e. the concerted focus on a learning target and on activities to practise and reinforce learning. Both kinds of intensity affected children's learning. Amount of exposure within a session dramatically reduced the number of sessions needed for print knowledge development. Children benefited as much from a high amount of exposure twice a week as from a moderate amount of exposure four times a week. If we are certain we can provide highly structured and focused input within each teaching session, we are likely to need to provide fewer sessions per week. However, be cautious: it is not known if the same applies to phoneme awareness and alphabet knowledge instruction as to the development of print knowledge. Again, there are implications here for the need for ongoing informal assessment of children's learning, which provides information as to the effectiveness of teaching.

Building on these solid foundations: teaching to develop phonological recoding skills

Knowledge of phonics is one essential element in developing phonological recoding processes. In England, phonics teaching begins in the Reception year, the final year of the EYFS. In the USA, it can sometimes begin in pre-kindergarten (equivalent to Reception in England), but more frequently begins in kindergarten (Year 1 in England). As well as learning phonic correspondences, children need to be shown how written words can be segmented into the graphemes and onset-rime segments that map on to phonological segments, and taught to blend phonological segments into whole word pronunciations.

A plethora of terminology is used to describe different approaches to phonics teaching, so we will start by clarifying terms (see Table 5.5).

Table 5.5 Different kinds of phonics teaching

Term	Term is used to mean
Synthetic (small unit) phonics	Children are taught small unit grapheme-phoneme correspondences in a pre-determined order, starting with single letter-sound correspondences, and gradually introducing consonant and then vowel digraphs. Once children have learned at least one vowel and a couple of consonant letter-sound correspondences, they are taught to translate graphemes in words into phonemes, sequentially from left to right across the word, and to blend the phonemes into a pronunciation of the word.
Analytic (or analytical) phonics	Children are again taught small unit grapheme-phoneme correspondences. However, teaching starts with the whole word, and children are taught to analyse the phonemes in the word. For example, teacher and pupils discuss how the following words are alike: *pat*, *push* and *pen*; *man*, *tin* and *sun*; *bad*, *can* and *sat*.
Analogy/onset-rime (large unit) phonics	Onset-rime phonics, which uses large units of rime correspondences, is the basis of analogy phonics. Children are taught rime families (e.g. the -an family: can, ban, man, etc.) and encouraged to read an unknown word by analogy to a known word (knowing 'park' allows you to read similarly spelt words, e.g. 'lark' and 'bark'). The analogy is based on the shared rime correspondence (-ark). However, grapheme-phoneme correspondence knowledge is needed to read the word's onset.
Implicit (or 'embedded') phonics	Embedded phonics instruction teaches either large (rime) or small (grapheme-phoneme) correspondences, but teaching is in the context of literature rather than in separate lessons, and the skills to be taught are identified opportunistically rather than systematically.
Systematic phonics	This includes any kind of phonics programme that delineates a planned, sequential set of phonics elements and teaches these explicitly and systematically. The requirement for explicit, sequential, planned teaching means that implicit (embedded) phonics does not meet the criteria for systematic teaching.

Is the Reception year too early to start teaching reading and phonics?

In the UK, children start school and are taught to read earlier than in many other countries, leading to worries that teaching in the UK starts when children are too young, which might have detrimental effects on their progress. Cunningham and Carroll (2011) provide some evidence that this is not the case. Exploiting the fact that in Steiner schools children are not taught to read until they are age 7 years, they compared the reading skills of children in Steiner schools and those in standard educational settings. Children were assessed three times during their first year of reading instruction (when Steiner children were 7–8 years old, and standard educated children were 4–5 years old), with a follow-up assessment at the end of their second year in school. No significant differences in word reading were found between the two groups of children at the end of their first or second year in school, nor in reading comprehension at the end of their second year in school. Standard educated children were significantly better spellers at the end of both years than Steiner educated children. The two groups of children made equally good progress despite the fact that standard educated children were two years younger than their Steiner educated counterparts. The early start had not had detrimental effects on their progress, and appeared to have had beneficial effects on their spelling, which the authors attribute to the 'more consistent and high-quality synthetic phonics instruction' they had received in school.

What type of phonics should we teach?

The Rose Review (Rose, 2006) recommended:

> ...the case for systematic phonic work is overwhelming and much strengthened by a synthetic approach, the key features of which are to teach beginner readers grapheme-phoneme ... correspondences ... in a clearly defined, incremental sequence [and] to apply the highly important skill of blending ... phonemes in order, all through a word to read it [and] to apply the skills of segmenting words into their constituent phonemes to spell...
> (Rose, 2006: 20)

Following government acceptance of Rose's recommendations, synthetic phonics teaching was adopted in schools in England, and there is now a statutory requirement in the Programme of Study for English in the latest version of the National Curriculum (Department for Education, 2014) that children should be taught GPCs and phoneme blending. This has caused some disquiet in certain quarters in the UK. For example, Wyse and Goswami (2008) cite the US National Reading Panel Report (NICH & HD, 2000) to support their argument that while there is a wealth of research evidence demonstrating the value of *systematic* phonics teaching, there is less evidence that teaching *synthetic* phonics is the best way to implement systematic phonics teaching. The dispute largely concerns the linguistic units to be taught in a systematic phonics program: small, grapheme-phoneme correspondence (GPC) units, as in synthetic phonics programmes, or large, rime units, as in onset-rime analogy phonics programmes. The National Reading Panel report concluded 'systematic phonics instruction makes a bigger contribution to children's growth in reading than alternative programs providing unsystematic or no phonics instruction' (National Institute of Child Health and Human Development, 2000: 2–92), but found no significant difference in effect sizes on reading growth of three different types of phonics programme: small-unit synthetic phonics programmes (effect size 0.45), large-unit programmes (effect size 0.34), and 'miscellaneous' programmes which did not fit into either of the other two categories (effect size 0.27).

Very few studies have explicitly compared effects on reading growth of teaching word reading skills through either exclusive synthetic (small-unit) or exclusive onset-rime analogy (large-unit) phonics. One study included in the NRP report (Foorman, Francis, Fletcher, Schatschneider & Mehta, 1998) did achieve a nice clean comparison of onset-rime and GPC phonics. Working with low-achieving children in Grades 1 and 2, they found significantly more and faster growth in phonological awareness and word reading in children in their small-unit GPC group than their large-unit onset-rime analogy group.

As in many of the studies included in the NRP report, most of the more recent studies we have found tend to inadvertently introduce some small-unit teaching into the large-unit condition, and vice versa, rendering comparisons between conditions unreliable. Moreover, some studies do not report effects on reading. We have found only two adequately controlled studies published since the National Reading Panel report which have succeeded in directly comparing the relative efficacy of synthetic small-unit phonics and onset-rime analogy large-unit phonics in promoting reading growth. Results from these studies are presented in Table 5.6: both conclude that teaching small units is more effective than teaching large units.

Table 5.6 Two further studies comparing relative effectiveness of synthetic (small-unit) and onset-rime analogy (large-unit) phonics teaching in promoting reading growth

	Christensen & Bowey (2005)	**Hatcher, Hulme & Snowling (2004)**
Children	7-year-olds in 2nd year at school	410 children from 20 Reception classes 1/3rd identified as 'at risk' of reading failure at start of intervention
Teaching conditions	Small unit synthetic phonics vs Large unit onset-rime phonics vs Control (implicit phonics)	Reading with Rhyme vs Reading with Phoneme vs Reading with Rhyme and Phoneme vs Reading

	Christensen & Bowey (2005)	**Hatcher, Hulme & Snowling (2004)**
Teaching amount	20 minutes per day for 14 weeks	14 months across Year R and Year 1
Results	Small and Large unit groups significantly better word readers than control group. Small unit group significantly faster and more accurate than large unit group in reading unfamiliar untaught words, and higher scores on comprehension test.	All four conditions are equally effective in typically developing children. In 'at risk' children, Reading with Phoneme and Reading with Rhyme and Phoneme are significantly more effective than Reading with Rhyme or Reading.
Authors' conclusions	For relatively early readers, a programme focusing attention on individual grapheme-phoneme correspondences and encouraging analysis of every grapheme in a word is superior to one that encourages them to focus on larger orthographic units, specifically rimes.	Teaching small unit phonics (synthetic phonics) is more beneficial than teaching large unit phonics (onset and rime phonics) for young children at risk of reading failure.

Further support for the decision to teach grapheme-phoneme correspondences rather than onsets and rime correspondences comes from analyses of the relative numbers of each type of correspondence required for children to be able to read the words they typically encounter in their reading materials, which we reported in Chapter 4: children need to know almost five times as many onset and rime correspondences as grapheme-phoneme correspondences to read all monosyllabic words in the early version of the Children's Printed Word Database (Stuart, Dixon, Masterson & Gray, 2003). It is simply more efficient to teach children grapheme-phoneme correspondences.

Which is more beneficial to *learning* phonics: whole-class, small-group, or one-to-one teaching?

Phonics teaching has been successfully implemented in all three situations. However, it is a truism that children learn at different rates, and require different amounts of repetition and practice to gain complete mastery of the material being taught. Thus, whole-class phonics teaching requires considerable skill on the part of the teacher to differentiate teaching so that all children benefit. This is forcibly brought home in a study by Shapiro and Solity (2008). They describe whole-class synthetic phonics teaching implemented in line with current knowledge about effective learning. Drawing on research by Seabrook, Brown and Solity (2005), which found that teaching letter-sound correspondences for three two-minute sessions daily promoted more learning than teaching a single daily six-minute session, Shapiro and Solity incorporated this 'spaced sessions' technique into their study. They also incorporated 'incremental rehearsal' into the teaching. This involves interspersing known items among the new items being taught, a practice shown to promote better learning of the new items (e.g. Burns, 2004). This effect might depend on the boost to children's motivation to learn that is provided by knowing they already know some of what is being taught – an 'I can learn this!' effect.

> ### Teaching phonics in several short sessions spaced through the day
>
> Each whole-class session lasted 12 minutes and was delivered by the children's normal class teacher three times a day.
>
> Within these sessions, children practised four skills (phoneme synthesis, phoneme segmentation, phonic skills and sight vocabulary) for two minutes each.
>
> Teachers mixed new material with older, more familiar material when practising each skill.
>
> In addition, all skills were taught to high fluency levels, with children only taught skills that are explicitly used when reading, writing and spelling.
>
> For the final four minutes of each session, teachers read to children from large books and demonstrated how the skills they had been practising applied to reading.

Differentiation within each two-minute teaching slot for each of the four skills practised was achieved by dividing the class into high-, middle- and low-achieving groups, and devoting time *in each two minute slot* to teaching aimed at the skill level of each group. Shapiro and Solity (2008) illustrate this using a word reading task in which children were required to sound out and blend words. The high-achieving group might be asked to sound and blend CCVCC words (e.g. <PRINT>); their responses modeled these skills for children in middle and low groups. The middle achieving group might be asked to sound and blend CCVC words (e.g. <SPIN>), with their responses providing further modelling on easier material for the low-achieving group, while the high-achieving group are asked to do the task in their heads. The low-achieving group might be asked to sound and blend CVC words (e.g. <PIT>), with children in the other two groups asked to do the task in their heads. Teaching like this requires a high degree of organizational competence and minute knowledge of children's differing skill levels. But Shapiro and Solity (2008) demonstrated that their whole-class intervention resulted in faster acquisition of fluent word reading skills compared to children in control classes.

How many GPCs should we teach?

It is not always necessary to teach children every last grapheme-phoneme correspondence: once typically-developing children have a firm grasp of the alphabetic principle and can apply the grapheme-phoneme correspondences they have learned to read and write words, they begin to self-teach, to infer new correspondences from experiences of reading texts. But how many GPCs should we ideally teach to give children the best chance of becoming able to read appropriately levelled texts independently, and thus begin to self-teach?

As stated in Chapter 4, Shapiro and Solity (2008) claimed that teaching children the most common pronunciation of a set of 64 frequently occurring graphemes (listed in Table 5.7) plus 100 very high frequency words (including 61 irregular words) allowed children to read 90% of words in texts they read, and this was enough to set most children on the road to self-teaching.

Table 5.7 GPCs taught in the Shapiro and Solity (2008) programme

Single-letter	Pronunciation	Multiple-letter	Pronunciation	Suffix	Pronunciation
b	bed	ai	aid	ed	t or d
c	kiss	air	chair	s	s or z
d	dog	ar	barn		
f	fish	au	cause		
g	golf	aw	claw		
h	help	ay	bay		
j	jump	ea	beam		
k	kite	ear	clear		
l	lamp	ee	creek		
m	man	er	fern		
n	nip	ew	screw		
p	pad	ey	key		
q[1]	quick	igh	fight		
r	run	oa	float		
t	tap	oi	foil		
v	van	oo	food		
w	wet	oor	door		
x	ox	or	born		
y	young	ou	bound		
z	zap	oy	toy		
a	cat	ur	blur		
e	bed	ch	chip		
i	sit	ck	buck		
o	log	kn	know		
u	sun	ph	photo		

(Continued)

Table 5.7 (Continued)

Single-letter	Pronunciation	Multiple-letter	Pronunciation	Suffix	Pronunciation
a_e	make	qu	quick		
e_e	eve	sh	shop		
i_e	life	th	thin		
o_e	code	wh	what		
u_e	mute	geminate as single			

[1] q is represented as a single letter in the original 2008 paper. This is unusual.

Can phonics teaching be delivered effectively by teaching assistants?

The answer to this is a qualified 'Yes'. In research studies, learning support assistants have successfully delivered intervention programmes designed to teach phonics to young children (e.g. Hatcher, Hulme, Miles, Carroll et al., 2006; Savage & Carless, 2004, 2005). It is clearly not good practice to hand over teaching materials to learning support assistants and expect them to use these effectively without specific training. Learning support assistants who have been well trained in the specifics of programme content and delivery, and have access to ongoing support and monitoring, can provide effective teaching. In the Hatcher et al. (2006) study, learning support assistants were given four days' training in programme delivery, and during the intervention were provided with ten fortnightly tutorials with one of the researchers. In the Savage and Carless (2004, 2005) studies, they were trained to administer screening tests and deliver intervention, with weekly visits from one of the researchers during the intervention period.

Fidelity to the programme

In research studies, considerable efforts are made to monitor programme delivery, to ensure teachers or learning support assistants are teaching the programme exactly as it was designed to be taught. This is known as 'fidelity to the programme'. Children's learning is better when teachers and learning support assistants adhere precisely to a programme's teaching structure and sequence, to timings suggested for sessions and activities within sessions, and to a faithful implementation of the programme's teaching and learning activities. The requirement to adhere so closely to a pre-designed programme might seem to challenge the importance of teachers' professional judgement. Professional judgements about phonics teaching should be based in knowledge and understanding of the need for and place of this in the teaching of reading. We have tried to provide the kinds of evidence-based information that will help inform professional judgement. But, research evidence suggests that fidelity to the programme matters in phonics teaching. The combined professional judgement of teachers in the school will have contributed to the selection of the phonics programme used in that school. The children will learn more, and more easily, if that programme is taught exactly as it was intended to be taught. Moreover, this saves teacher time: the phonics lessons are pre-planned, and by faithfully following the sequence of lessons, all necessary content of the programme will be covered *systematically* which, as we have seen, has proven beneficial effects on children's learning. Professional judgement is nonetheless important: for example, in noting and recording children's learning, so that teaching can be adapted to individual learning needs by providing additional teaching and practice for children whose learning is relatively slow. Don't let them fall behind!

Does use of decodable texts enhance the growth of word reading skills?

There is little solid research evidence on this, and findings from studies have produced mixed results. There are difficulties in defining 'decodable texts', in terms of both the text and the phonic knowledge of the reader. No text is entirely decodable by the application of phonic rules, however skilled and knowledgeable the reader: how many times in this book have we required you to read the word 'THE'? Such highly frequent, irregular words appear constantly in all texts. So, decodability can never be absolute: texts can only be more or less decodable. What is decodable for a 6-year-old is markedly different from what is decodable for an 8-year-old. Some studies do not take reader-knowledge variation into account when assigning texts to 'decodable' and 'non-decodable' categories.

Juel and Roper-Schneider (1985) taught first-graders the same phonics programme but assigned them to 'more' or 'less' decodable book reading groups. They found significant beneficial effects of reading decodable text on children's word and nonword reading skills, but not on their scores on a standardized reading test. Jenkins, Peyton, Sanders and Vadasy (2004) describe a well-designed study in which 'at-risk' first-graders were taught the same phonics programme four days a week for a period of 25 weeks. Half the children read 'more decodable' books: 'storybooks that were consistent with the phonics programme'. The other half read 'less decodable books': 'storybooks written without phonetic control'. For the first 30 lessons, texts read by children in the 'more decodable' group were 85% decodable, compared to the 11% decodability of texts read by children in the 'less decodable' group. At the end of the programme, there were no significant differences between the 'more decodable' book group and the 'less decodable' book group on measures of nonword and word reading, passage reading and passage comprehension.

However, given the evidence (e.g. Hatcher, Hulme & Ellis, 1994) that phoneme awareness and phonics teaching is more effective when children are given immediate opportunities to apply their new knowledge and skills to reading and writing, it would seem sensible to provide absolute beginner readers with texts where they can work out the words in the text using such phonic rules as they have been taught. Providing specially prepared sentences that allow beginners to practise in this way can be useful: the 'Letters and Sounds' programme provides examples of these. Some commercially produced phonics programmes also provide texts for children at different programme levels to practise their new-found knowledge and skills. Children gain a sense of mastery from being able to read texts independently, a sense of 'I can do this!' which is so important in motivating them to read. However, the down sides of a carefully controlled vocabulary include limitations to the richness of the story, which might have negative effects on motivation. This can and should be counteracted by making sure we read *to* and *with* the children those rich and rewarding stories that are as yet beyond their own capacity to read, but not beyond their capacity to understand and enjoy, given the opportunity.

And, children will not be able to 'self-teach' if they are only ever exposed to texts where they can already work out most of the words using rules they have been taught. Again, professional judgement is called for in deciding what kinds of material are best suited to further developing the reading skills of each child. In our broad professional judgement, 'more decodable' texts are probably essential and motivating for beginners and for children who need more practice in developing phonological recoding skills, but once children have got a head start in reading, artificial restrictions on texts should no longer be necessary. Solity and Vousden (2009) provide some support for this view. They analysed vocabulary in three sets of books: two reading schemes (Oxford Reading Tree, Rhyme World) and one set of 66 story books commonly available in EYFS and Key Stage 1 classrooms. The analyses focused on the proportion of monosyllabic words in each set of books that would be readable by children who had learned the set of 64 GPCs taught in the Shapiro and Solity (2008) study. They found similar proportions of different words that were decodable by children who knew these 64 GPCs across the three sets of books (about 75% in each case), but these different decodable words occurred relatively more frequently in the two reading schemes.

Is phonics teaching equally effective with English Language Learners?

Studies have shown that phonics teaching is equally effective in developing the word reading skills of monolingual English-speaking children and English Language Learners (e.g. Stuart, 1999, 2004; Vadasy & Sanders, 2012, 2013). Furthermore, no significant differences have been found in the word and non-word reading performance of monolingual English-speaking children and English Language Learners in the Phonics Screening Check (administered to all children in England at the end of Year 1).

However, the research studies cited above differ as to the effects of phonics teaching on the reading *comprehension* of English Language Learners. Vadasy and Sanders (2013) found lasting effects of a kindergarten phonics programme on reading comprehension as well as word reading and spelling skills. Stuart (2004) found lasting effects of a 12-week phonics programme delivered in the Reception year on word reading and spelling, but differences in reading comprehension just failed to reach statistical significance (p= .06). These different findings are likely due to demographic as well as instructional factors. Almost all the children in Stuart's study (86%) were English Language Learners, with the vast majority speaking Sylheti as their first language. Thus, the lingua franca among the children was Sylheti, at school as well as at home. At pre-test, their scores on the British Picture Vocabulary Scale (BPVS) (Dunn, Dunn, Whetton & Burley, 1997) were almost two standard deviations below the mean for all children, and almost one standard deviation below the separate mean for English Language Learners. Thus, in addition to phonics training, these children urgently needed teaching to develop their knowledge of English vocabulary and sentence structure. Dockrell, Stuart and King (2011), working with EYFS children in the same locality, successfully implemented developmentally appropriate language learning activities that impacted on both these aspects of English. In terms of instructional differences, Vadasy and Sanders (2012) found that English Language Learners whose teachers emphasized word-level work in Grade 1, and meaning-oriented work in Grade 2, achieved higher reading scores at the end of Grade 2.

How long-lasting are the effects of phonics teaching?

Long-term follow-up studies are relatively rare, but tend to show the effects of early phonics teaching can be long-lasting. Vadasy and Sanders (2013) reported persisting benefits to word reading, spelling and reading comprehension up to the end of third grade for at-risk children given phonics intervention in Grade 1. Johnston and Watson (2005) and Johnston, McGeown and Watson (2012) both reported persisting benefits of early synthetic phonics teaching on reading, spelling and reading comprehension up to the age of 11.

Effects of phonics teaching on reading comprehension can be explained in several ways. First, word reading skills account for a larger proportion of the variation in reading comprehension among young readers than do language skills, such as oral vocabulary. In these early stages, being able to read the words at all is of paramount importance, and being able to read them accurately and fluently frees the child to devote more attention to understanding the text. Second, good word reading skills help motivate children to read more; reading more exposes children to a wider range of vocabulary and syntactic structures, which serves to increase children's oral language comprehension, which feeds into reading comprehension. Thus, the effects of phonics teaching on reading comprehension are indirect – but they have been shown to exist.

It is not the case that a brief phonics intervention at the start of reading tuition will inevitably result in a child with no further word reading problems. Research interventions tend to be brief because they are costly to set up. Classroom programmes as now taught in England typically continue to teach phonics throughout Key Stage 1, that is, until children are at least 7 years old (or, we hope, until children have learned all that they need to be taught in the programme).

And phonics for older struggling readers?

Phonics teaching has its largest effect on word reading when it is introduced at the start of reading tuition: the National Reading Panel report (NICH & HD, 2000) showed mean effect sizes for phonics taught in kindergarten (0.54) or first grade (0.52) were significantly greater than the mean effect size (0.27) for phonics taught from Grade 2 up to Grade 6. It is still necessary to teach phonics to older children with insufficient phonics knowledge and skill to support the development of efficient phonological recoding processes, because these processes are an essential part of word reading skills: if they are not developed, the child will not become a fluent word reader.

Researchers constantly develop and test programmes specifically designed to address the learning needs of these older struggling readers. For example, McCandliss, Beck, Sandak and Perfetti (2003) worked with 7- to 10-year-old children with phonological recoding difficulties. They implemented a programme called 'Word Building', adapted from materials designed by Beck and Hamilton (2000). Initial assessments of the children's phonological recoding skills (McCandliss et al., 2003) showed they could accurately sound out the first grapheme in a word or nonword, but performance on subsequent graphemes was poor. The word building intervention directed children's attention to each grapheme position in a word, through an activity they call 'progressive minimal contrasts', described in the next two suggested activities.

Description of 'progressive minimal contrasts' activity

This activity provides a chain of words that differ by a single grapheme.

A child forms the words in a lesson with letter cards by stepping through a scripted set of transformations that change one word into the next by changing a single grapheme at the beginning, middle, or end of the word.

After each transformation, the child reads the new word, which looks and sounds similar to the previously decoded word.

This activity is designed to help children attend to the subtle impact of a single grapheme change on the appearance and pronunciation of each word.

Focusing attention on each individual letter sound unit within words may play an important role in developing fully specified representations of printed words.

(McCandliss et al., 2003: 78)

This illustrates the progression of word transformations in the word-building activity: children are instructed to add or change or take away a certain letter, and to read the resulting new word.

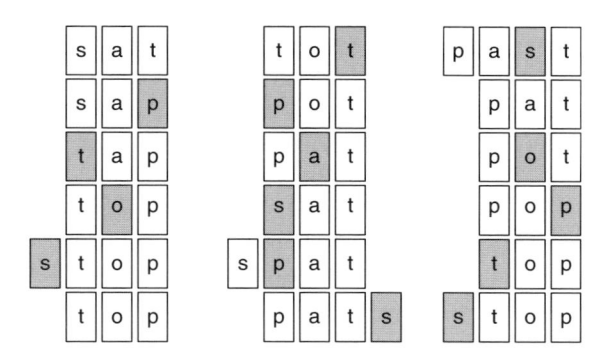

Figure 5.1 Illustration of 'progressive minimal contrasts' activity (McCandliss et al., 2003: 84)

Children were taught individually by trained undergraduate students, working through a series of 77 lessons over 20 weeks, with up to three 50-minute sessions per week. Words used in the word-building activity became progressively more complex in terms of GPC and word form difficulty. GPC difficulty progressed from short vowels to split digraphs, to vowel digraphs, to vowel pronunciation changes in different contexts. CV structure progressed gradually from CVC items (e.g. <TOP>) to CCCVCCC items (e.g. <SCRIMPS>). Children were given a small set of letter cards to use in word building. Materials also included flashcards for each of the words in each lesson, and sentences containing a high proportion of words used in each lesson. After each word chain was completed, children were asked to read each word shown on flashcards. If they were 80% correct, a new chain was started. If not, the current chain was used again. At the end of each lesson, children read the sentences.

Children's ability to decode the vowel and coda of words (e.g. the <I> and the <MPS> in <SCRIMPS>), the second consonant letter in an initial consonant cluster (e.g. the <T> in <STAMP>), and the first consonant letter in a final consonant cluster (e.g. the <M> in <STAMP>) improved over the course of the intervention, and they performed significantly better than the control group on a standardized test of nonword reading.

Teaching to develop orthographic representations

In Chapter 3, we saw that in skilled reading, lexical processes giving direct access from the orthographic representation of a word to its phonology and meaning typically operate faster than phonological recoding processes. Thus, in skilled reading, visual word recognition is usually achieved through lexical processing. It is therefore important that children develop the orthographic representations linked to phonology and word meaning that are required for direct access through lexical processing.

We saw in Chapter 4 that orthographic representations are more rapidly acquired if some of the letters in the written word can be linked to their corresponding phonemes, if the child can form partial links from orthography to phonology as well as links from orthography to semantics. We saw that absolute beginner readers need to experience large numbers of repetitions of a written word before an orthographic representation of the word is reliably stored, and that the most efficient way of providing these multiple repetitions is by presenting words on flashcards rather than by repeated reading of the words in texts. We saw that by Grade 2, many fewer repetitions are needed before children show signs of orthographic learning, of having stored the orthographic representation of a word. We might think of this as children having learned how to learn.

Research studies have shown that, for young readers, word reading is slower as the number of letters in the word increases (e.g. van den Boer, de Jong & Haentjens van Meeteren, 2013). This letter-length effect indicates sequential processing of the letters in words, and sequential processing is the hallmark of phonological recoding processes. In contrast, in lexical processing, all the letters in a word are processed simultaneously: whether a word has three or nine letters does not affect the time taken to read it. Thus, the absence of letter-length effects in word reading is one indication that orthographic representations are available to and used by the reader.

Progress towards fluent word reading involves a transition from more reliance on phonological recoding processes to more reliance on lexical processes – but at what point does this transition occur, and what causes it? Rau, Moeller and Landerl (2014) provide some information about the likely point of transition for the German schoolchildren in their study. German is a more regular and consistent language than English, so in theory there is less need to develop orthographic representations than in English. Rau et al. (2014) asked children in second grade (7-year-olds), third grade (8-year-olds) and fourth grade (10-year-olds) to read a set of 72 single-line sentences presented on computer. Each sentence contained a target word or nonword, varying in length from short (3–6 letters) to long (7–10 letters). Rau et al. (2014) used an eye-tracking apparatus to measure children's gaze duration on the target word or nonword. They concluded that from Grade 3 onwards, lexical processing becomes increasingly dominant, as gaze duration for words became similar from Grade 3 onwards, regardless of letter length, and fourth-graders only showed letter-length effects for nonwords.

Converging evidence comes from a study by Schmalz, Marinus and Castles (2013), using a lexical decision task with 8- and 9-year-old Australian children in Grades 3 and 4. In this task, words and nonwords were displayed in random order on a computer screen, with children asked to press the space bar when they saw a real word. Real words were either high or low in frequency, and regular or irregular. Children in both grades responded equally accurately and fast to high frequency regular and irregular words: there was no regularity effect. Schmalz et al. (2013) conclude that from about the age of 8, children rely largely on lexical processes in silent reading of highly familiar words.

Can we assume that, as phonological recoding becomes increasingly fast and fluent, children will automatically create orthographic representations of words they can read? There is some evidence this might be the case. De Jong and Share (2007) showed that children who are fluent nonword readers (indicating well-developed phonological recoding processes) perform better on the orthographic learning tasks described in Chapter 4. In these tasks, good performance depends on forming an orthographic representation of the words to which participants have been exposed.

What teaching practices might help children develop orthographic representations?

One implication of the de Jong and Share (2007) study is that we need to ensure children develop fast and fluent phonological recoding processes, which seems to lead us back to phonics teaching. When discussing phonics teaching, we did not emphasize the importance of activities to develop children's speed: speed of recalling grapheme-phoneme correspondences, and speed in applying phoneme blending processes. You cannot develop fluent phonological recoding processes if you are slow to translate graphemes to phonemes, or slow to blend phonemes into words. If the school's chosen phonics programme does not include activities likely to develop speed, it needs to be supplemented with some such activities. Fortunately, help is at hand. The Florida Center for Reading Research provides downloadable resources, designed in 2005–06 by a team of teachers following a review of current research. Downloadable activities to develop speeded recall of grapheme-phoneme correspondences can be found at www.fcrr.org/curriculum/PDF/G2-3/2-3Fluency_1.pdf and to develop speeded recall of words at www.fcrr.org/curriculum/PDF/G2-3/2-3Fluency_2.pdf. These might need some adaptation (for example, by selecting more appropriate items to incorporate into an activity).

Closing words

We hope you have not found this chapter as exhausting to read as we did to write. We imagine by now you might be thinking back fondly to the uncomplicated diagram of the Simple View of Reading presented in Chapter 2. Word recognition processes have turned out to be fiendishly complicated – in fact, it may now seem miraculous to you, as it does to us, that anyone ever succeeds in learning to read the words on the page. We should not be surprised that some children find this difficult: the surprise is that so many children find it so easy. We also hope the material we have covered so far in this book will help teachers become ever more able to provide effective teaching to the children who do find this learning to read business difficult and dispiriting. Those are the children who really need knowledgeable and inspiring teachers. We return to them in Chapter 9.

PART 3
Understanding spoken and written language

PART 3

6
Comprehension of oral and written language

Summary

In Chapter 1, you learned about the phonological and orthographic systems of language. In this chapter, you will learn about the other language systems involved in the comprehension and production of spoken and written discourse: vocabulary, morphology, syntax, pragmatics and semantics. This will provide you with firm foundations upon which to build your understanding of language comprehension. You will also learn about reading comprehension as the active construction of a mental model of the text, and the processes that are involved in this construction.

The language comprehension dimension of the Simple View of Reading

We now turn to the vertical axis in the figure of the Simple View of Reading: language comprehension processes (Figure 6.1). That we are considering this *after* we have considered word reading skills in no way implies that word reading skills should be taught first before we trouble ourselves about teaching comprehension. You will be developing the language comprehension abilities of the children you teach while they are still learning to read the words on the page. But, with the youngest and most inexpert readers, much of this comprehension teaching will be accomplished through oral language work: reading texts to and with children, and discussing the texts you read.

The Simple View of Reading makes clear that a person cannot be said to be reading effectively unless both word reading processes *and* language comprehension processes are brought into play simultaneously. In order to understand what we are reading, we have to be able to decode the words on the page *and* access the meanings that are locked in the language. We can only understand texts if our language comprehension processes are well developed and functioning adequately. As we explained in Chapter 2, the same language comprehension processes are involved in both oral

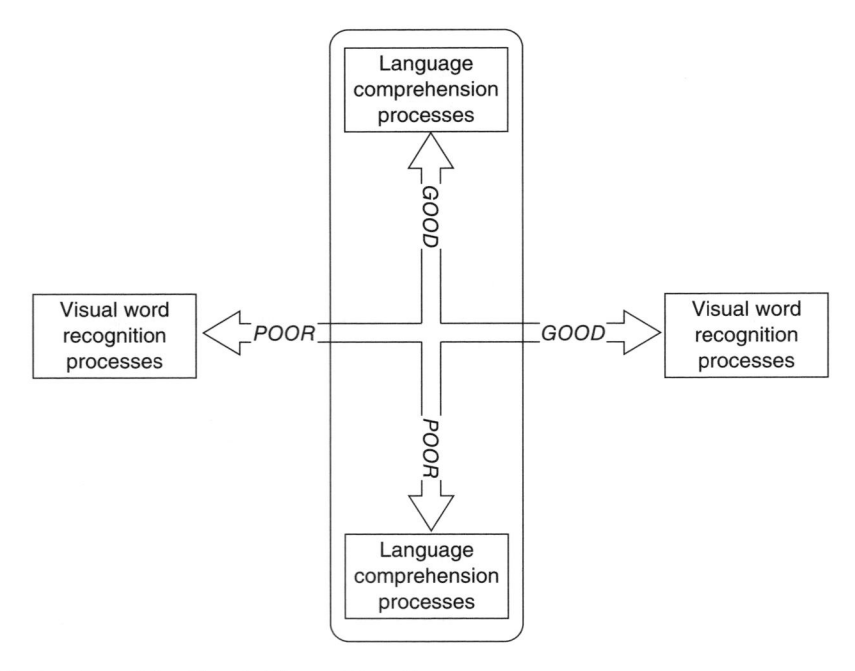

Figure 6.1 The Simple View of Reading

and written language comprehension. However, as we shall see, the discourse style of the written form is different from that of spoken language. Structures may be more complex, and vocabulary is frequently more varied but less common than in spoken language. Therefore we cannot assume that children will automatically be able to understand the texts they can decode. This is not a trivial observation. To help children become truly literate, we need to understand what is involved in comprehending language, so that we can teach them what they need to know.

Language

Language is an aspect of mind and brain that appears to be a unique characteristic of being human. We use language to communicate with other people and with ourselves. There are well over 6,000 different languages used by humans, all of which are composed of a set of systems. To understand language comprehension processes, we need to know about these systems that all languages share (see Table 6.1).

We covered phonology extensively in Chapter 1. Here, we will cover the other language systems: vocabulary, morphology, syntax, semantics and pragmatics.

Vocabulary

Vocabulary can be subdivided into *receptive* vocabulary and *expressive* vocabulary. Our receptive vocabulary is the set of words that we understand but may not actually

Table 6.1 The systems of language

Language system	Description
Phonology	The sound system of language
Vocabulary	The words and their meanings
Morphology	The system for combining meanings within words
Syntax	The system of rules for combining words into phrases or sentences
Semantics	The system for creating meaningful utterances (or texts) that go beyond the individual words
Pragmatics	This is language in use. It involves aspects of meaning that are dependent on the speaker. It also includes the context in which communication is taking place, such that skilled people are able to tailor their language to the social settings in which they find themselves.

use in everyday speech. Having an extensive receptive vocabulary means we can understand a wide range of communications both in spoken and written form. Our expressive vocabulary is the words that we do use. Having an extensive expressive vocabulary means we can convey our meanings accurately and precisely. Vocabulary grows with age, but does not simply unfold with age: it is not of itself a developmental skill (Paris, 2005). As children grow older, they come across more and more words which are added to their vocabulary, and this continues throughout life. Languages also are constantly evolving and new words are added all the time. Not only that, but the meanings of words and their usage may change over time as well. This is illustrated in the next box.

Novel words and changes in usage: Hoover, Laser, Ebook, Wicked

- *Hoover* (other vacuum cleaners are available): This was first the trade mark name of the manufacturers of a well-known vacuum cleaner in the 1920s. In England the word came to be synonymous with the class of cleaners themselves. Then, arising from this new noun, the new verb *to hoover* began to be used. Initially it meant 'the act of using the vacuum cleaner', but now it includes its use as a transitive verb followed by the preposition *up* meaning 'to dispose of something quickly and completely' as in: 'They hoovered up their breakfast.' This last use of the verb can be considered to be metaphorical because obviously no vacuum cleaner was involved! As we shall see, the ability to recognize and understand metaphor is important for language comprehension.

(Continued)

(Continued)

So much of English usage is metaphoric, which can lead to confusion for English language learners.

- *Laser*: This is now a noun meaning 'a device that produces a nearly parallel, nearly monochromatic, and coherent beam of light by exciting atoms to a higher energy level and causing them to radiate their energy in phase'. It has also come to be used as a verb as in '*to laser*': for example, when doctors laser people's eyes to correct a detached retina. When scientists developed the device in the late 1950s they were writing about Lightwave Amplification by Stimulated Emission of Radiation and used the acronym LASER. The word is now in common usage and many people will be unlikely to be aware that it was originally an acronym.
- *Ebook*: This is an electronic/digital form of a paper book with pages. Obviously the word has only been used as long as the device has been in existence, but it has rapidly been assimilated into everyday usage. If you think about your own language you will recognize how many words in your vocabulary are now new or adapted to communicate about modern technology. *Electronic, digital, computer, tablet, twitter, blog, text, mobile*: the list is not endless but it is ever growing.
- *Wicked*: Of all the words in this list, *wicked* is the only one that would have been recognized by people in the nineteenth century, but they would have been very confused if they were around today to hear someone saying: 'Those trainers are wicked.' Wicked has taken on a new meaning, which is the exact opposite of the original usage.

Early vocabulary

The words children first acquire are those that they hear most often in their verbal environment: high frequency words such as the noun MAMA and the verb DRINK. These are words needed to convey the meanings they want to express. They learn first to express their immediate needs e.g. MORE! and comment on things that are happening in their immediate environment e.g. ALL GONE. Much early vocabulary is common across different cultures and languages. We will consider word classes later, but for the moment we will note that nouns and verbs are an *open class* of words; 'open' indicates that new nouns and verbs can be created to accommodate new concepts; they are content words. We all have thousands of these open class content words in our vocabularies, and children seem to add examples of them daily as their early language develops.

Children's early vocabularies also include words which serve to structure the language. These are the very small set of words, known as *closed class*, that do not carry meaning *per se*, but have the function of structuring the language to support meaning. As children's language develops they begin to use these words to produce grammatical utterances. Closed class words include articles, e.g. THE, A, AN; verb auxiliaries, e.g. CAN, IS; prepositions, e.g. ON, UNDER; and conjunctions, e.g. AND.

The two 'sentences' in the next box show the difference between structural or function closed class words and content open class words. In the first one, all the **content** words have been replaced by nonwords, and in the second one all the **function** words have been replaced by nonwords.

'Sentences' illustrating the difference between open and closed class words

1 The flantmet are lariton their mavrim montep rotup because it is slem, but the tarithone for lomanple is for waght so they will have to narit corine.

2 Wap children pog eating risam lunches outside today sladump os ux warm, leb wap forecast dit tomorrow ux sil rain pu wimt spom poch ir stay inside.

You will be able to reconstruct the original sentence easily enough. You should notice that, although it is not possible to understand sentence 1, it has the feel of being a grammatical English sentence. On the other hand, sentence 2 seems just like a list of words, but you can get the gist of it because you understand the content words. Those of you who are modern text message users should be able to introspect that texters (a very new word!) cut many of the function words out of messages. A message might read: MEET 2PM CAFE QUEENS ROAD. Though it is possible to convey straightforward immediate meanings without structural words, it is not possible to convey more complex meanings, so it is important that children's vocabularies include all these essential words. In fact, without the structural words, meaning can be obscured. In sentence 2, without the structural words, it could be that the day was warm or the lunches were warm. There is no structure to tie the meaning of warm to the weather and not the food.

Although we have both structural and content words in our vocabularies, it is the content words that form the vast majority of words we know and use. These are the nouns, verbs, adjectives and adverbs (defined below) that we continue to add to throughout our lives. By the time children begin school, they have vocabularies of around 10,000+ words (Anglin, 1993) that they have learnt from being in an oral/aural environment. It is essential that children engage with people who provide them with a rich conversational background in order to build up their language skills and extend their vocabularies. Children start school from very different backgrounds and the level of their vocabulary acquisition is very variable. Children with larger vocabularies are likely to understand more of what is said to them in the classroom than children with impoverished vocabularies. But for all children, the more words they encounter, the better their language development will be and the more they will understand. Once they have learned to read, their vocabularies extend through exposure to the wider vocabulary of the written form. Eventually children will end up with the typical vocabulary of an adult, which is estimated at around 50,000 words. We can do a simple illustrative calculation starting at age 2 years and ending up at age 18 years. There are 5,844 days in 16 years. Eighteen-year-olds are near adulthood, and if vocabulary development were smooth and linear (which it obviously isn't) they would have to learn 8.5 words a day every day for the whole 16 years.

A limited vocabulary hinders many aspects of life, including educational progress and social interaction. It is really frustrating for children when they know what they want to say but do not have the words to express their thoughts. Their understanding, not just of language in general, but of much of the content of the curriculum is compromised when they do not understand the words.

Vocabulary can also be considered in terms of its *breadth* and its *depth*. Breadth refers to the number of words that an individual knows the meaning of. It is not difficult to see how this could be an important parameter in comprehension. If we do not know the meaning of individual words, then our understanding of what we hear or read may be compromised. A typical example of an assessment of vocabulary breadth frequently used in schools, by educational psychologists, and in research is the *British Picture Vocabulary Scales III* (Dunn, Dunn, Styles & Sewell, 2009). Children are shown pages containing four pictures and asked to point to the one that best represents the word spoken by the tester. The vocabulary items assessed in this test must, by its very nature, be pictureable, but through ingenuity it is not just concrete nouns that are covered, but other parts of speech, including verbs and adjectives. Another procedure for assessing breadth of vocabulary is to ask people to choose the correct synonym from a set of potential alternatives. These breadth of vocabulary measures identify whether children know the meaning of individual words, but they do not provide any insight into the depth of their word knowledge. Vocabulary depth refers to the richness of the semantic interconnections between words. There is evidence (Ouellette, 2006; Tannenbaum, Torgesen & Wagner, 2006) that vocabulary depth is more important than vocabulary breadth for understanding written texts.

Depth of vocabulary means that people can define words, they can provide attributes of the word and supply examples of other semantically related words. When a person's vocabulary is embedded in a rich network of semantic connections, there is a fluency which supports comprehension. Knowing the meaning of one word may support the understanding and acquisition of a new related word. This can be particularly important in school when children come across new curriculum-specific words, or words that are common but used in a curriculum-specific way; below we illustrate this with the word VOLUME.

Curriculum-specific meanings of common words
Volume

- The likelihood is that children will have encountered this word on their many electronic devices as the button to change the sound level. They may well have been told to 'turn the volume down!'

- Eventually they will encounter it in relation to maths and science as capacity, or the quantity of three-dimensional space. This may include the equation length times breadth times height (L × B × H).

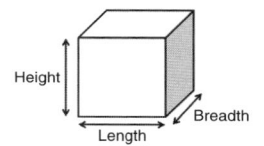

- They may also encounter the word in English, where it is a book.

Three very different meanings.

Depth of vocabulary implies knowing about different meanings of the same word. It also implies knowing different usages for the same word. You will be able to notice this in the example of BOOK below. Although the meanings of BOOK are not the same, at some level it is possible to detect the semantic relatedness between the words.

One word, different meanings
Book

Book: as in 'A thing to read' (noun)

Book: as in 'The book department is smaller than the kitchen department' (adjective)

To book: as in 'I want to book a room for tonight' or 'We want to book you to sing at our concert' or 'The police will book you for speeding' (verb)

Depth of vocabulary implies the ability to recognize a word as (in our case) an English word; to provide a definition which includes the defining features of the concept; and to use the word in a meaningful sentence context. We can all do this for thousands of words in our vocabulary, but as they get rarer (for us) we find there are some words that we recognize as being English despite not knowing what they mean.

You might like to investigate your own vocabulary depth with this list of words:

- Chore
- Chord
- Radix
- Radius
- Synchrony
- Syncope

Do you recognize each word as being English? Do you know something about the meaning of each word so that you can vaguely give some definition or can you define it completely? Can you use it in a sentence? And can you give any possible synonyms for each word?

Try to do this without the temptation of looking up each word in the dictionary. But then, of course, check your knowledge through the dictionary.

A good game to play which taps vocabulary breadth and depth through semantic networks is to get from one word to another seemingly completely unrelated word in a specified number of turns – the longer the better.

Here is an example:

Snail to bike in 9 moves

Snail → shell → peas → carrots → orange → marmalade → jam → traffic → car → bike.

Morphology

Morphology is the way words, as units of meaning, may contain roots and affixes assembled in a rule-governed way to form other acceptable recognizable words. Thus, morphology is intimately involved in vocabulary and its development, supporting both breadth and depth. For example, BOOKS is a single word with two units of meaning: 'Thing with words printed on paper' and 'more than one'. The morphological rule is that the unit of meaning that signals 'more than one' is added to the end of the noun. It cannot occur at the beginning or in the middle. Within morphology there is also the possibility of compounding words: for example, BOOKSHELF. This is a word composed of two separate words each with a specific meaning. The meaning of the compound word is obviously related to the meaning of both the constituent words, but goes beyond both.

Next, we look at some further aspects of morphology using the root word TEACH. By root, we mean the single mono-morphemic word that has no prefixes or suffixes.

Morphological affixes can indicate related meanings

- *Teach* is a verb meaning 'to impart knowledge to or instruct someone as to how to do something'. This is part of a family of words that all share some aspect of meaning.
- *Teacher*. This is a noun that has two morphemes – the root: *teach*, plus the derivational suffix *–er*. Together they create the new word that is a noun meaning 'one who teaches'. The suffix *–er* means an agent who does the action of the verb. Think of all the other words you know that end in this suffix. There is *skater, reader, writer*, and thousands more.
- *Teachable*. This is an adjective with two morphemes. Again the root: *teach*, plus the derivational morpheme *–able* meaning capable of being taught. The suffix *–able* means there is a person or thing that has the characteristic of receiving the action of the verb. A book may be said to be *readable*. You will be able to list many more words with *–able* at the end. Try to unpack them to identify the two units of meaning. Be warned that often in affixation, the root word is modified. For example, *edible* is a word meaning 'having the characteristic of being eaten'. It therefore can be deconstructed into *eat* and *–able*. You will begin to see how interesting affixation can be. Discussions about this can be very stimulating with children, particularly in Key Stage 2.
- *Unteachable*. The root *teach* plus the suffix *–able*, plus the prefix *un-* meaning 'not' – in this case, not capable of being taught.

All the examples here are of *derivational* morphology where a new word is derived from an old word by the addition of affixes. There is also *inflectional* morphology where a suffix is added to the root to create an inflected form of the same word: e.g. TEACH + ES – root plus third person singular affix; TEACH + ING – root plus the present participle. These are all different aspects of the same verb.

Very early in their language history, children are able to use and understand inflectional morphology. They know that when they hear the sound /s/ or /z/ or /iz/ added to the end of a noun then there is more than one: CATS, DOGS, HORSES. They are also able to use this to express more than one: DOLLS, TEDDIES, EYES … FOOTS!? It is very common for young children to overgeneralize their morphological knowledge. Use of incorrect plural forms such as FOOTS and SHEEPS and MOUSES, and past tense forms such as I RUNNED, I WRITED IT, indicate implicit understanding of the rules of the morphological system. Children eventually learn the exceptions to rules and use FEET, SHEEP and MICE; RAN and WROTE successfully. They need support with this. Adults understand the meanings of overgeneralized forms, and can value the child's contribution by accepting the meaning (e.g. 'I writed it'; 'Yes, that was very clever of you!') and providing expanded language with the standard form in contingent conversation ('Do you want to add that to the story you wrote yesterday?'). In this way, children hear the conventional form which will stand them in good stead for developing their literacy skills.

You will note that the affixes we have used as illustrations so far are all 'bits' of words that can only exist in combination with root words: so they are *bound* morphemes. There are rules for combining these with roots. Some affixes are prefixes: e.g. UN– (UNLIKE, UNTIE) and PRE– (PREFIX, PRECEDE). They have to come before the root. Others are suffixes: e.g. –ING (EATING, SINGING), –FUL (BEAUTIFUL, THOUGHTFUL), –LY (GENTLY), –NESS (KINDNESS, SWEETNESS). They have to come after the root.

It is possible for a root to have a number of different affixes added to it either as prefixes or suffixes. There is a syntax for the order in which this may occur. For example, we can add the suffixes –LY and –NESS to KIND to create KINDLINESS but the order is fixed. We do not say KINDNESSLY. Right from the early stages of language development, children are good at affixing words in the correct sequence. Using affixation to support vocabulary extension in school can be very productive and fun and has the benefit of supporting spelling skills as well.

When talking about vocabulary size, we should note that we are talking about root words and not all the additional words that are created through affixation. However, when considering vocabulary depth, we may well be interested in all the words that are derived from the root.

Syntax
Word order

Syntax is the system for ordering words into sentences. Syntax is commonly known as grammar: the way words are combined in sentences in a rule-governed way to produce utterances that are recognized by other speakers of the language as being acceptable. 'The little children were running' is recognized as an acceptable English sentence, but 'Children little the running were' is recognized as unacceptable in English. Why do you think this is not acceptable? Here are some more unacceptable English 'sentences'.

- Dogs big the playing are.
- Football best the team won.
- The babies crying hungry were.

Rearrange the words to form acceptable English sentences. You will have no difficulty doing this. However, try to state what the rules are before you read on.

Perhaps you stated that in English, THE always comes before a noun and not after it; that if there is an adjective modifying the noun, it has to come before the noun but after THE; and auxiliaries to the verb, such as ARE or WERE, always have to come before the main verb not after it.

Rules for word order vary from language to language and within languages. For example, in French, some adjectives come after the noun (e.g. *la porte verte*, the green door), but others come before it (e.g. *un grand repas*, a big meal). This means that there is nothing immutable about word order. All we can say is that each language has its own way of doing things. Each language has its own syntax.

Sentence structure

A *sentence* can be defined as a sequence of words that is complete in itself and that conveys a statement, question, command or exclamation. The most common form of sentence in English is composed of a subject and a predicate. The *subject* of the sentence is the noun or noun phrase that comes before the predicate. The *predicate* is the rest of the sentence, including the verb. The subject always has to agree with the verb for the sentence to be considered grammatical. Thus, in Standard English, we say: 'the dog barks' and 'the dogs bark', not 'the dog bark' or 'the dogs barks'. There are likely to be dialects or other forms of English where the rules are slightly different.

Probably the most frequent sentence form in English is when the predicate is composed of a Verb and an Object. This is called a Subject-Verb-Object sentence. The subject performs the action of the verb. The *object* is the noun or noun phrase that is said to receive, or be affected by, the action of the verb.

Take the sentence illustrated in Figure 6.2.

 Susan   eats   pears
 Subject **Verb** **Object**
         _____Predicate_____/

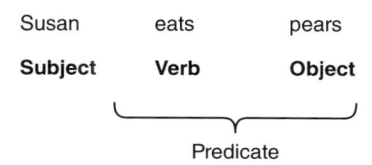

Figure 6.2   Subject-Verb-Object sentence

SUSAN is the subject, EATS is the verb, and PEARS is the object. SUSAN is the subject because she performs the action of the verb, i.e. she eats. The thing that is affected by this is the PEARS, so they are the object. This is obviously a very short sentence where each element of the sentence, the subject, the verb and the object, are all single words. However subject, verb, and object are grammatical units that do not have to be single words. This is illustrated in Figure 6.3.

The very happy young children are carefully picking the delightfully perfumed roses.

Subject   **Verb**   **Object**

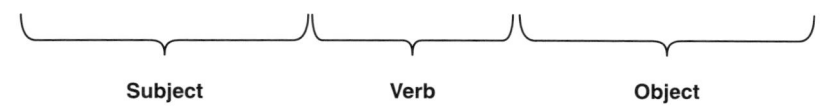

Figure 6.3   Grammatical units of Subject, Verb and Object

We can see that it has the same grammatical form Subject-Verb-Object as 'Susan eats pears', but the subject now is composed of five words, the verb is two words, and the object is four words. In this sentence, the grammatical unit subject is 'The very happy young children'. The five words are parsed together as one unit to form a noun phrase.

We should quickly define *phrase* and *clause* here for completeness. A *phrase* is a group of words that can be parsed together but which do not form a complete unit, a phrase needs some more words to complete the sentence. This contrasts with a *clause,* which is a group of words that form a complete unit and which contain a verb. Some clauses are also simple sentences, but many sentences (like this one) contain more than one clause.

According to linguists, there is a hierarchy of units that goes:

word → phrase → clause →simple sentence → complex sentence → compound sentence.

This is illustrated in the next box.

Hierarchy of units and sentences

- Caretaker (*word*)
- The caretaker (*phrase*)
- When the caretaker arrived (*clause*)
- The caretaker arrived. (*sentence*)
- When the caretaker arrived, he unlocked the school. (*complex sentence*)
- The caretaker arrived and he unlocked the school.(*compound sentence*)

Unlike vocabulary, syntax is a system of language that definitely is developmental, and unrolls over time. Children begin speaking using single words, but then start combining words into longer units to convey more complex meanings. They extract the rules for combining words from the language they are exposed to, again emphasizing the importance of a rich language environment for good language development. Syntactic development continues well into the secondary school years so it is important that language is part of the school curriculum: an object of study in its own right. Though the processes for understanding syntax are the same for both spoken and written language, there are many more complex forms of syntax that children are primarily exposed to in their written texts. Teaching reading comprehension involves helping children to unpack different syntactic structures. The most effective way to do this is through talking about the language itself.

Syntax provides a bridge between vocabulary and meaning: sentence structure and word order are essential to the meaning of sentences. Take the sentences:

- The dog chased the children.
- The children chased the dog.

The words are the same, but the meaning is different. The meaning of each sentence is mediated by the word order. Underlying understanding of both sentences is also knowledge of vocabulary and world knowledge, as we can see if we think about the next two sentences:

- The dog ate the bone.
- The bone ate the dog.

Both sentences are grammatically acceptable. They both have the same Subject-Verb-Object syntactic structure. However, the first sentence is the only one that makes real-world sense because we know that, in the real world, inanimate objects do not eat. They do in books and they do in cartoons. Authors and animators make full use of this for comic or for scary effect.

Parts of speech

All words have a number of different identities: their meaning or meanings, their syntactic status and their phonology. As syntax is the system for combining words into meaningful units, words themselves are units of syntax and have their own syntactic status: e.g. *noun, pronoun, verb, adjective, adverb, preposition, conjunction, determiner*. These are known as *parts of speech*. The syntactic rules of a language relate to the order in which different parts of speech may be combined to form meaning. We will introduce you here to just enough about parts of speech to support your understanding of how this impacts on comprehension. We have already been using the words for parts of speech earlier in this chapter, but now we will provide specific definitions.

Nouns

Nouns are open class words (new nouns can be created). They are frequently defined as the class of words that refer to a place, person or thing but we can also add an event, substance, quality or quantity. Strictly speaking, this is a semantic definition relating to the meaning of words. Syntactically, nouns generally occur at the end of noun phrases, e.g. 'the brown bear'; after adjectives, e.g. 'brown bear'; after determiners, e.g. 'the bear'; and before verbs, e.g. 'bears eat'.

Nouns can be further classified into *count* or *mass* nouns. A count noun refers to an entity that can be counted. *Book, bone, party* are all count nouns, which can be used in plural as well as singular form: e.g. BOOKS, BONES, PARTIES. They can be preceded by a *determiner* (defined below), such as *a, two* (or any number), SEVERAL, EVERY: e.g. A CHILD; TWO BONES; SEVERAL PARTIES; EVERY OCEAN.

Mass nouns have none of these properties and so cannot co-occur with quantifying determiners. We do not put A, TWO, SEVERAL, EVERY before a mass noun such as WATER or FURNITURE. Although, because language is so creative and exciting, we can say 'a stretch of water' or 'several pieces of furniture'. This means we can add a count noun to a phrase containing a mass noun.

Nouns are very important parts of speech for enabling us to understand about things. As English-speaking children develop their vocabularies, nouns are the largest group (Dhillon, 2010), much larger than verbs. Nouns feature very largely in written texts, so children need to develop their noun vocabulary in order to understand what they are reading. However, because nouns form the largest group, each individual noun is not necessarily likely to be repeated very often in any one text. This is in contrast to the function words, which are few in number but very high in frequency. Nouns are very large in number but also very variable in frequency. This inverse relationship between number and frequency impacts on learning to read words, as we have seen.

Pronouns

Pronouns are related to nouns. This is the very small set of words that stand for nouns or noun phrases in phrases, clauses and sentences. Examples are: I, ME, YOU, SHE, HE, WE, THEY, IT, HERSELF, HIMSELF, EACH, FEW, SOMEONE, WHO, WHOSE, etc. The list here is not exhaustive, but serves to show this is a small set of words that are very high in frequency. We can identify whether a word is a noun, or a phrase is a noun phrase, by replacing it with a pronoun. We can also replace a pronoun by a noun or a noun phrase.

Take the sentence we presented earlier (Figure 6.3):

- The very happy young children are carefully picking the delightfully perfumed roses.

The noun phrases can be replaced by two pronouns: THEY and THEM to give the sentence:

- They are picking them.

In real language interactions, the noun or the noun phrase is usually always mentioned before it can be replaced by a pronoun. This is because without the nouns having been specified, we do not know to what or to whom the pronouns refer. This is particularly the case with written language where there is no face-to-face communication, and no possibility of using gesture or pointing to clarify the meaning.

One of the authors of this book learnt about pronouns a very long time ago in a *Happy Grammar* book that had pictures and rhymes all about the parts of speech. Not everything stuck, but the rhyme about pronouns went:

Now, if WE were asking Miss Martin to tea,

We shouldn't keep saying 'Miss Martin', YOU see,

But would ask HER to come

If SHE possibly could,

And say WE would all be so pleased if SHE would.

The linguistic point being made in this jingle is that constant repetition of the noun or noun phrase makes for poor communication. Pronouns may be few in number, but they are complex words. As we shall see when we consider reading comprehension *per se*, understanding the noun to which a pronoun refers is crucial for both literal and inferential comprehension.

Verbs

After nouns, the next most plentiful words in English are verbs. These are also an open class of words: new verbs can be created. As shown in the next box, they express states, physical actions, mental actions, or occurrence.

Categories of meaning expressed in verbs

- State: *I am happy* – the verb is TO BE
- Physical action: *She throws* – the verb is TO THROW
- Mental action: *They think* – the verb is TO THINK
- Occurrence: *Events happen* – the verb is TO HAPPEN

Verbs are the only class of word that is compulsory in sentences. Single word sentences can be formed using just a verb: commands like 'Go!', 'Stop!', 'Think!' are all considered to be well-formed English sentences, even if not very polite. As we said above, the verb forms part of the predicate in a sentence and the predicate is the only part of a sentence that is required to make it grammatically acceptable.

Verbs are more complex parts of speech than nouns and there is a considerable amount of morphology associated with them. A verb on its own is called the infinitive form of the verb. In English, the infinitive form is always two words: the word TO plus the verb itself, as in TO GO, TO THINK. This is different from French, where the infinitive form is just one word: ALLER, PENSER.

An example of the morphology of verbs is in the specification of tenses. The *tense* of a verb indicates when the action happened, or whether or not it will happen at all. We will not list all possible tenses here, but just illustrate tense with past, present and future of the action verbs TO TALK and TO RUN.

We will use the following set of sentences:

- They talk to their teacher.
- They talked to their teacher.
- They are talking to their teacher.

- They will talk to their teacher.
- They run to school.
- They ran to school.
- They are running to school.
- They will run to school.

The verb TO TALK is a regular verb. The past tense form of regular verbs is marked by the inflectional suffix –ED. In the present continuous form, we have to use a form of the modal auxiliary verb TO BE and add the suffix –ING. In the future tense, the modal auxiliary verb WILL is inserted before the verb. All regular verbs take these forms.

The verb TO RUN is an irregular verb. This means that its past tense form is phonologically different from, but related to, the infinitive form. There is no past tense marker. It takes the same form as the regular verbs in the present continuous and the future tenses.

We will not cover every possible verb tense, but we will note that modal auxiliary verbs are few in number but enable us to create many more tenses. The modal auxiliaries are:

- CAN and COULD
- MAY and MIGHT
- SHALL and SHOULD
- WILL and WOULD
- MUST

Try creating as many sentences with the verb *to talk* as you can, but with each one having a different tense.

Verb word forms also change according to the subject of the verb. The subject of a verb can be one of six forms: three singular and three plural. When the verb word form changes relative to the subject it is known as conjugation. This is illustrated below, using TO TALK and TO BE.

Conjugation

Singular	First person	*I talk*	*I am*
	Second person	*You talk*	*You are*
	Third person	*He/She/It talks*	*He/She/It is*
Plural	First person	*We talk*	*We are*
	Second person	*You talk*	*You are*
	Third person	*They talk*	*They are*

You may notice that all the subjects are pronouns. It is only in the third person that the pronoun can be replaced by nouns and noun phrases. Just try it.

The remaining parts of speech we will cover are adjectives, adverbs, prepositions, conjunctions and determiners.

Adjectives

These are open class words that modify nouns or pronouns. In our previous sentence, (The very happy young children are carefully picking the delightfully perfumed roses), HAPPY and YOUNG are both adjectives that modify the noun CHILDREN, and PERFUMED modifies ROSES.

Adverbs

VERY, CAREFULLY and DELIGHTFULLY are the adverbs in our sentence. VERY modifies the adjectives HAPPY and YOUNG; CAREFULLY modifies the verb TO PICK; and DELIGHTFULLY modifies the adjective PERFUMED.

If you think back to our discussion about morphology, you will note that the two words CAREFULLY and DELIGHTFULLY have the same morphological structure. They each have a root, CARE and DELIGHT respectively. The derivational suffix –FUL has been added to the root to create an adjective and then a further suffix –LY has been added to create the adverb. We hope that you will appreciate how introducing children to word morphology can help you to extend and deepen their vocabularies. They will learn about word families and the semantic relations between them.

Prepositions

Prepositions are the closed class of words that generally precede nouns, noun phrases, or pronouns to show their relation to other parts of the sentence. For example, in the sentence, the children played: THE CHILDREN PLAYED IN THE PLAYGROUND, IN is the preposition that informs us where the children were playing. The relationship it indicates is *place*. Other prepositions of place are BEHIND, UNDER, BESIDE. Prepositions can convey a number of other relationships, *time* (AT, BEFORE, AFTER); *direction* (TO, TOWARDS, THROUGH); *agency* (BY); *possession* (OF); *purpose* (FOR); *source* (FROM, OUT OF).

Prepositions are powerful in supporting the construction of mental models of the meaning of what we read and hear. Think about the mental images created by the following sentences:

- The Queen sat ON the throne.
- The Queen sat UNDER the throne.
- The Queen sat BESIDE the throne.
- The Queen sat BEHIND the throne.

There is just one word change in each case, but your mental image should change each time.

Conjunctions

Conjunctions are another closed class of words that connect phrases, clauses and sentences. Conjunctions that join units of the same level are called co-ordinating conjunctions. For example: AND, BUT, SO, OR.

Think about this sentence:

- Susan AND John watched the tennis finals AND they clapped at all the good shots.

The first AND connects the two nouns that form the noun phrase that is the subject of the first clause. The second AND connects the two clauses so that they become one sentence. In this sentence both the clauses are main clauses: they can both stand on their own without the conjunction:

- Susan and John watched the tennis finals. They clapped at all the good shots.

Conjunctions that connect a dependent clause to a main are called subordinating conjunctions. For example: BECAUSE, BEFORE, HOW, IF, ONCE, SINCE.

- Susan and John clapped BECAUSE the tennis was great.

In this sentence, the second clause is said to be dependent because we would not say 'because the tennis was great' on its own. It needs the main clause to complete the meaning. Subordinating conjunctions 'introduce' the content of the subordinating clause and always occur at the beginning of them. However, the subordinating clause does not have to come after the main clause. Our sentence could have read:

- BECAUSE the tennis was great, Susan and John clapped.

Realistically, in spoken language, the main clause usually comes at the beginning of a sentence, but in written language, this is not the case. Often, for reasons of style and impact, authors will move the subordinate clause to the beginning of the sentence. We have already mentioned that the style of written language is different from that of spoken language and this is one example of this.

Determiners

The last part of speech we will consider is *determiners*. These are a closed class of words that come at the beginning of a noun phrase. They serve to express the referent of the noun or the noun phrase. For example, they may indicate whether the noun is referring to a definite member of a class: e.g. THE pupil; or to an indefinite member: e.g. A pupil. THE is called the definite article, and A or AN is the indefinite article. Determiners may also be possessive pronouns: e.g. MY book, YOUR pen, THEIR shoes. They may be quantifiers: e.g. MANY chairs, FEW crayons, THREE desks. And they may be demonstratives: e.g. THIS photo, indicating a photo that is near to the speaker, or THAT photo, indicating a photo that is further away from the speaker.

The correct use and understanding of determiners is essential for understanding the aspect of language called *deixis*. This applies to the use of expressions where the meaning can be traced to when and where an event happened, who was speaking and who was being spoken to. Figure 6.4 illustrates an early study of children's understanding of deixis by Clark and Sengul (1978).

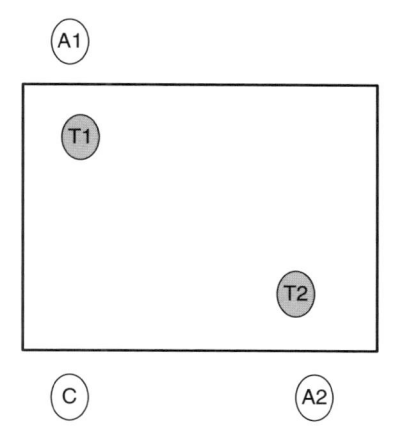

Figure 6.4 Children's understanding of deixis

Figure 6.4 illustrates an interaction between a child (C) and an adult who could either sit opposite the child (A1) or beside the child (A2). Two identical toys were in positions T1 and T2. The two toys were always exactly the same distance from the child, but one was close to the adult and one was away from the adult. In the study, when the adult gave the children instructions, she did not use any pointing or gestures. It might seem obvious to us that if the adult says to the child 'Make that toy dance', she intends the child to jiggle the one that is furthest from her, and we do not need gesture to help us understand this. Thus, if the adult is in position A1, she expects the toy in T2 to be jiggled. This is because 'that' indicates far from the speaker. Additionally, if she says 'Make this toy dance', she means the one nearest to her. If she is in position A2, she expects T2 to dance. Clark and Sengul (1978) found that children's awareness of the distinction in meaning between this and that and other deictic pairs such as here–there and come–go was still developing during the pre-school years if the adults did not use pointing and gesture. Children need to have complete command of these determiners to enable them to build up mental models of what they are reading. They do not have the support of gestures to help them understand what they are reading.

Pragmatics

This system is concerned with our use of language in a social context. It is the ways that people produce and understand meanings through language. This helps us to understand why written language is so different in style, structure and vocabulary from spoken language. Enabling children to learn to understand and control the written form of language is a major part of the teaching of reading and something that cannot just be left to chance.

Pragmatic skill enables us go beyond the words to take account of speakers' intentions: what they mean and not just what they say. In a face-to-face context we have many additional clues from the speaker, including tone of voice, facial expression, gestures and body posture, that all help us to get to their intended meaning. However, when we are reading someone's language we have none of the non-verbal cues that help us go beyond the surface to the intended meaning.

Take this extract from *Calling Doctor Amelia Bedelia* by Herman Parish (2004):

'Amelia Bedelia!' said Nurse Ames. 'You are a sight for sore eyes.'

'How terrible,' said Amelia Bedelia. 'I am sorry that your eyes hurt.'

'My eyes are fine,' said Nurse Ames. 'But I am up to my eyeballs in patients. Dr. Horton had to visit the hospital. Would you give me a hand until she gets back?'

'No,' said Amelia Bedelia. 'Both my hands are attached to me, but I would be glad to help you.'

The conceit of many of the Amelia Bedelia books is that she is a little girl who takes language literally. The books rely on children being aware of the ambiguities and metaphors that we use constantly in everyday language. Pragmatic skill involves understanding how meaning often lies beneath the surface of the words, and a deep knowledge of words, their usage and syntactic structure is necessary for understanding. Explicit knowledge is not necessary for generally going about our lives: we do not need to contemplate our language as we are engaging in conversation. However, teachers *do* need explicit knowledge in order to support children's learning. They need to be able to modify their own language as they are interacting with children to ensure that they support language development. Learning about language in its own right is as valuable as all the other curriculum subjects and children's literacy development can be enhanced by learning how language works.

Reading comprehension

You will have noticed that throughout our discussion of the different systems of language it has been impossible to separate any one system completely from any other. In particular, meaning seems always to inform discussion of vocabulary and syntax. Semantics, meaning, will form the main focus of our consideration of reading comprehension.

Comprehension of written texts requires readers to orchestrate at least three aspects of language: their wide vocabulary knowledge, including the ability to parse words into their morphological structures; their command of syntax; and their ability to go beyond the surface of the language in order to build up mental models of the meaning. So we now turn directly to reading comprehension: the process whereby the words in their syntactic context within the discourse are interpreted.

As we explained in Chapter 2, studies have shown that different abilities underlie the development of word reading skills from those that underlie the development of reading comprehension. The important predictors of reading comprehension in these studies were the ability to draw inferences, an understanding of story structure, and comprehension monitoring ability (Oakhill, Cain & Bryant, 2003), vocabulary knowledge and grammatical skills (Muter, Hulme, Snowling & Stevenson, 2004).

All these abilities are essential for understanding texts. Once children have mastered the time-limited skill of word reading, they can tackle any text. But without good language skills and extensive experience of print, they may not understand what they are reading. Language skills continue to develop well into the secondary school years. Fortunately, once word reading processes are fluent and automatic, more and more processing capacity is freed up to support comprehension.

This is an important issue. When children first begin to read, they should be given texts with a familiar content and structure, so that even when considerable effort is devoted to reading the words, there is likely to be enough processing capacity available for understanding what is being read.

Many of the paralinguistic cues which support spoken language comprehension are absent from written language. We use verbal emphasis, prosody and intonation patterns to support meaning. In English English, a rising intonation at the end of a sentence indicates a question. This can be the case even when the sentence construction is not in question form. Thus 'Coming' with rising intonation is interpreted as a question, just the same as 'Are you coming' – also with rising intonation. You will note that we have not included the question mark in the two examples. Children have to learn that punctuation replaces some aspects of intonation. There is no rising intonation on a page, just 'Coming?' or 'Are you coming?' It is the question mark which signals that coming is a question. The reason that we specify English English in this context is because this is not the case for Australian English where a rising intonation marks the end of a sentence regardless of whether it is a question or not. Reading, however, is a one-sided conversation – the writer is not present to clarify intended meanings, or to notice that there may be puzzlement or a lack of comprehension. Fortunately, in the early years of reading instruction, children read aloud and teachers are attuned to when children do not understand what they have just read.

Producers of printed texts use many graphic devices to capture meaning beyond the words themselves. There are headings, paragraphs, extra lines, changes of font, underlining, italics and the punctuation marks themselves. Novice readers have to internalize these conventions of graphic design in order to support their construction of the meaning of the text.

Construction of the meaning of the text

Comprehension of texts, whether spoken or written, is an active process which requires the attention of the listener/reader. It is generally agreed that when readers comprehend texts, they represent the meaning of the text to themselves through the construction of a mental model (Johnson-Laird, 1983) or situation model (Kintsch, 1998). For our purposes, it is possible to treat these as providing similar accounts of comprehension.

Mental models

Kintsch and Rawson (2005) argue that for skilled readers comprehension is largely smooth and effortless. They cite the classic work of Bransford, Barclay and Franks (1972) to support this. They presented adults with one or other of the following sentences.

- Three turtles rested beside a floating log and a fish swam beneath them.
- Three turtles rested on a floating log and a fish swam beneath them.

Both sentences express a relation between the log and the turtles: the turtles are either ON or BESIDE the log. They also express a relation between the turtles and the fish: the fish swim BENEATH the turtles. Bransford et al. (1972) found that the mental model constructed on reading the two sentences was different. Those people who read the sentence containing the preposition ON were more likely to accept the novel sentence 'Three turtles rested on a floating log and a fish swam beneath it' as the one they had read. Their explanation for this was that people use the linguistic input to create a mental model, which then is not wholly reliant on the exact wording. In this case, the mental model includes the idea that, since the turtles are on the log, when the fish swims beneath the turtle, it inevitably also swims beneath the log. Bransford and Johnson (1972: 717) furthermore said that 'Comprehension ... involves the recovery and interpretation of the abstract deep structural relations underlying sentences'. They reported a study where secondary school-age participants listened to a tape recording of a passage, and were subsequently asked to judge how easy the passage was to comprehend, on a seven-point scale from 1, very difficult, through to 7, very easy. They were also asked to recall as much of the passage as they could.

We cannot provide you with a tape recording, but we can provide you with the whole passage to read. We will not expect you to memorize it. We invite you to read it carefully.

> If the balloons popped, the sound wouldn't be able to carry because everything would be too far away from the correct floor. A closed window would also prevent the sound from carrying, since most buildings tend to be well insulated. Since the whole operation depends on the steady flow of electricity, a break in the middle of the wire would also cause problems. Of course the fellow could shout, but the human voice is not loud enough to carry that far. An additional problem is that a string could break on the instrument. Then there could be

Comprehension of oral and written language   121

no accompaniment to the message. It is clear that the best situation would involve less distance. Then there would be fewer potential problems. With face-to-face contact, the least number of things could go wrong.

You will not be surprised that rated comprehension and memory for the passage was low in the groups that did the auditory equivalent of what you have just done. However, there were a number of different conditions in this study. One group were able to listen to the passage twice. This group may have been in a position more like you: we suspect you may have read the passage at least twice in order to try to work out the meaning. A third group were given a picture to look at *after* they had listened to the passage that accurately depicted the scene described in the passage. A fourth group were given a picture to look at *before* they heard the passage that contained all the same elements as the other picture, but was constructed in such a way that the relationships were not defined. Finally, a fifth group were given the accurate picture to look at *before* they heard the passage. Results are shown in Table 6.2.

The two pictures are available on the next page.

Table 6.2 Results of comprehension experiment

	No context		Context		
	Hear the story once	Hear the story twice	Full context *after* hearing the story	Partial context *before* hearing story	Full context *before* hearing story
Participants' mean comprehension rating (maximum score 7)	2.30	3.60	3.30	3.70	**6.10**
Participants' mean memory score (maximum 14)	3.60	3.80	3.60	4.00	**8.00**

The fifth group (who saw the picture which was a true reflection of the scenario described in the passage *before* they heard the passage) rated it *easy* to *very easy* to comprehend. Their mean comprehension rating was 6.10. All the other groups rated the passage hard to comprehend, with significantly lower ratings than the fifth group. These four groups also recalled far less than the group who saw the true picture beforehand.

Below you will find the true picture (Figure 6.5) and the one which contains all the elements, but not in the relationships described in the passage. Figure 6.5 shows the two pictures. The top one is the true picture. The bottom one contains all the elements but not in the relationship described in the passage.

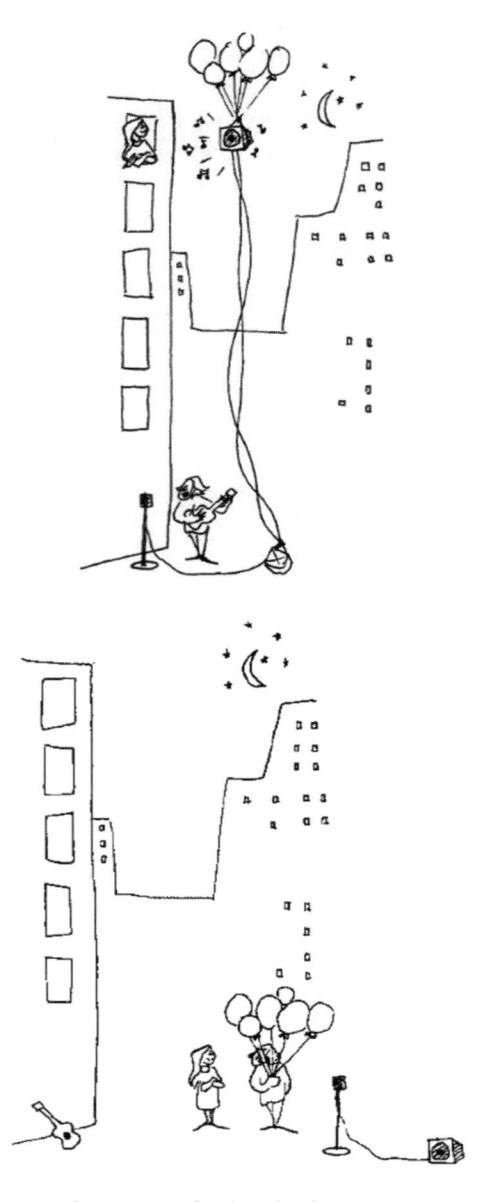

Figure 6.5   Illustration from Bransford and Johnson, 1972

People often experience an 'ah-ha' phenomenon when they see the picture. Suddenly everything makes sense. Just having the words, none of which would be unfamiliar to teenagers, in appropriate syntactic form, was not enough to aid comprehension: they needed the semantic context to build a mental model of the scene.

Realistically, children are not presented with texts that are deliberately designed to obscure meaning. They are presented with texts where the language is designed to support the building of a mental model of the content. In order to do this, readers need to understand the separate words and phrases individually. They also need to understand these severally and collectively to begin to build their mental models, but beyond the surface of the text they need to bring in their previous knowledge, and knowledge of the world, to gain a deeper comprehension of the text.

Inferencing

An inference is a conclusion reached on the basis of evidence *and* reasoning. Inferencing skills enable us to draw inferences from texts we listen to or read. As we mentioned above, Oakhill et al. (2003) and Muter et al. (2004) found that ability to draw inferences is a significant predictor of ability to comprehend texts.

Below is a simple text from Charniak (1972).

> Jane was invited to Jack's birthday party. She wondered if he would like a kite. She went to her room and shook her piggy bank. It made no sound.

Before you read further, introspect on the mental model that you built up when reading the four sentences. In this short passage, there is no intention to deliberately obscure the meaning, and you do not need a picture to build up your mental model.

Most people report that they assume that Jane and Jack know one another. They are children rather than adults. This is because Jack is having a birthday party; the present is a typical toy for a child; and Jane keeps her money in a piggy bank rather than a high street bank. We infer that the reason she goes to her room is to find her piggy bank. We also infer that she does this because she has the intention to buy the kite, she does not already have one that she could give him. Furthermore, there is the realization that Jane will be disappointed because the piggy bank is empty. We deduce this because our real-world knowledge tells us that piggy banks generally contain coins that rattle when the piggy bank is shaken. We know in British culture that children have parties when they have birthdays and that birthday guests are expected to turn up with a gift.

We build up a mental model that goes beyond the words and that subsequently supports our comprehension. Additionally, we can see that comprehension is further supported by the linguistic syntactic cohesion of the text. These are not four unrelated sentences. The use of pronouns ties the sentences together. The personal pronoun SHE refers to Jane, as does the possessive pronoun HER, HE refers to Jack, and IT refers to the piggy bank.

These pronouns are examples of *anaphoric reference*. An anaphoric reference is when a word is used to refer to ideas and concepts that have been mentioned previously in the text. If you refer back to the discussion of pronouns, you will remember that we said pronouns should only be used once the noun to which they refer has been mentioned. The way the pronouns are used in Charniak's example supports understanding. They help to tie the meanings and events together. The psychological process that enables us to identify the concept specified by a previous noun, the referent, is called *anaphoric resolution*. Use of anaphoric resolution enables you to establish that JANE and SHE refer to the same entity.

The mental model you will have built up situates Jane as the main protagonist on the scene. This means that even if we substituted Jill for Jack, so that all the pronouns were feminine, the passage would probably not be ambiguous. The second sentence would read 'She wondered if she would like a kite', but anaphoric resolution enables us to work out that the two pronouns refer to two different entities.

However, this is not always the case and it is important that writers are careful about their use of anaphoric reference so that meaning is not obscured. Using a growing understanding of anaphoric reference to build up a mental model of a text is not trivial and children may need support to begin to work this out.

In order to understand texts completely, we have to build mental models that go beyond the surface structure of written or auditory texts to infer elements of meaning that are not specified. This shows us that comprehension is not a passive process, but an active one. By active here, we do not mean to imply that it is always effortful, explicit or deliberate. Much of the time, the inferences we make, as you saw in Charniak's 'party' text, seem to be almost automatic. We often do not realize that we have been making inferences until this is pointed out to us. As we shall see, this can have important implications for teaching comprehension. Teachers need to be conscious that at word, sentence and text level, children will need to be able to make quite complex inferences drawing on their vocabulary, syntactic, and world knowledge in order to comprehend seemingly obvious texts.

One way to check children's comprehension of texts is to ask them questions. However, we need to be careful about the types of question we ask. It is possible to be misled into thinking that children understand what they have been reading by asking them *literal* questions.

Read the following passage.

> Mary's New Year's resolution was to get fit and lose weight so she joined a gym not far away from her house. She thought it would be a good idea to cycle to the gym so that she could double her fitness regime. Unfortunately, she got a puncture, so she began to drive instead. Then a café opened just next to the gym car park. The smells coming from its bakery were very tempting. All her best resolutions went up in smoke and when she weighed herself at the end of February she was horrified. She tried to tell herself that her scales were faulty, but then she had to admit that cars and delicious cakes might have something to do with it.

Now answer these questions:

1. Who made a New Year's resolution?
2. What was her resolution?
3. Where was the café?
4. When did she weigh herself?
5. Did Mary stick to her New Year's resolution? How do you know?
6. Do you think Mary bought anything from the café? Why?
7. How was Mary getting to the gym at the end of February?

The first four questions can be answered by using words or phrases lifted directly from the text.

1. Mary
2. To get fit and lose weight.
3. Next to the gym car park.
4. At the end of February.

These are all literal answers requiring no inferencing skills. As long as one can read back over the text or remember what was said the answers are there explicitly.

The next three questions cannot be answered in this way. Though this is not a challenging text for you, you will have had to use your inferencing skills to provide satisfactory answers.

1. No, because it says her resolutions went up in smoke. Also, she was horrified by her weight so she must have put some weight on, or certainly not lost any.
2. Yes, because the smells from the café's bakery imply they cooked lovely cakes and she felt that cakes were one of the causes for her not losing weight.
3. She was driving there in her car.

A child who could only answer literal questions and not inferential ones could not be said to have sufficiently good comprehension skills to support learning through independent reading. As we shall see in Chapters 7 and 10, it is important to enable children to practise their developing inferencing skills in order that they may become independent learners. All but the very basic texts require a degree of inferencing, and without this major linguistic skill learning and progress are likely to be compromised.

Understanding story structure

There is a general view that all stories can be deconstructed into three parts:

- The introduction where the main characters are introduced and the plot may be set up;
- The exposition where the main events occur, which drive the story forward. Here there may be complications or obstacles which the protagonists have to overcome as the story begins to reach a climax;
- The resolution where the threads are drawn together and all is resolved.

Put more simply, story structure involves a beginning, a middle and an end. There is considerable evidence that children who have extensive exposure to stories internalize an awareness of structure that helps them anticipate and understand the ongoing events in stories. Studies (e.g. Cipielewski & Stanovich, 1992; Stainthorp, 1997) have shown that children who have greater exposure to print have higher levels of comprehension. Even before beginning literacy instruction, they can begin to extract the event patterns that occur and so they already have in place the experience of building up mental models of texts.

The literary language used in stories not only supports vocabulary development, but helps to draw attention to the patterns of event. A child who has heard 'Once upon a time…' or 'In the beginning…' a thousand times has the comfort of knowing that a tale is about to be told. Children begin to recognize when the setting and the characters have been introduced so that the plot can begin to unfold. They can also begin to anticipate when the resolution is upon them so that the final words '…And they all lived happily ever after' come with feelings of satisfaction. Part of the story structure is also the title, and experienced children are able to predict something about what the story will involve from the title.

We do not mean to imply that everything children read should be predictable. Their interest thrives on novelty and surprise. However, without an internalization of basic structure, surprise does not work and comprehension is compromised.

Though much of the print in the early stages of learning to read involves stories with chronological narratives, it is important that children have a wide experience of many different types of expository texts so that they can begin to learn about the wider curriculum through independent reading. We sometimes forget that when children read about history, geography, science, mathematics, cookery, religion, music, sport they have to engage in at least the same level of inferencing skills as when reading stories. They also have to learn about the different forms of the different genres to enable them to build up the necessary mental models of the texts. This is really important because they are likely to be having to understand content that is new to them and which may be cognitively challenging. This adds a further level of demand from the text. We refer you back to the discussion of the importance of vocabulary. When children are faced with reading subject textbooks independently, the content of the texts may be presented to them in the form of new subject-specific vocabulary, or known vocabulary that is being used in a subject-specific way. Nagy and Scott (2000) estimated that children need to understand around 90% of the words if they are going to have a chance of comprehend the text.

Comprehension monitoring

Oakhill, Cain and Bryant (2003) found that individual differences in monitoring one's own comprehension while reading significantly affected comprehension. Markman (1979) was one of the earliest people to investigate this. She gave children passages to read that may or may not have involved logical inconsistencies.

The reasoning was that, if readers are monitoring their understanding as they progress through a passage, the mental model they build up should not support any inconsistency, so they will notice this.

Read the following text, which was one of the expository texts that Markman developed for her work.

> Ants
>
> Everywhere they go they put out a special chemical from their bodies. They cannot see this chemical, but it has a special odour. An ant must have a nose in order to smell this chemical odour. Another thing about ants is they do not have a nose. Ants cannot smell this odour. Ants can always find their way home by smelling this odour to follow the trail.

We alerted you to the fact that the text contains inconsistencies, but we hope you would have thought there was something wrong by the time you read the fourth sentence. Markman worked with 10–13 year-olds and found that even some of the older readers simply accepted the texts as being fully comprehensible.

It should not surprise us that Oakhill et al. (2003) found the ability to monitor comprehension is an important factor in understanding. If one does not notice inconsistencies then one may not be building a sufficiently effective mental model of the text to support comprehension. This is likely to hamper the ability to learn from expository texts and therefore compromise educational progress.

Closing words

If you have been reading this chapter effectively and building up a useful mental model about comprehension, it will not surprise you that children's comprehension of texts is something which cannot be left to chance. They need their teachers to support vocabulary growth, syntactic skills, and ability to draw inferences from text – all to support the construction of mental models which will enable them to understand what they are reading. The knowledge and understanding you have gained from reading this chapter provide the basis for effective teaching of reading comprehension – the topic of our next chapter.

7

Teaching reading comprehension

Summary

Having read Chapter 6, you will be fully aware that teaching children to understand what they are reading is a complex task requiring sophisticated knowledge and skill on the part of the teacher. In this chapter, you will learn about the kinds of teaching that have been shown to be helpful in developing reading comprehension: ways of improving children's vocabulary, and of teaching comprehension strategies such as monitoring comprehension, making and using graphic organizers, and summarization. This is set in the wider context of reading as the active construction of a mental model of the discourse.

Introduction

Teaching children to understand what they read requires a considerable degree of multitasking, both in preparation and execution. In the past – for example, when the authors of this book went to primary school – the 'academic subject' called 'comprehension' was often taught through books that consisted of comprehension exercises. Pupils were given short passages to read, followed by questions relating to the texts. These were solitary exercises: there was unlikely to be any discussion about the texts or their meanings. Right answers would get a tick; wrong answers would get a cross. The questions would largely be literal questions where the answer could be found by reading back in the text. In the light of current knowledge and understanding, it seems positively bizarre that this was considered to be teaching comprehension as such. There was no real linkage between comprehending spoken language and comprehending written language, no discussion about the differences and similarities between the two, and no idea that the reader might be actively involved in interpreting the text. Things were not always better in the past.

There was a step change in thinking about comprehension in reading in the 1970s when people began to think about the processes involved in comprehension.

Two definitions of reading comprehension provided by Harris and Hodges (1995) illustrate the contrast between the older view of reading comprehension as being largely passive and the current view that the reader is an active participant in the process.

Reading comprehension is:

1. The reconstruction of the intended meaning of a communication; accurately understanding what is written or said. Note: The presumption here is that meaning resides in the message awaiting interpretation, and that the message received is congruent with the message sent.
2. The construction of the meaning of a written or spoken communication through a reciprocal, holistic interchange of ideas between the interpreter and the message in a particular communicative context.

(Harris & Hodges, 1995: 39)

This second view of reading comprehension arises from understanding that readers actively construct mental models of texts, creating representations which can be stored in memory. By engaging actively and constructively with texts, readers can use what they have read to expand their knowledge and understanding of what they subsequently read.

The Simple View of Reading deconstructs reading into word reading processes and language comprehension processes. As we saw in Chapter 5, developing fluent word reading skills depends on the development of both phonological recoding and lexical processes. When considering teaching comprehension, Figure 7.1 (adapted from Perfetti (1999) for inclusion in Appendix 1 of the Rose Review (Rose, 2006)) identifies the different elements of language which are necessary to enable children to build up effective mental models of texts.

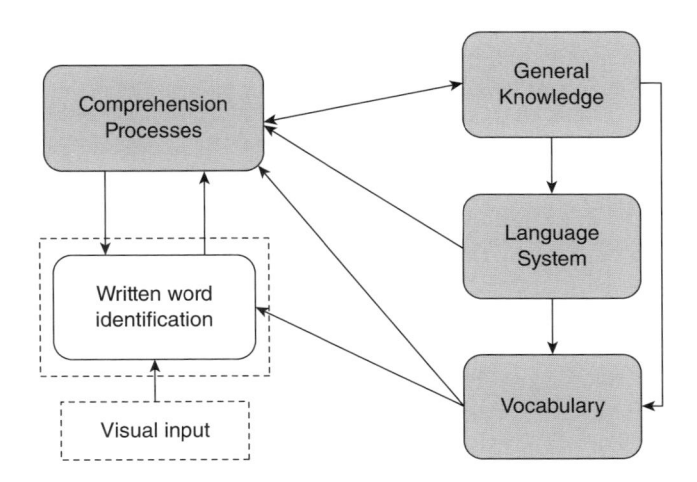

Figure 7.1 The components of the comprehension system

The four boxes with a shaded background relate to comprehension of language be it oral or written. The additional two boxes summarize the word recognition processes necessary for comprehension of written language through reading. To generate a mental representation of a text, the comprehension processes use information from the language system, vocabulary and general knowledge of the reader/listener. Improvements in all these areas are likely to underlie improvements in comprehension. However, becoming literate has the potential to extend both vocabulary and general knowledge and thereby to accelerate improvements in language comprehension. This emphasizes the importance of teaching children to understand texts and not just leaving it to chance. In the final analysis, 'comprehension is the essence of reading' (Durkin, 1993).

Within most educational jurisdictions, teaching reading comes within the domain of the language of instruction: for example, in the UK, it is included in the National Curriculum for English (Department for Education, 2014). However, it is a mistake to think of comprehension as being solely the purview of English (or whichever language is the language of instruction). Reading is essential for all curriculum areas. We need to ensure children have a generalized ability to understand texts so they can build up mental models of the content regardless of which curriculum area is involved. This is embodied in the expectation that children progress from learning to read to reading to learn. Reading is an essential life skill: skilled readers, particularly those in affluent technologically advanced countries, read every day of their lives. They see texts all around them and use their word reading skills, vocabulary knowledge, general knowledge and language comprehension strategies to build mental models of these texts, without any conscious awareness of what they are doing. Texts come in multiple forms: books, handwritten lists, newspapers and magazines, text messages and emails, timetables, adverts, product information in shops, road signs, etc., and in both private space and in the public domain: the personal and the communal. Texts inhabit the domains of education, work and leisure. And increasingly they come in multiple modes: both hard copy and electronic. For all this multitude of engagement with texts, vocabulary, language processes and knowledge of the world must be orchestrated to enable understanding.

Vocabulary

We begin with vocabulary. The impact of vocabulary knowledge on reading comprehension has been known for almost a century (Whipple, 1925) and in truth it would be peculiar if this were not the case. As we saw in Chapter 6, the more extensive the breadth and depth of one's vocabulary, the better one's comprehension of texts is likely to be. The larger the vocabulary, the greater the chance that meanings of words in texts are already known.

When children begin to learn to read, they already have an extensive oral vocabulary which supports their understanding of what they are reading. In this early stage, transforming the letters on the page into the phonological forms of the words they represent allows children to access words that are already in their oral vocabulary. Oral vocabulary smooths the transition from understanding spoken language to understanding written language. As Perfetti, Landi and Oakhill (2005) suggest: 'Not knowing the meaning of words in a text is a bottleneck in [reading] comprehension.' However, though there is evidence that reading ability and vocabulary size are related, there is no evidence that this is actually a *causal* relationship, i.e. that teaching vocabulary *per se* actually improves reading ability (NICH & HD, 2000). However, given we know there is this relationship between the two and given that vocabulary involves meaning, albeit at the word level, it is reasonable to assume that there is a place for vocabulary teaching within the context of teaching reading comprehension: without knowledge of word meaning it is difficult to see how text meanings might be accessed. Beck, McKeown and Kucan (2002) showed that most everyday conversations are composed of words that are generally in the oral vocabularies of children when they start school. This means that the conversations they hear around them are unlikely to be a source of vocabulary extension. Schooling becomes the vehicle for this, and particularly the written texts to which children are exposed.

Though no causal relationship has been demonstrated between vocabulary size and reading ability, there is a robust relationship. Early vocabulary during preschool years is predictive of later vocabulary up to the age of 10 years (Storch & Whitehurst, 2002), showing that those with a larger vocabulary have an early and lasting advantage. In particular, a number of studies have shown that oral vocabulary predicts comprehension (Davis, 1942; Just & Carpenter, 1987; Ricketts, Nation, & Bishop, 2007; Whitehurst & Lonigan, 2001).

A recent longitudinal study by Lee (2011) investigated the relationship between early oral language ability at the age of 2 years and literacy development up to the age of 11 years. The data came from a large longitudinal data set collected for the National Institute of Child Health and Human Development (NICH & HD) Study of Early Child Care and Youth Development (SECCYD) (2000, 2005). Lee examined data from 1,137 typically developing children from nine US states. Vocabulary size at the age of 2 years was found to be a good predictor of reading comprehension at the age of 9 years and 11 years, after controlling for individual differences in terms of parental socio-economic status, gender, birth order and ethnicity. She further analysed data from a subset of 311 children with large vocabularies (> 460 total words at the age of 2 years) and compared their performance with a subset of 312 children with small vocabularies (< 230 total words at the age of 2 years). Children in the large vocabulary size group significantly outperformed those in the small vocabulary size group on all literacy and language measures at both 9 years and 11 years. Her analyses confirmed established findings that socio-economic status, gender, ethnicity and birth order all significantly affect vocabulary development and attainment in literacy, but even when all these variables were accounted for, there was still a significant effect of early vocabulary development on later reading comprehension. The logical conclusion is that, even if the causal relationship between vocabulary development and comprehension has not been firmly established, it would seem negligent not to include vocabulary teaching as part of one's teaching of reading comprehension.

Implicit vocabulary teaching: vocabulary learning through listening to stories

There is a long tradition of teachers in pre-school settings and primary schools (particularly in the Key Stage 1 years) reading stories to children. This tradition stems from social and aesthetic judgements that this is a 'good' thing. However, there is now solid evidence that it has a positive impact on children's vocabularies (e.g. Leung, 1992 (kindergarten); Nicholson & Whyte, 1992 (8–10 year olds); Robbins & Ehri, 1994 (kindergarten); Sénéchal & Cornell, 1993 (4–5 year olds)).

While reading stories to children has a beneficial effect on their vocabularies, related activities can further enhance this. Dickinson and Smith (1994) found that when teachers encouraged the children to talk about the stories they were hearing there was a significant impact on vocabulary. Sénéchal (1997) also found that kindergarten children learned more from answering questions about stories than they did from simply listening to them without any active engagement. Furthermore, she found that repeated readings of the same text were particularly effective in supporting vocabulary learning. The effect has also been noted by Leung (1992) with children in Grade 1 in the USA (aged 6 years). This all fits nicely with the view that comprehension is an active process. By talking about the stories they listen to, children can also build up mental models of stories and story structure which adds to their general knowledge.

The studies of Robbins and Ehri (1994) and Nicholson and Whyte (1992) both found the positive impact on vocabulary of listening to stories was greatest for those pre-school and primary-aged children who already had larger vocabularies. They benefited most from the incidental learning made possible by encountering new vocabulary in meaningful contexts while listening to stories. This is an example of what Stanovich (1986) called 'Matthew Effects in Reading'. The rich get richer and the poor get poorer ('For unto every one that hath shall be given, and he shall have abundance: but from him that hath not shall be taken away even that which he hath' (Matt. 25: 29)). This does not mean that those children with poorer vocabularies should miss out on story reading – far from it. However, it does suggest that we should also provide other activities to ensure vocabulary growth (see below).

The National Curriculum for English in England (Department for Education, 2014) makes specific reference to teachers reading a wide range of stories, poetry and non-fiction books to children. Though less prominence is given to this for the later primary years, it is still there. The expectation is that teachers will be reading quality texts to support children's vocabulary development. Reading books to a class of children requires considerable preparation. For example, teachers need to be conscious of the vocabulary used by authors in the texts they select, so that they are prepared to engage children in discussions about word choice and meanings to support the development of vocabulary.

Explicit vocabulary teaching

As with story reading, teachers have often engaged in teaching vocabulary directly. A common procedure has been to introduce new vocabulary that will be subsequently encountered in texts. The belief is that by introducing children to the meaning of new words beforehand, when they come across them in texts they will already be primed, thus making the texts less cognitively demanding and therefore easier to understand. In keeping with the ethos of this book, we need to consider whether there is any evidence that this direct teaching of vocabulary is effective – both for vocabulary development *per se* and for reading comprehension. And there is indeed evidence that pre-instruction of new words that will be encountered in texts facilitates both vocabulary acquisition and comprehension, in both story and non-fiction contexts. In a study involving fourth grade children (age 10 years), Brett, Rothlein and Hurley (1996) found that giving pre-instruction on meanings of unfamiliar target words in the story increased pre-instructed children's vocabulary relative to children who were given no such instruction. In an earlier study, Carney, Anderson, Blackburn and Blessing (1984) pre-taught vocabulary related to social studies content to fifth grade (11-year-old) pupils. They found that this priming of vocabulary had a significant effect both on vocabulary retention and acquisition of the content of the topic.

Kameenui, Carnine and Freschi (1982) found that instruction on the meaning of difficult words helped vocabulary learning in an experimental study with 10- to 12- year-olds. Children were given contrived passages to read aloud. They either read a passage with easy everyday words or low frequency, more difficult words. A further group read the passage with the difficult words but were given additional redundant information in brackets. The next box gives an example of the contrived texts.

Example of a passage from Kameenui, Carmine and Freschi (1982)

Target words in bold

Easy words

> Joe and Ann went to school in Portland. They were **enemies**. They saw each other often. They had lots of **fights**. At the end of high school Ann **said bad things about Joe**. Then Ann moved away. Joe stayed in Portland. He **worked for a judge**. One day Joe was working, and he saw Ann. Ann did not see Joe. Ann looked **afraid**. She was **under arrest**.

Hard words

> Joe and Ann went to school in Portland. They were **antagonists**. They saw each other often. They had lots of **altercations**. At the end of high school, Ann

(Continued)

(Continued)

> **maligned** Joe. Then Ann moved away. Joe stayed in Portland. He got a job as a **bailiff**. One day Joe was working, and he saw Ann. Ann did not see Joe. Ann looked **apprehensive**. She was **being incarcerated**.
>
> Hard words with redundant information (in brackets)
>
> Joe and Ann went to school in Portland. They were **antagonists**. They saw each other often. They had lots of **altercations**. (They just didn't get along very well.) At the end of high school, Ann **maligned** Joe. Then Ann moved away. Joe stayed in Portland. He got a job as a **bailiff**. One day Joe was working, and he saw Ann (talking to a policeman, afraid and answering questions). Ann did not see Joe. Ann looked **apprehensive**. She was **being incarcerated**.

A further element of the study was that some of the children who read the hard words were given specific training on their meaning. This training either took the form of pre-training or pre-training plus integration of the meaning when the pupils read the hard words.

After reading the passages, children were given a set of literal and inferential questions to answer and were asked to retell the story. Children who read the passage with easy words did significantly better than those who read the passage with difficult words. This alone suggests that texts containing unknown words can compromise comprehension. However, since we want to expand children's vocabularies, we need to go beyond this. While having prior instruction on the meaning of the difficult words significantly aided comprehension, the most effective condition was where there was contingent discussion of the meaning of the hard words at the point when they were encountered in the passage.

Implicit and explicit vocabulary instruction combined

In reviewing the evidence for approaches to teaching vocabulary as part of teaching comprehension, the Comprehension panel of the National Reading Panel in the report on teaching children to read (NICH & HD, 2000) felt unable to suggest there was evidence for any single approach as the best way to support vocabulary learning. This was because the majority of studies do not focus on just one approach. The NRP proposed the following:

1. Vocabulary should be taught both directly and indirectly.
2. Repetition and multiple exposures to vocabulary items are important.
3. Learning in rich contexts is valuable for vocabulary learning.

4. Vocabulary tasks should be restructured when necessary.
5. Vocabulary learning should entail active engagement in learning tasks.

(NICH & HD, 2000: 4–27)

The study by Sénéchal (1997), referred to above, investigating the effect of multiple story readings on vocabulary learning, exemplifies this multiple approach. The children taking part in the study were 60 3- and 4-year-olds attending a Canadian kindergarten. Children were pre-tested on their knowledge of ten target words before the study and then post-tested at the end of the study. The target words were embedded in a story, with illustrations that represented each target. These target words were low frequency synonyms for high frequency words that were known to the children. The items were:

- Angling (fishing)
- Fang (tooth)
- Fedora (hat)
- Gazing (looking)
- Goblet (cup)
- Infant (baby)
- Sash (window frame)
- Satchel (purse)
- Skiff (boat)
- Vessel (bucket)

The adult read the story, pointing to the picture of the target word as it was read. Non-target word illustrations were also pointed to. In the post-test for each target word, the children were presented with four illustrations and asked to choose the one that represented the target. In each case the illustration of the target was not identical with the one that had been used in the story, so they could find out if any learning was related to the generalized meaning of the word and not the specific instance from the story.

The 60 children were randomly allocated to one of three conditions. In one, each child listened to the story being read aloud once. They were pre-tested on their knowledge of the target words first, listened to the story and were then post-tested. In the second condition, each child listened to the story three times. On the first day they were pre-tested on the target vocabulary, listened to the story and were then asked if they would like to hear the story again because it was so good. None of them declined. The next day they listened to the story a further time and were then post-tested on the vocabulary. In the third condition, the procedure was the same as for the second condition except that during the second reading the adult asked a 'what' or a 'where' question after each target word. If the children used the target word this was acknowledged. If the children did not use the target word in response to the question they were then asked, 'Can you tell me the word I used when I was reading the book?' If this did not elicit the correct target word, then the illustration was labelled for the child. The pointing and questioning behaviours used in this study had ecological validity because they are the types of interactive behaviour that parents use when reading to their children (Sénéchal, Cornell & Broda, 1995). Sénéchal reported that what- and where-questions accounted for 85% of all the questions used by parents when reading to their 27-month-old child. These types of verbal interactions by parents have been found to have a positive beneficial effect on vocabulary development (Whitehurst et al., 1988).

The results obtained showed that listening to the same story three times had a significant positive effect on learning both for receptive and expressive vocabulary. In addition, the use of questions had a particularly beneficial effect on expressive vocabulary. The simple fact that multiple readings supported vocabulary development shows story books can be a rich source of vocabulary for children, but they need the repetition in context to support this learning. The additional evidence about the positive benefit of questioning on targeted vocabulary shows us that we can directly impact vocabulary development through our interactions with children.

Teaching vocabulary

The approaches to teaching vocabulary we have covered may well seem like common sense and there is certainly nothing radical about them. One might expect to find teachers using any one or indeed all of the approaches. The important thing is that teachers should be conscious of the implications of the approaches they are using, and be able to articulate their reasons for so doing. This then ensures that teaching about vocabulary is strategic and not random.

As an exercise you might like to find a story book for a chosen age group of children and analyse all the words in it. There are likely to be some words which will prove tricky for your chosen age group. Think about the types of question you might use for supporting the acquisition of these words. What strategies might you use for effectively re-reading the story? There are also likely to be some words where it is possible for some children to infer the meaning from the context, but some children will need more direct support. Thinking about the questions you might develop for supporting vocabulary development will help you to provide this support. Sénéchal (1997) found that the best effects were where the children had used the target words themselves: that is, your questions should support children in using the new words in their expressive answers. In the early years, the vocabulary you might want to target is likely to be that found in everyday speech, but with the capability of extending oral vocabulary: just like Sénéchal's substitution of *angling* for *fishing*. With a whole class it is possible to elicit multiple synonyms. Actively engaging children in introspection about unusual vocabulary through questioning, discussion and synonym provision would seem to map on to the National Reading Panel finding that vocabulary should be taught both directly and indirectly.

Right from the start of education, children will be being introduced to subject-specific vocabulary or vocabulary that is used in a subject-specific way. It is this type of vocabulary that may benefit from pre-teaching so that when it is encountered in context it is already in the children's oral vocabulary. Much of the vocabulary used in curriculum areas outside English is less frequent than the general spoken vocabulary of everyday speech. The evidence about the effectiveness of pre-teaching vocabulary suggests that when introducing a new topic, the children's learning will benefit from a teacher identifying all the new vocabulary and all the regular vocabulary that is used in a subject-specific way. These words and their meanings can be presented to children so that the comprehension of any exposition on the part of the teacher and/or any reading of texts will be supported by the vocabulary having become familiar.

This is not a recommendation for children simply to be presented with lists of words to learn. Learning in rich contexts is valuable for vocabulary learning. It is important to provide activities which require the active engagement of children as you pre-teach the vocabulary before introducing it in expositions and texts. As children become more proficient at word reading and so able to read longer texts independently for accessing content, it is likely to become more important that pre-teaching of vocabulary takes place: Nagy and Scott (1990) estimated that readers need to know at least 90% of the words in a text in order to comprehend it. In order for children to work on a topic independently and access information through texts, they need high levels of content vocabulary at their fingertips. You might like to try the exercise shown below:

> Identify a topic area from science, mathematics or the humanities. Take a selection of books that are relevant to the topic and analyse the vocabulary for words that are likely to be new to the pupils of your chosen age group. Remember to be on the lookout for common everyday words that are being used in a subject-specific way (e.g. *higher*, *lower*, *note* in music) as well as subject-specific vocabulary *per se* (e.g. *clavichord*, *timpani*, *viola*). Think about how you would pre-teach this vocabulary to aid comprehension of the texts by young readers. Also think about how you might further support comprehension and vocabulary learning by preparing questions about the difficult vocabulary as it comes up in exposition or in texts.

Teaching comprehension strategies

The theoretical approach, supported by research evidence, that comprehension is an active process of building mental models has led to the view that children need to be taught strategies that will enable them to understand what they are reading. This meant that different approaches to teaching were needed, because it was recognized that simply providing children with 'comprehension' exercises would not do the job. Teaching comprehension strategies gives children tools to enable them to understand the texts they are reading and so use reading for the purposes of learning and studying more effectively. It also supports their ability to take more from the reading they do for leisure and entertainment. Some of the guiding principles for teaching comprehension strategies include teachers actively modelling the strategies for their pupils and talking to them about what they are doing. The activity that takes place when one is reading is not open to public scrutiny because it takes place in the brain. Children need their teachers to explain and discuss what is going on in their heads, and they need to be helped to introspect about what is going on in their own heads. The rule should be first externalize and make explicit and then give much practice to enable the internalization of the strategies so that they become skilful and implicit (Palincsar & Brown, 1984; Pressley, Almasi, Schuder, Bergman & Kurita, 1994; Rosenshine, Meister & Chapman, 1996). Internalization of strategies must be the end goal, because thinking about what we are doing when we are doing it takes processing capacity away from what we are trying to do. This poses an interesting problem for teachers. By becoming teachers, they have necessarily succeeded in the education system and therefore, by definition, have shown that they can understand complex academic texts. In order to teach children the cognitive strategies needed for comprehension they have to be able to verbalize for the children what is going on in their heads and how they are using this to help them build a mental model of the text to understand it.

We hope the content of this book is challenging but accessible. We also hope that the writing style is supportive to aid comprehension. However, we now invite you to read at least the first few pages, if not the first chapter, of Stephen Hawking's book, *A Brief History of Time* (1988). The book was written to make the complex ideas about the origins of the universe accessible to non-specialists. You may have read the book, but many people own it without actually having read it. The words, on the whole, are in common use. Where technical terms are used, they are explained. From what we have said about the importance of vocabulary to comprehension you might expect this. But nevertheless, the ideas are complex. Try reading the chapter and at the same time try to make your comprehension strategies explicit. Keep a note of these and see if they map on to the strategies we are now going to consider.

Monitoring comprehension

Monitoring one's own comprehension of what one is reading is a useful cognitive strategy for ensuring that comprehension proceeds smoothly. This involves recognizing when the mental model one is constructing does not make sense, when comprehension has failed. Children who are good at self-monitoring are able to recognize their own comprehension breakdowns and implement repair strategies. Teaching comprehension monitoring involves helping children to notice when things have gone wrong and giving them the confidence to do something about this. If we just alerted children to becoming aware that they might not understand everything, we would be in danger of producing learned helplessness (Seligman, 1975). The point of comprehension monitoring is to ensure children do not blithely continue reading the words on the page, but actively engage in constructing a mental model of the text.

Markman (1979) found that children of junior school age were not good at noticing inconsistencies in texts. This suggested that they may not be monitoring their comprehension spontaneously and therefore could in some cases build up poorly specified mental models of the text. In order to monitor comprehension, we have to be able to store the information we have been reading and make inferences about meaning as we progress through the text. This is cognitively demanding. However, Markman found that, with support, children could be taught to monitor their comprehension. Teaching comprehension monitoring can be done through teachers modelling their own comprehension by thinking aloud in front of a class. If children learn how to do this from an early stage, they are more likely to become active readers from the start and will be less likely to feel helpless when they do eventually realize that they have not understood (Baumann, Seifert-Kessell & Jones, 1992). The research evidence for the effective use of comprehension strategies comes from the use of experimental texts where pupils have to detect inconsistencies. However, it is possible to model the behaviours that support comprehension modelling with both specially developed texts and authentic ones.

The types of strategies that can be modelled and taught to aid comprehension monitoring include reading aloud and listening to see if it makes sense to the reader and the listener; checking for internal consistency to identify where the problem might be; looking back through the text; asking questions and restating the topic in one's own terms.

With younger children, modelling by the teacher can successfully be done through the use of puppets. The puppet can demonstrate misunderstandings which are very obvious to the children, giving them a sense of control and superiority. The puppet can then show how to use the strategies to repair the error. As the lesson continues, the children can suggest which strategies will work and help the puppet come to a good understanding. By having the puppet ask the children what to do, they can rehearse strategies and see them being effective.

In addition to the use of magical talking puppets, the modelling that teachers themselves engage in with children can develop more systematic strategic comprehension monitoring. The next box gives an example of how this might be done.

Modelling comprehension monitoring

Select a text from any curriculum area that you might read to the pupils. Begin by reading aloud, but pause regularly at appropriate places, such as the end of a paragraph and ask does it make sense. Show how you can retell the text you have just read in your own words, including checking the meaning of difficult vocabulary, and this helps to literally monitor comprehension. In other words literally *think aloud*.

Then model strategies that can be used when comprehension breaks down.

(Continued)

(Continued)

These can include:

- re-reading the section, slowing down to re-read it carefully
- going back in the text and taking a run at the problematic section
- reading on to see if the meaning becomes clear, all the time asking yourself questions through thinking aloud
- identifying the words that may be causing the problem and seeing if the surrounding text helps to work out the meaning
- using a dictionary
- showing where inferences had to be made from earlier parts of the text
- possibly creating diagrams or drawings to help you map concepts, events and actions (see 'graphic organizer' below)
- asking someone to help you
- having to hand another text which might help.

After your modelling, you will need to provide the children with opportunities to do this themselves. This can be done with whole classes and then in groups or pairs. A sheet with all the questions and strategies is useful as an aid. Elliot-Faust and Pressley (1986) successfully trained 8-year-olds to take control of monitoring through the use of questions like 'What am I supposed to do?', 'What's my plan?' and 'Am I using my plan?' Children may need years of reminding to use their comprehension monitoring skills before they use them spontaneously to support comprehension. They need plenty of practice with active participation. The activities suggested here in thinking aloud are also called *metacognitive strategies* (Boulware-Gooden, Carreker, Thornhill & Joshi, 2007). The modelling externalizes the metacognitive activity of thinking about thinking.

Graphic organizer instruction

This approach is where children are taught to use some form of external diagrammatic representation of the text (Armbruster, Anderson & Meyer, 1991; Baumann, 1984). Various names are given for the same thing: webs, maps, story boards, frames, charts, graphs. These techniques require readers to externalize concepts, themes, events, causal links, etc. in texts and to begin to see how they relate to each other. In some sense it is like a restating of the text in summary form, but using graphics to link elements helps children build up a representation of the whole text.

Children have to be taught some of the conventions of graphics, such as putting information in boxes, using arrows to indicate time or causality and using some form of graphic or layout to represent different parts of the text, such as topic, main theme, subordinate theme, resolution. This technique has been found to be particularly useful for curriculum subjects but also works well with stories, where children can identify the theme of the narrative, the setting, the protagonists, the problem, the events, sub-events and the resolution. There are plenty of commercially available sheets with pre-prepared maps and frames, but it does not take much imagination to use packages like PowerPoint to create frames, such as those shown in Figure 7.2.

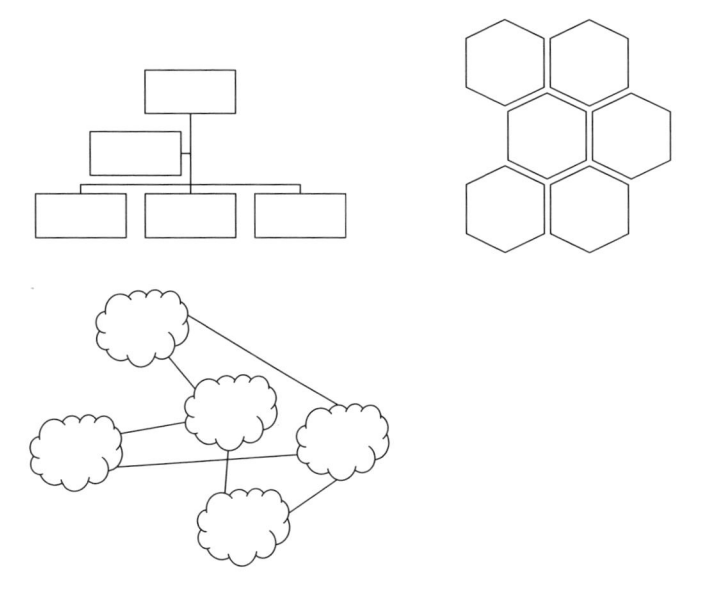

Figure 7.2 Examples of graphic organizer frames

These can be used to show children how to map concepts. It is important children begin to create their own, because no text is likely to generate the same set of boxes or relationships. Also, generating their own will support their understanding of the elements and relationships in the text.

You will be aware that non-fiction texts, including, or indeed especially, those for schools, make use of graphic organizers such as headings, subheadings, activity boxes, diagrams, graphs. In modelling thinking aloud when using expository texts, it is important to discuss how these are used: this is not necessarily obvious to young learners. If during modelling children are questioned and asked to generate ideas about graphic organizers, they will begin to appreciate how these can be useful for aiding comprehension. Try this for yourself:

> When you have finished reading this chapter, you might like to try to generate some different webs and maps to encapsulate the themes. By using different graphic organizers you will be able to find out whether some work for you and some don't.

Then take two classic children's stories, such as 'Goldilocks and the Three Bears' and 'The Little Red Hen', and create graphic organizers for them. How are they similar and how are they different?

Questioning

Questioning as an effective comprehension strategy includes both the generation of and response to questions. There is a very important approach to teaching reading called *reciprocal teaching* (Palincsar & Brown, 1984), which we focus on in greater depth in Chapter 10: here we simply note that questioning is one of the suite of strategies in reciprocal teaching. Andre and Anderson (1978–79) suggested that asking oneself questions for clarification, interpretation and prediction improved comprehension and supported comprehension monitoring strategies. Question generation is not an easy strategy and, as we shall see when we consider reciprocal teaching, Palincsar and Brown (1984) found that often, even after teacher modelling, children would be asking essentially non-questions. However, with extensive modelling and scaffolding they can learn to use this technique to good advantage to support comprehension. Questions may relate to the structure of the content: who, where, when, why, how. They may also relate to thinking aloud: 'How do I know this?' and 'What does this tell me?'

Summarization

One aspect of questioning is to identify the main ideas and themes in texts and paragraphs. A strategy to take this further is to teach children how to summarize what they have been reading. This is more easily achieved through writing and so has been found to be particularly effective with children in the later primary years and beyond.

Summarization is not an easy thing to do, but if children are taught how to do this effectively, it helps them to develop a coherent mental model of the text, which improves memory of what the text is about (Baumann, 1984; Brown, Day & Jones, 1983; Carnine, Kameenui & Woolfson, 1982; Taylor, 1982). This is an important element in learning the content, not just understanding the text *per se*. The central aim of most summarization instruction is to teach the reader how to identify the main or central ideas of a paragraph or a series of paragraphs. Summarization training has the effect of making readers more aware of how the text is structured and has the added benefit of incidentally teaching note-taking skills.

Activities that support summarization involve identifying the main ideas of paragraphs and deleting all extraneous and redundant information. Children are taught to try to identify one sentence in the text which encapsulates the paragraph. Where no such sentence exists, they have to generate their own. Children begin with summarizing single paragraphs and then move on to summaries of summaries, to generate summaries of longer texts. At the end of this chapter you might like to try summarizing the content.

Multiple strategy use and classroom organization

We suspect that as you have been reading this chapter you will have had the occasional feeling of *déjà vu*. Each strategy we have covered seems to rely on aspects of other strategies. This is indeed the case. Indeed, in the analysis of effective comprehension teaching, the National Reading Panel (National Institute of Child Health and Human Development, 2000) suggested that learning multiple strategies was desirable. For young learners, it may be easiest for them to practise one strategy at a time and gradually learn to integrate their skills for optimum success. The evidence does seem to be that teacher modelling is an essential starting point. This can obviously be done with whole-class teaching, but it is very effective with groups and even for individual support.

Story structure

All the reading strategies we have covered so far imply that interactions with texts are essential for developing good comprehension. Let us now make this explicit. Those children who have had the chance to listen to many stories and poems being read to them and who have multiple opportunities for handling books are at an advantage when they come to learn to read. They seem to absorb the vocabulary and the characteristics of many different genres and so reap a positive benefit when they begin to become independent readers (Elley, 1989; Hargrave & Sénéchal, 2000; Robbins & Ehri, 1994).

They may not have the technical language, but they know about plot and characters and settings; they know about the *who*, the *what*, the *where*, the *why* and the *when*. They are able to recognize how stories develop; they know about the problem solving that goes on in the lives of the protagonists; they understand about their goals and achievements. They are likely to have empathized with emotions and feel satisfaction about resolutions. *Who*, *what*, *where*, *when*, *why* and *how* questions figure largely in the interactions that parents have when reading to their children and are found to support comprehension (Bus, van IJzendoorn & Pellegrini, 1995; Phillips, Norris & Anderson, 2008; Scarborough, Dobrich & Hager, 1991).

Explicit instruction about story structure may not seem warranted for children who arrive in school with a hinterland of story experience, but it is helpful to give them the language to discuss stories explicitly (Hargrave & Sénéchal, 2000). Those children who are not so advantaged clearly benefit from this. Stories are used extensively in primary schools, particularly in the early years, to support learning across the curriculum, not just in English. This means it is important to give all children the tools to understand their structure.

The following five questions characterize teaching about story structure:

1. Who is the main character?
2. Where and when did the story occur?

3. What did the main characters do?
4. How did the story end?
5. How did the main character feel?

> We hope you have already tried mapping stories through graphic organizers. Now try asking the essential *WH*-questions of the same books to externalize your own implicit understanding of story structure.

Closing words

The strategies discussed in this chapter have all resulted from theory-driven research projects designed to help children improve their active comprehension behaviours. There is empirical evidence that they work with typical children in mainstream settings. However, they arise from research projects, and it is up to teachers to teach these strategies within the context of their own curriculum. The point to remember is that in mainstream settings we know children need to be guided towards being actively engaged in their own comprehension and learning. It is also important to remember that vocabulary training will need to be integrated and articulated with comprehension strategies.

In this chapter, in terms of language processes, we have concentrated largely on vocabulary. In Chapter 10, where we begin to address issues relating to children who have specific difficulties in comprehending texts, we devote more time to the essential language processes of syntax and inferencing.

PART 4
Assessment and intervention

8

Assessing reading: from international comparisons to individual processes

Summary

This chapter marks a transition from considering typical to considering atypical reading development. You will learn about different types of assessment of reading and the rationale for each of them, at international, national, school and classroom levels. You will learn a little about the statistics underlying standardized tests, and about the kinds of information you need to consider in selecting a test appropriate to your purposes. Assessment is essential to identification of children with reading difficulties: you will learn how to identify these children. You will also learn the importance of identifying their individual strengths and weaknesses, as the basis for designing targeted intervention programmes.

Introduction

It is a truism that today's children are some of the most tested there have ever been in history. This is a worldwide phenomenon. Educational assessment has a long and not uncontroversial history in the United Kingdom. However, local authorities and national governments need evidence about attainment for effective planning and provision. Without effective assessment regimes, teachers are unable to gain an objective picture of the levels of attainment of individual children in their classes, or of the levels of attainment across school years and whole schools. Although testing *per se* does not raise reading standards, the evidence collected from testing can provide data from which to plan and to develop more effective teaching strategies at national, regional, school, class and, ultimately, individual level.

There should always be strong educational reasons for children to be subjected to assessment. However, these do not always relate to the direct wellbeing of the child being assessed. Contemporary assessment of school children ranges from the international through to the individual, with a considerable amount of assessment conducted for research purposes. Ethics committees vet research plans and protocols to ensure no harm is done, that schools and parents understand the purpose of the proposed testing and that, where appropriate, children themselves give informed consent. Testing for research purposes has indirect benefits for education: knowledge and insights gained inform practice for the children who come afterwards. Much of the research reported in previous chapters has involved testing children, enabling us better to understand how children learn to read, and also sometimes leading to the development of theoretically sound tests and interventions.

In considering the assessment of reading, we begin with international studies and work through to the classroom. This will lead us to the individual so that we can focus in depth on the assessment of processes involved in reading.

International studies

Since 2001, the International Association for the Evaluation of Educational Achievement (IEA) has conducted a series of studies every five years. These Progress in Reading Literacy Studies (PIRLS) (PIRLS 2001, PIRLS 2006, PIRLS, 2011) investigate how well fourth-grade students read and how their reading habits and attitudes compare from one country to another. Publication of results necessarily lags behind implementation of assessments (scoring, analysis and interpretation take time), with results published in 2003 (Mullis, Martin, Gonzalez & Kennedy, 2003), 2007 (Mullis, Martin, Kennedy & Foy, 2007), and 2012 (Mullis, Martin, Foy & Drucker, 2012). The PIRLS consortium defines reading literacy as 'The ability to understand and use those written language forms required by society and/or valued by the individual. Young readers can construct meaning from a variety of texts. They read to learn, to participate in communities of readers, and for enjoyment.'

Reading assessment for all three studies was based on children's written responses after reading carefully-constructed passages. A range of reading comprehension strategies were assessed when reading for both literary and informational purposes. There are major obstacles to overcome in conducting such international studies if comparisons are to be meaningful. First and foremost, there is the issue of different orthographies which, as we have seen, pose different challenges for learners. Then, there is the issue that different countries have different starting ages for reading instruction. The majority of 10-year-olds assessed were in their fourth year of formal schooling. Because of the earlier starting age of children in England, the English 10-year-olds were in their fifth year of formal schooling.

Individual children could achieve scores ranging from 0 to 1,000. Comparability across jurisdictions and over time was enabled by establishing 500 as the average scale score for participating countries, with 100 set as the standard deviation. Most actual scores achieved by children ranged from 300 to 700. This is to be expected: with such a large number of children being tested, the scores follow a normal distribution. The percentage of a population falling within 2 standard deviations either side of the mean of a normal distribution is 95.4%, and the range of PIRLS scores between 300 and 700 is 2 standard deviations either side of the mean of 500.

Patterns of performance: The normal distribution

It is not possible to talk about assessment without providing some information about the statistics and expected characteristics of the patterns of performance which underlie tests.

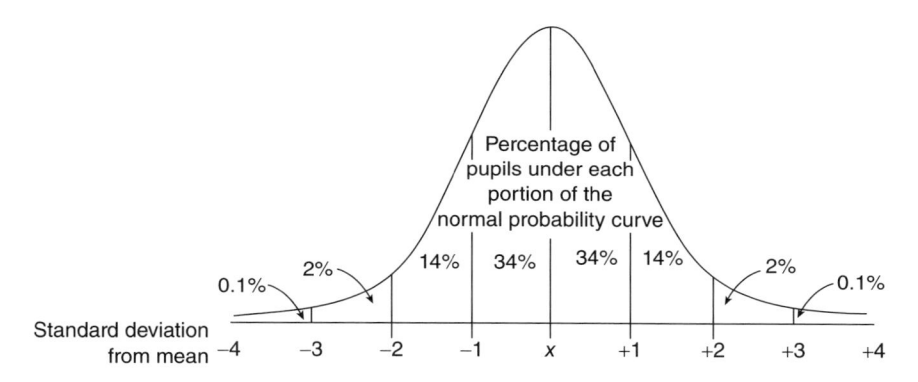

Figure 8.1 The normal distribution

Figure 8.1 illustrates a normal distribution. This is also called the 'bell curve' because it resembles the shape of a bell. If we measured every adult's height and plotted the results in a histogram we would find that the data would look very much like Figure 8.1. The top of the curve is where the average of whatever is being measured occurs. This is also the *mode*: the most frequently occurring measure. For example, the average adult female height is 5ft 5in (165cm) and this is also the most frequently occurring height. There are more women who are 5ft 5in than any other height.

If you inspect the figure you will see that there are lines descending from the 'shoulders' of the curve. These lines are placed at 1 standard deviation from the mean. The percentages tell us that approximately 68% of the measurements fall between -1 and +1 standard deviation from the mean. The standard deviation of women's heights is 3.5in. This means that 68% of women are between 5ft 2.5in and 5ft 8.5 in. There are also lines placed at -2 and +2 standard deviations. The percentage of the population who fall between -2 and +2 standard deviations around the mean is approximately 95%.

Knowing about height is important for clothing manufacturers. To ensure they are not left with too many frocks of the wrong size, they need to produce numbers which mirror the normal distribution of female height. However, it turns out that those things that psychologists and educationalists might want to measure also fall on a normal distribution curve. If we measured the reading performance of thousands of children at the age of 9 years 6 months and plotted the number achieving each score, scores would be 'normally distributed' and fall on a bell-shaped curve.

In terms of educational assessment, children who are assessed as achieving below -2 standard deviations are considered to have significant difficulties. There is an equal percentage of children who achieve more than 2 standard deviations above the mean: their significantly advanced abilities should also be addressed. In practice, within mainstream educational settings, we should be concerned about those 13.59% of children who achieve between -1 and -2 standard deviations on any assessment. Their performance is poor relative to their age and their life chances are likely to be increased if their reading skills are improved.

We will return to some more statistics of measurement later. For now, you need to remember that for most standardized assessments, the mean performance for age is a standard score of 100 with a standard deviation of 15. However, in the PIRLS study, performance has been normed with a mean of 500 and a standard deviation of 100.

PIRLS results

In the first (2001) PIRLS study (Mullis, Martin et al., 2003), 23 of the 35 participating countries had average levels of reading literacy achievement significantly above the international average (500), two performed about at the international average and ten had average achievement below the international average. National average scores ranged from 561 to 327 (a 234 scale score point difference between first and 35th rank). There were very small differences in achievement between the 23 countries achieving above average scores (a 52 scale score point difference from first to 23rd rank) and a much wider spread of scores between countries whose children performed below the international average (a 167 scale score point difference between 24th and 35th rank).

English children were third in the international ranking, with an average scaled score of 553. Sweden came first with 561 and the Netherlands second with 554. Scottish children were 14th with 528. One possible conclusion to be drawn from these data is that the teaching English children had received in their primary schools between 1996 and 2001 had enabled them to develop reading skills which were among the best in the world. This is not a message generally highlighted in the media.

By 2006, the number of participating jurisdictions had grown to 45: 40 countries, including Belgium's two education systems, and five Canadian provinces. The range of scaled scores achieved was wider than in 2001, between 565 and 302. Thirty-two jurisdictions achieved above average scores; three achieved at the average and ten performed below the international average. Performance of the high achieving countries was within the same range as in 2001, but the range for low achieving countries appeared to be wider. This change could be accounted for by the participation of South Africa in this second study: South Africa had an average scale score of 302 but had not participated in 2001.

The relative positions of jurisdictions in these 'international league tables' changed from 2001 to 2006. By 2006, the Russian Federation was first, with an average scale score of 565, Hong Kong next with 564, and then the Canadian province of Alberta with 560. Alberta had not been an individual participant in 2001 but the Russian Federation and Hong Kong had been, respectively, 16th and 17th, both with 528. They had significantly improved both attainment and 'ranking'. England, Sweden and the Netherlands had all dropped in the 'rankings'. Sweden was 10th with 548, the Netherlands 12th with 547, and England 19th with 539. Scotland came 26th with 527.

By 2011, 49 countries participated (Scotland did not). Scores ranged between 571 and 310 (a 261 scale score point difference from first to 49th rank). Scores of the 32 participating jurisdictions scoring above the international average were again between 571 and 506 scale points (65 scale score point difference from first to 32nd rank). Again, the range of low achieving jurisdictions was greater, between 488 and 310 (178 scale score point difference from 33rd to 49th rank). Two of the top achieving participants remained the same: Hong Kong with 571 and the Russian Federation with 568. However, this time one of the top three participants was Finland, taking part for the first time, with an average scale score of 568.

What of the original top three participants: Sweden, the Netherlands and England? In 2011, England was 11th with 552; the Netherlands 13th with 546; and Sweden 15th with 542. Note that the average scaled score of English children in 2011 was just one point less than it had been in 2001. Children in the Netherlands showed a remarkable degree of consistency with average scaled scores over time of 554, 547 and 546. Despite variability in the relative standing of the high achieving jurisdictions, the differences are fairly small overall. The case of England illustrates this well. If, on an objective assessment, a score of 553 was considered to be quality performance in 2001, that same score must also indicate quality performance in 2011, even though the score now ranked 11th as opposed to third in 2001. Unfortunately, politicians and newspapers tend to take the bald headlines and ignore the details of the reports. We have shown you that children in England always perform above the international average, which is a positive finding.

The PIRLS reports always show an ordered attainment list of all the participant jurisdictions relative to the average scaled score for all participating children, leading inevitably to an interpretation that the relative positions are significant. However, this is not necessarily the case and the authors of the PIRLS reports are very careful to enable a more nuanced reading of the data. Fortunately, the reports are freely available on the web so you can make your own in-depth analysis of these international data. The reports' urls are:

http://timssandpirls.bc.edu/pirls2001i/PIRLS2001_Pubs_IR.html

http://timssandpirls.bc.edu/pirls2006/intl_rpt.html

http://timssandpirls.bc.edu/pirls2011/international-results-pirls.html

In addition, teams from the National Foundation for Educational Research (NFER) in England have produced commentaries to the main PIRLS reports, focusing specifically on performance in England (Twist, Sainsbury, Woodthorpe & Whetton, 2003; Twist, Schagen & Hodgson, 2007; Twist, Sizmur, Bartlett & Lynn, 2012). These are also freely available to download. The urls for these publications are:

http://files.eric.ed.gov/fulltext/ED504613.pdf

www.nfer.ac.uk/publications/PRN01/PRN01.pdf

www.nfer.ac.uk/publications/PRTZ01/PRTZ01.pdf

Drilling down into the data beyond the national average scores reveals some interesting facts about the relative performance of boys and girls: internationally, girls consistently outperform boys. In 2001 the difference between girls and boys was statistically significant in every country. When Spain began to participate in 2006, it was the only country where boys performed as well as girls. By 2011 four countries – Columbia, Italy, France and Israel – had reduced their gender gap so that it was no longer significant and Spain again did not have a gender gap. The gender gap in England has been consistently large, with only Trinidad and Tobago and New Zealand showing a greater gap. These data serve to show that international data can provide useful information for policy makers, but they do not tell us how to address the issue of raising boys' performance in reading.

National assessment

In national assessment, the unit of interest can be the whole nation, within-nation administrative districts, the school or the individual. National testing in England illustrates this well. Following the statutory introduction of the National Curriculum in 1988, reading has been assessed as part of assessing levels of achievement in English. Before that, schools and local education authorities had their own testing arrangements, but there were no arrangements for systematically monitoring performance nationwide. Children's levels of reading achievement have been assessed in England at age 7 (at end of Year 2/Key Stage 1, first introduced in 1991); at age 11 (at end of Year 6/Key Stage 2, first introduced in 1995) and, between 1998 and 2013, at age 14 (end of Year 9/Key Stage 3). The assessments, originally called Standard Assessment Tasks, soon became known as SATs, with the T widely assumed to stand for Tests. Though part of the assessment arrangements included teacher-based assessment for the younger ages, schools were required to administer the national assessment during a specified period each year. Children's attainment was then classified relative to criteria set out in the National Curriculum, with the expected levels being 2 at Key Stage 1; 4 at Key Stage 2; and 5/6 at Key Stage 3. As we write, this system is being changed and we do not as yet know what the assessment criteria will be (or even if there will be any nationally set criteria) after 2015.

Assessing reading: from international comparisons to individual processes

Reading assessment in KS2 SATs is similar to that in PIRLS. Children read narrative and non-narrative texts silently and write answers to questions about the texts. Questions are designed to assess both literal and inferential comprehension. The stated purpose of introducing SATs was to monitor performance and progress at national and local levels. This is necessary, and could have been both positive and benign: parents had access to objective information about their children's achievements; schools had access to information about children's progress and the efficacy of their teaching; local authorities had access to data to help them plan; and central government had data about national levels and patterns of performance. Unfortunately, because the SATs data have been used to generate league tables of school performance, what could have been a progressive development to provide useful data for monitoring and planning has turned into a process widely distrusted by teachers and often misunderstood by parents and politicians alike.

Nevertheless, some objective data have emerged from national assessments. Figure 8.2 shows the national percentages of children achieving level 4 for reading in Key Stage 2 SATs for the years 1997–2013.

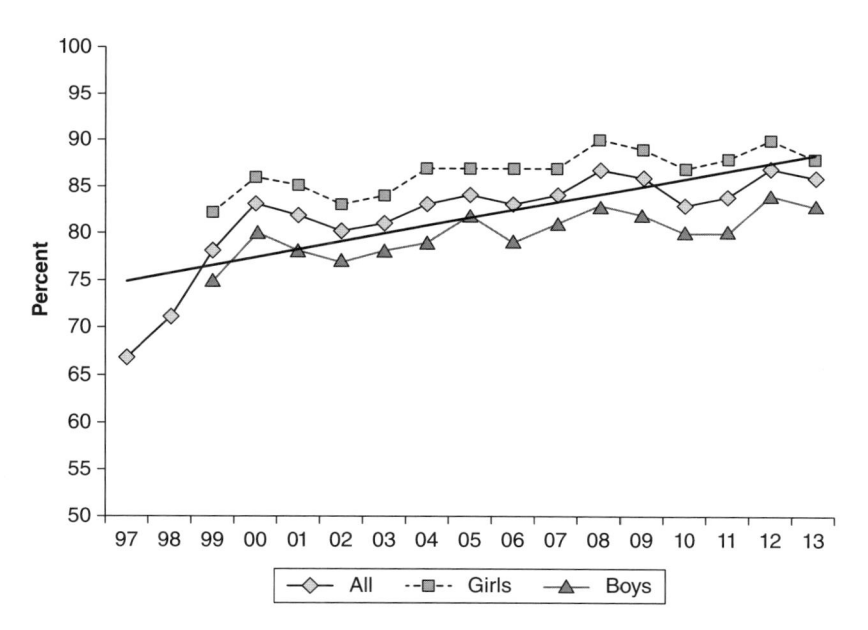

Figure 8.2 Percentages of children achieving level 4 for reading in KS2 SATs, 1997–2013 (The solid line shows an overall rising trend)

Over time, there has been a steady increase in the numbers of children achieving the expected levels, with the gap between boys and girls slightly decreasing. While objective and positive, these data take no account of different starting points. Governments soon recognized that a school's performance profile needed to be calibrated relative to its intake: the data are now qualified with reference to some school and child characteristics. We are now able to interrogate the national data with reference to socio-economic measures of the school's population, and assess the 'value added' the school has been able to achieve throughout the time of the children's stay in any one Key Stage. These data are available and schools have access to their profiles, but after nearly 20 years of publishing tables of children's performance, the Key Stage 1 data no longer have to be reported, and Key Stage 3 assessments have ceased.

The tests and marking protocols are developed by agencies of central government: in 2014 this was the Standards and Testing Agency (STA). Every child in the age group does exactly the same test as every other child in the age group. In this sense there is a level playing field. However, children's age is not taken into account when marking the response sheets. Unsurprisingly, there is evidence (Crawford, Dearden & Meghir, 2010) that 'summer-born' children perform less well than those born in the autumn: there can be as much as 11 months' age difference between autumn- and summer-born children. This summer lag decreases by Key Stage 3, but nevertheless, it is important that within schools the month of birth of a child is borne in mind when considering the SATs scores that are reported to the next Key Stage. A child born in August may achieve a lower level of performance than a child born in September, but they may well both have the same relative ability.

Test materials sent out to schools by the STA are newly developed each year. This can have advantages: the materials are secure, children will not have seen them before, and schools are not able to 'teach' directly to the test. Again this provides a level playing field. The STA and their predecessors take great care to ensure that each annual test is equivalent to those of previous years, but there are inevitable differences. Having a different test each year makes it impossible to make absolute year-on-year comparisons. These annual assessments also only provide a single metric of the level of achievement by each child in relation to reading comprehension: they provide no information about which areas of comprehension a child finds easy or difficult, or about the processes involved in reading.

Since 2012, a further assessment has been introduced in England for even younger children. This is the Phonics Screening Check, administered in the final half term of Year 1 when children have had up to almost two years of reading instruction. This assessment provides information about how well children have learned the grapheme-phoneme correspondences in their phonics programme, and how well they have learned to blend phonemes into words and pronounceable nonwords. Individual school data from the Screening Check are not reported publicly, but parents are given information about their child's performance.

The Screener consists of 20 real word items and 20 nonwords. All the real words have regular transparent spellings which can be read successfully through phonological recoding processes. The items get progressively more difficult, ranging from simple CVC nonwords to bisyllabic real words. Each page contains just four items. Real words and nonwords never occur on the same page, and there are pictures of monsters on the nonword pages to remind the children that these are made-up words. For the first three years of the Screener, the expected level of performance has been 32 out of 40 items correct. Children not achieving this are supposed to receive additional support in word reading over Year 2 and the school is required to administer the Screener again in Year 2 to check their progress.

The inclusion of nonwords in a national assessment was a brave move. There were claims children would be confused by the inclusion of these items and that it is questionable to require children to read nonsense. However, from Chapter 4 you will be aware that reading nonwords provides a pure measure of the degree to which a child has learned to use phonological recoding processes in reading. Additionally, of course, children have always been presented with nonsense words in literature: think of the Grinch, the Quangle Wangle, and the Jabberwocky: 'T'was brillig and the slithy toves did gyre and gimble in the wabe'. The Phonics Screener is definitely not literature, but it does enable teachers to identify those children who have difficulty in establishing the phonological recoding processes that are the foundation of word reading skills.

The first year the Screener was administered just 58% of Year 1 children achieved the benchmark of 32 items correct. In line with other assessments, the percentage of girls was higher, at 62%, than boys, with 54%. In 2013, there was an increase overall with 69% of children achieving the 32 items correct benchmark. By 2014, the percentage achieving the benchmark level had risen to an overall 74%, with 78% of girls and 70% of boys achieving the standard. The chart in Figure 8.3 shows the yearly percentage of children achieving the benchmark relative to ethnicity, language status (English first language: EL1; English as an

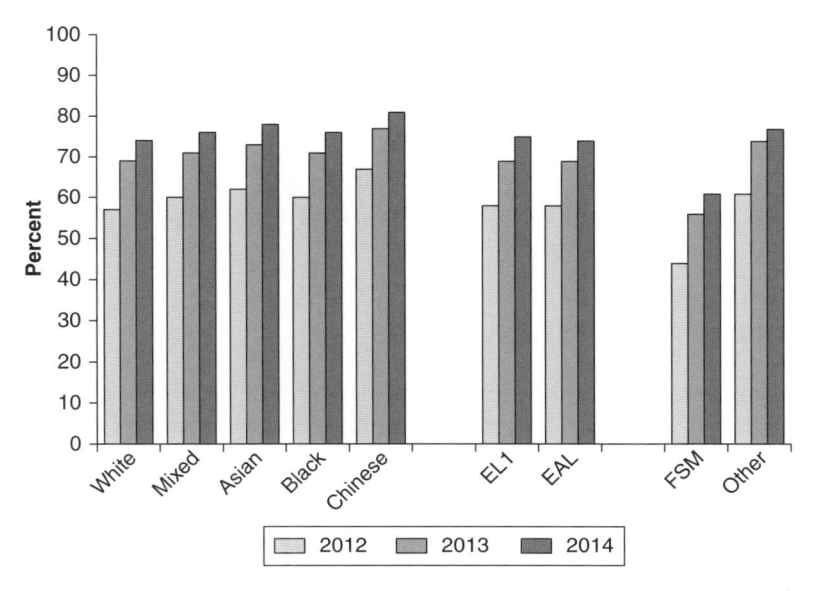

Figure 8.3 Percentage of children achieving the expected level in 2012, 2013 and 2014, by ethnicity, language status and free school meals

additional language: EAL), and whether the child had free school meals (FSM) or not. The figures show that having English as an additional language was no barrier to success, but that overall, the poorest performers were white boys from economically poorer backgrounds. The pattern of improvement was more or less uniform for each category.

Some issues were raised about the scoring after the first iteration of the Screener, because teachers who administered the Screener knew that 32 was the expected level. As you can see in the histogram in Figure 8.4 of the numbers of children achieving each of the different possible marks from zero to 40, there was a dip between 30 and 32 marks, with a very sharp rise in numbers of children achieving 32 in 2012 and 2013.

From the histogram, it is clear that the pattern of performance in the first two years was substantially the same, with a long tail of children not able to achieve 32. In both years there is a dip at 31 and a dramatic steep climb at 32. However, unlike 2012, when teachers were told in advance that the benchmark would be 32, in 2013 teachers did not know what the expected performance level was going to be until *after* the children had been assessed. The fact that performance patterns were nonetheless similar across these two years casts doubt on the view that at the margin between 'success' and 'failure', teachers gave children the benefit of the doubt. A more likely explanation lies in the nature of the Screener, where the final eight stimuli are particularly challenging items containing both initial and final consonant clusters, and bisyllabic words. The data could be interpreted as showing that children who have developed secure phonological recoding processes are able to read regular words and nonwords. Children with less secure skills cannot read the more challenging items. Overall, performance in 2013 was significantly better than in 2012, with more children gaining marks between 32 and 40. The pattern in 2014 was different, with another rise in performance and a general shift to more children scoring 32 and above. The curve is smooth and skewed towards the maximum performance. This suggests that a programme of teaching phonics systematically, as recommended by the Rose Review (Rose, 2006), has begun to pay off in terms of giving children the skills they need to begin to develop independent accurate word reading skills.

Assessment of individuals

In the UK and most other developed countries, teachers have for decades used standardized assessments of reading to monitor individual achievement as children progress through school. Such assessment can be helpful and informative in providing teachers with objective information about the individual children in their class. This can help them to plan their provision and provide them with dispassionate information to discuss with parents. In an ideal world the national programme of SATs testing would have provided this type of information. However, though the SATs are called Standard Assessments, they are not standardized in the sense in which that term is used by educational psychologists.

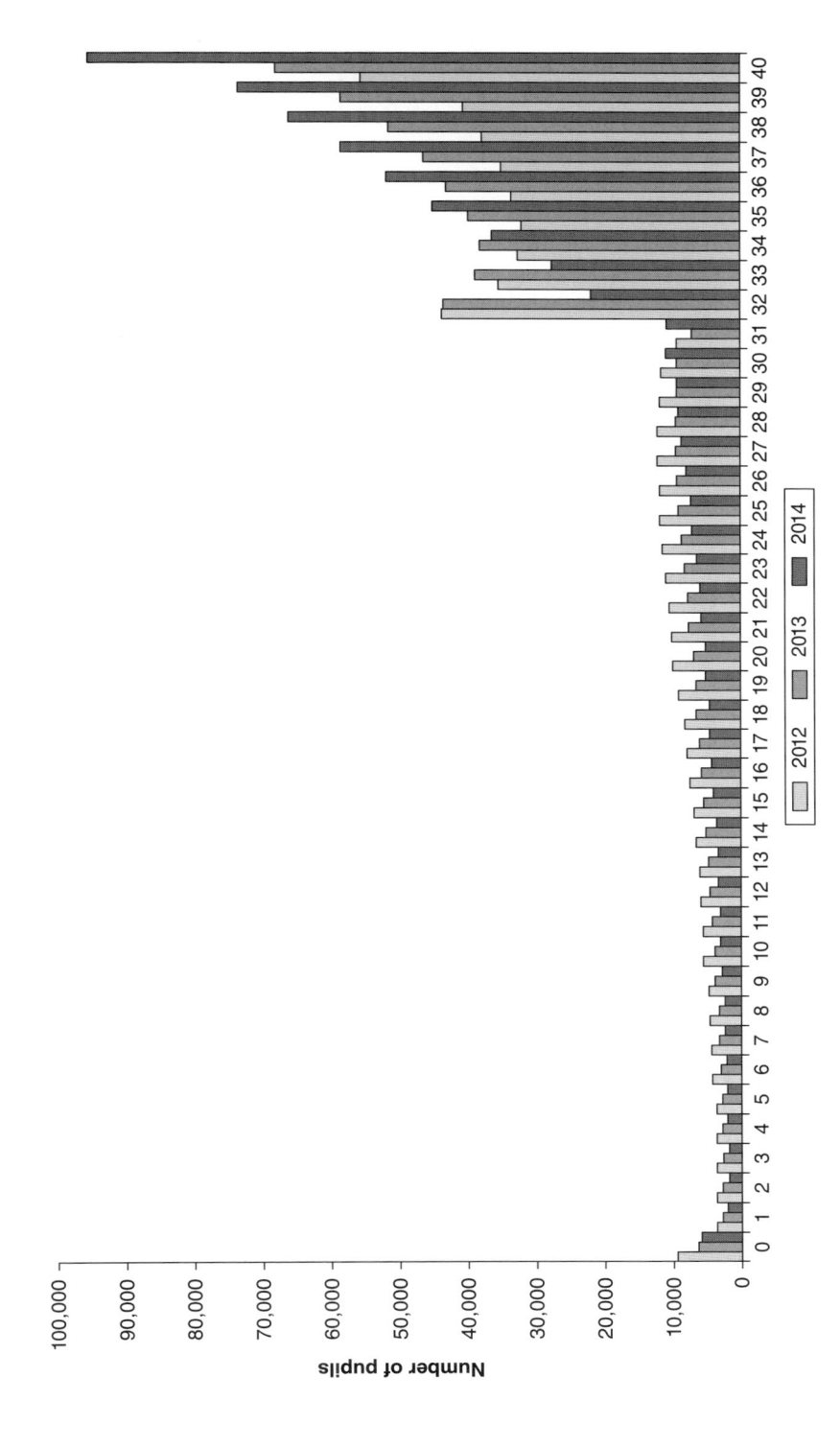

Figure 8.4 Numbers of children achieving each of the different possible marks

What then are standardized assessments? These are tests developed to assess performance in an objective manner in an attempt to obtain an unbiased measure of achievement at the time of testing. Standardized tests require all the testees to answer the same bank of questions. The instructions for answering the questions are given in a standardized way, as laid down in the manual accompanying the test. This is to ensure that as near as possible the conditions for doing the test are the same for all testees regardless of where or when or by whom they are tested. The responses are then marked in a standard way. This ensures that there is no bias in marking. The same test or an equivalent form of the test will be used. Tests may be used for many years, which can be useful because teachers and other professionals will be able to judge performance over a number of years without worrying that the test might have changed. Eventually, tests can get out of date and they may well need to be re-standardized or redeveloped. It is always important that teachers take note of the edition of the test that they use, and which might have been used by others to assess children.

Standardized tests are usually norm based. This means that during development of the test, the developers collected performance data from a sample of people drawn from the population who will eventually be the target population for the test. For example, if the test is being developed to assess the reading attainment of primary-school age children in the United Kingdom, the developers would have to first identify a norming population. These should be children representative of the population of the UK as a whole: children from the different geographical regions, an appropriate balance of girls and boys, and children representative of the ethnic profile of the UK population as a whole. And because reading performance changes as children get older, the norming population should include enough children at each age range (usually broken down into six month groups) across the complete age range of the target population.

A bit more on test statistics

We need to know a little more about assessment statistics. From the performance of the norming population, the test creators calculate raw scores by adding up the marks achieved by each age group, and use these to generate standard scores for each level of performance at each age group. The standard scores are usually generated with a mean for each age group of 100 and a standard deviation of 15 points. This process allows the performance of an individual to be compared with the norm of the population in the relevant age band. It also allows comparisons to be made of children at different ages, or the same children at different phases of life. For example, one would expect a typical 7-year-old to score less on a reading test than a typical 10-year-old. If just raw scores were provided for a test, then this would be all the information one would have. Without any information about the population performance, we would not know how either the 7-year-old or the 10-year-old was doing relative to their age groups, and we could not make a meaningful comparison of their performance. However, by transforming raw scores into standard scores, it is possible to compare performance. Most commonly, the manuals of standardized norm based tests provide tables for converting the raw scores into standard scores for each age.

Let us imagine that a 7-year-old achieves a raw score of 28 on a test, which converts to a standard score of 100 for children aged 7 years. We would know that this child was achieving just what would be expected from a typical 7-year-old. If we assess our child again three years later as a 10-year-old and record a raw score of 45, we need to know whether this is evidence of making typical progress, accelerated progress or stalled progress. If the raw score of 45 converts to a standard score of 100 for children aged 10 years, then the child would have made typical progress. If on the other hand the raw score of 45 converted to a standard score of 80, then we would conclude that though the child was reading at a higher level than at the age of 7 years, progress had stalled. Reading performance would be judged to be now below that expected of a typical 10-year-old. Conversely, if the raw score of 45 converted to a standard score of 115, then we could conclude that over the three-year period, the child had made accelerated progress and was now reading at a high level for a 10-year-old.

Figure 8.5 shows the normal distribution we presented earlier, but this time three additional set of figures have been added: standardized scores, percentile ranks and stanines.

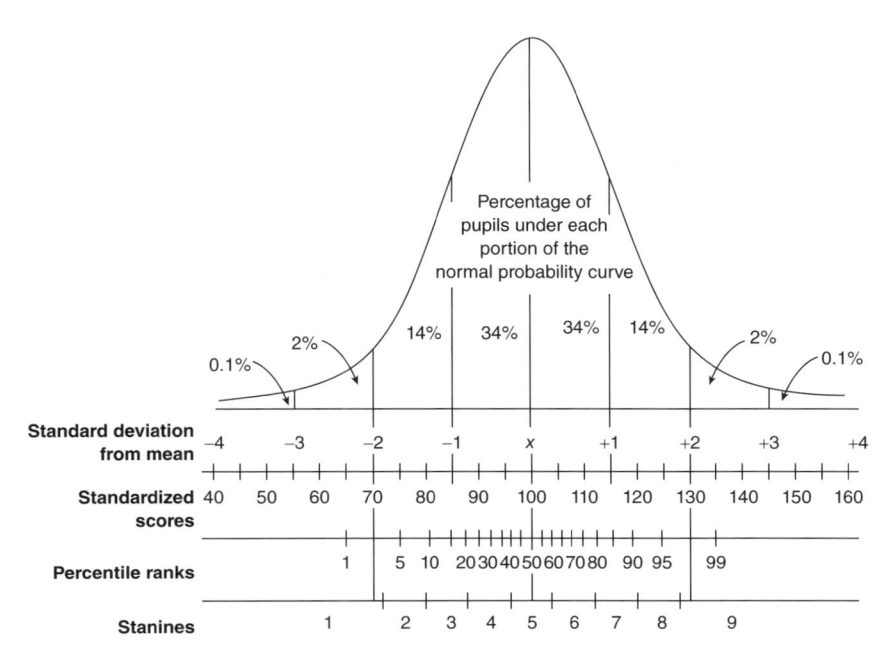

Figure 8.5 The normal distribution, showing standardized scores, percentile ranks and stanines

It is increasingly likely that test manuals provide stanine scores. This is a means of collapsing the range of scores for each age group into nine units related to the standard score. Table 8.1 shows the relationship between stanines and standard deviation scores, and the percentage of the population falling into each stanine.

Table 8.1 Relationship between stanines and standard deviation (SD) scores, with the percentage of the population falling into each stanine

Stanine	1	2	3	4	5	6	7	8	9
SD score	<−1.75	−1.75 to −1.25	−1.25 to −.75	−.75 to −.25	−.25 to +.25	+.25 to +.75	+.75 to +1.25	+1.25 to +1.75	>+1.75
Percentage of the population in each stanine	4%	7%	12%	17%	20%	17%	12%	7%	4%

Fifty-four per cent of the age group achieve stanines of between 4 and 6. This is considered to be normal or typical achievement for age group. Those achieving 7, 8 or 9 are considered to be high achievers and those achieving 1, 2 or 3 are considered to be comparatively low achievers. The usefulness of stanines is that they avoid the tendency to over-interpret small differences in standard scores.

Some test manuals will also give Reading Ages (or Spelling Ages). These are based on the scores achieved by each age group of the norming population. An argument for using Reading Ages is that reporting them to parents makes sense. However, a downside of this is that often spurious levels of accuracy are conveyed. Parent may feel that if their child of 9 years 10 months is said to have a reading age of 9 year 6 months, that child is not achieving sufficiently well. However, a four-month discrepancy is not significant in testing terms. It could be said that the problem with Reading Ages is not these numbers themselves, but the way they are reported. Using stanines, it is possible to say to parents, for example:

> Your child has gained a score of 6. This means that s/he is reading at a level we would expect at this age because children of this age typically score between 4 and 6.

or

> Your child has gained a score of 2. This means that s/he is reading well below the level we would expect at this age because children of this age typically score between 4 and 6.

It is to be expected that, where this is reported to parents or carers, the school will have in place a plan to ensure that the child receives targeted support.

Under the National Curriculum in England and Wales (Department for Education, 2014), there were statements to describe the levels of performance and these were given a number classification. The level expected of a child aged 11 years at the end of Year 6 was 4. These level descriptors were not the same as stanines because they did not arise from any performance data.

Norm-based standardized tests come in a number of different forms depending on how they are administered and what they are designed to assess. If we consider the Simple View of Reading, a test may be designed to assess word reading processes or reading comprehension processes.

Group tests

Group tests are tests administered to children in groups. The National Curriculum Key Stage 2 SATs are group tests, but not norm-based. Group tests are efficient to administer and therefore less costly in terms of teacher time and classroom disruption. Inevitably they are designed to assess silent reading performance. Group tests are generally recommended for obtaining, monitoring and screening data of whole classes and even schools. Data from annual administration of the same test enable reliable comparisons to be made of the performance of successive cohorts of children, and of the same cohorts as they progress through the education system.

These are usually pencil and paper tests, although increasingly publishers are developing tests which can be taken electronically. A well-designed group test will have a simple scoring procedure that does not require interpretation of individual responses. Thus the scoring of a group test should be highly accurate and reliable and does not require a professional to spend time logging the responses. Test publishers now offer electronic scoring services which are efficient and take away the need for human collation of data.

Group tests are not designed to be diagnostic in terms of drilling down to investigate the strengths and weaknesses of individual children's attainment. However, when they are standardized and norm-based they can be effectively used for identifying those children who fall outside the normal range of performance both in terms of the standardization population and more locally in terms of a school's population. These children can then have further more detailed diagnostic assessments which can be used to plan for any additional necessary intervention. These tests can also be useful for schools both to monitor each child's progress over the years, and to keep data on the standards achieved by the whole school year on year.

A well-designed standardized group test will include a manual giving full details of the theoretical framework which informed the creation of the test. There will be clear information about the construct of reading that is being assessed. This might be word reading processes or reading comprehension. Teachers need to know what the test was designed to do in the first place and also who the test was designed for. It is important to have details about the standardization population. Without doubt, the manual should include full details of how to administer and score the test, and it should also have user-friendly tables to enable raw scores to be converted to standard scores for each age group. Increasingly there will be tables of stanines and percentiles as well.

It can be very useful if a test includes an alternate form. This is a second version of the test which was developed in the same way and places the same demands on the testees, it just has different stimuli. An alternate form means that if some children are absent for whatever reason when a group test is administered, one can give them the alternate form without fear of them having discussed the test with their friends. Alternate forms also mean that one can administer the test to whole classes of children, with half of them taking one form and half taking the other. In this way the chances of inadvertent copying are greatly reduced so the scores will be more reliable.

The New Group Reading Test developed by the National Foundation for Educational Research (Burge et al., 2010) is an example of a well-designed group test. There are four different levels of the test designed for 6-year-olds, 7–9-year-olds, 10–13-year-olds and 14–16-year-olds. Each level includes different scales assessing different aspects of reading. Test 1, for the youngest children, focuses on word reading processes with phonics and decoding being assessed, but it includes some assessment of literal comprehension. Tests 2, 3 and 4 gradually include more scales for assessing comprehension, including inferencing and deduction skills, and eventually covering higher-order reading skills for the oldest children. Because the test assesses different aspects of reading, the manual gives details about calculating scores for the different scales. This is particularly useful for identifying those children who show uneven profiles.

A test like this should only ever be given once a year, or even only once every two years because it is a monitoring and screening test and not a diagnostic test. However, it does enable teachers to identify those children who need further more detailed assessment to identify their particular weaknesses.

Individual diagnostic tests

Where a child is showing weaknesses, or is not making acceptable progress, or has been identified as falling below what would be expected from administration of a test like the New Group Reading Test, teachers need to begin to drill down to identify where the problems lie. The best way to do this is to use standardized individual diagnostic tests. Such tests are not designed for monitoring whole groups of children. The Simple View of Reading is an excellent framework for considering which tests to use to help diagnosis. Where a child is showing difficulties, it is important to identify whether the problems lie with word reading processes, or language comprehension processes, or both.

Word reading processes

The Diagnostic Test of Word Reading Processes (DTWRP) is a test which *only* assesses word reading processes. There are three sets of single items to read: 30 regular words, 30 exception words, and 30 nonwords. As you will recall from

Chapters 3 and 4, nonwords can only be read accurately using phonological recoding processes, and exception words can only be read accurately using lexical processes. As with the Phonics Screener, the nonwords are accompanied by pictures of monsters to alert children to the fact that these are not real words. However, unlike the Phonics Screener, this test was designed and standardized for children between the ages of 6 and 12 years. The Phonics Screener only gives an overall score and does not separately record the number of real words and nonwords read accurately. This means one cannot identify specific weaknesses in phonological recoding processes directly from the Screener. In the DTWRP, when a child has a relative weakness in reading the nonwords, there is likely to be a weakness in developing efficient phonological recoding processes for word reading. This is different from the child who shows a relative weakness in reading the exception words. In this case the child is likely to have difficulty in establishing the orthographic representations that are required for lexical processing. Some children are likely to show weaknesses in reading all the items. The manual provides advice about identifying individual profiles and possible teaching approaches depending on the profile.

When a child shows a specific weakness in nonword reading, the next steps would be to investigate phonological processing using a test of phonological awareness, and grapheme-phoneme correspondence knowledge. This is because the development of phonological recoding processes for word reading may be compromised by both poor phonological awareness and inadequate knowledge of GPCs.

The Phonological Assessment Battery (PhAB2) Primary (2nd edition) (Gibbs & Bodman, 2014) is an example of a phonological awareness test. The battery includes 10 subtests, enabling teachers to make detailed assessments of childrens' phonological processing skills. These include assessments of ability to manipulate individual phonemes as well as the larger phonological units of rime. Single phoneme subtests include blending phonemes into words, deleting phonemes from words, segmenting words into their component phonemes. The battery also includes a working memory subtest to help identify whether the difficulty lies with memory. Finally, the battery includes a nonword reading subtest. This is particularly helpful if the PhAB2 is administered after having identified a child with phonological processing weaknesses from administration of the DTWRP. Having two measures of nonword reading provides a very useful reliability check.

We know of no standardized tests of grapheme-phoneme correspondence (GPC) knowledge, so assessment here depends on you to construct your own informal assessment based on the GPCs that have been taught under your chosen phonics programme. If you routinely collect these data from all the children in your class, you will over time become increasingly able to form a judgement as to the adequacy of an individual child's GPC knowledge. Remember, in Chapter 5, we emphasized that children not only need to be accurate in recalling grapheme-phoneme correspondences, they also need to be fast and fluent if word reading skill is not to be compromised. Children from the end of Key Stage 1 onward should have comprehensive, accurate and swift access to GPCs.

Reading comprehension

The comprehension dimension of the Simple View of Reading can be investigated using assessments that are specifically designed to assess children' comprehension of texts they are required to read. Individual reading comprehension assessments typically take the form of a series of short texts to be read (usually aloud), which are then followed by a set of questions designed to investigate understanding of the text just read. The York Assessment of Reading for Comprehension (YARC) (Hulme et al., 2009) suite of tests has been designed to do just this. The tests provide information about reading performance from age 4 years through to age 16 years. A very important feature of these tests is that the questions have been carefully designed to assess vocabulary knowledge, literal comprehension and different types of inferential aspects of comprehension. At the youngest age, the assessment includes measures of letter knowledge, phonological awareness and single word reading.

The Simple View of Reading and assessment

Tests of word reading processes are able to identify those children whose word reading skills are weak. These are the children who fall in the two left-hand quadrants of the Simple View of Reading diagram (Figure 8.6).

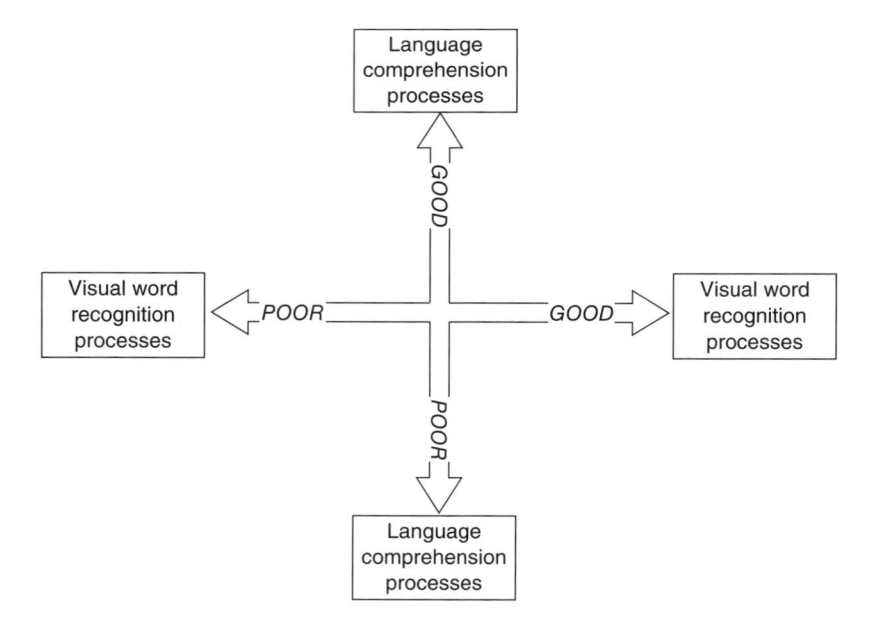

Figure 8.6 The Simple View of Reading

Tests of reading comprehension are able to identify those children whose linguistic comprehension processing skills are weak. These are the children who fall into the bottom two quadrants of the Simple View of Reading diagram. By assessing both word reading processes and comprehension separately, it is possible to identify which of the four quadrants a child falls into and therefore to begin to plan targeted support.

Closing words

What should schools assess? An ideal policy would be to have a programme of assessing children's reading skills annually by administering a group reading test. Children's scores would be entered into a database logging objective levels of skills of all children as they progress through school. Such data would be based on standardized norm referenced tests which the schools can use for monitoring their own effectiveness and for making decisions about provision for all children. These data of course would be owned by the school and not part of a system of national reporting or creating league tables. Assessment policy would also include specialist teachers being responsible for administering diagnostic assessments to those children identified as having difficulties. In an ideal world, schools would be able to identify those children in need of support as early as possible. However, because progress is not uniform, because children move schools, because some difficulties may not show themselves until the later years, good practice is to have an assessment policy that covers all the year groups in the school. It is also good practice to record the data from assessments very accurately and to share these data with the schools to which children move.

9
Teaching to overcome word reading difficulties (developmental dyslexia)

Summary

In this chapter you will learn about ways of assessing areas of weakness and strength in children's word reading processes, within the context of the Dual-Route Cascaded (DRC) model of reading. You will learn about ways of teaching to improve the word reading skills of children experiencing difficulty in developing these skills, and will come to realize that the kinds of teaching outlined in Chapter 5 serve both to prevent and overcome children's word reading difficulties. Effective teachers of reading can also effectively teach most children experiencing difficulty. For intractable difficulties, we need specialist teachers with a deep understanding of word reading processes, who are able to pinpoint precisely an individual child's processing weaknesses and design teaching that targets these.

Introduction

There continues to be argument as to whether all children experiencing difficulty in developing word reading skills should be accorded the label 'dyslexic'. We will not rehearse these arguments here, but refer to the recent six-point definition of 'dyslexia' provided in the Rose Report (Rose, 2009).

Definition of developmental dyslexia

1. Dyslexia is a learning difficulty that primarily affects the skills involved in accurate and fluent word reading and spelling.
2. Characteristic features of dyslexia are difficulties in phonological awareness, verbal memory and verbal processing speed.
3. Dyslexia occurs across the range of intellectual abilities.
4. It is best thought of as a continuum, not a distinct category, and there are no clear cut-off points.
5. Co-occurring difficulties may be seen in aspects of language, motor co-ordination, mental calculation, concentration and personal organization, but these are not, by themselves, markers of dyslexia.
6. A good indication of the severity and persistence of dyslexic difficulties can be gained by examining how the individual responds or has responded to well-founded intervention.

This definition is based in current knowledge about the existence and nature of developmental dyslexia, and was broadly agreed by the several different constituencies represented on the advisory group to the Rose Report (Rose, 2009), which included academics and researchers with backgrounds in education and/or psychology, those involved in training teachers and specialist teachers, representatives of dyslexia charities and specialist teachers. You can find and download a free copy of the Report by entering 'Rose 2009' into your search engine. Chapter 5 of the Rose Report contains useful information for classroom teachers about how to adapt the classroom environment and teaching procedures to assist children with any of the co-occurring difficulties associated with dyslexia. Here, we concentrate on the core reading difficulties.

The word 'dyslexia' comes from Greek '*dys*' meaning 'abnormal, difficult' and '*lexis*' meaning 'word, speech': thus, in point 1 in the box above, defining the *primary* problem in dyslexia as a difficulty in acquiring word reading and spelling skills perfectly embodies the etymology of the term 'dyslexia'. Word reading difficulty is present in every definition of dyslexia we have found, further emphasizing its importance as *the defining characteristic* of dyslexia. The term was first applied in the 1870s to adult formerly-skilled readers who, through various forms of brain injury, had lost some or all aspects of their ability to read words. Reports of this kind of loss date back to the seventeenth century. The first accounts of *developmental* dyslexia (i.e. of children who find it abnormally difficult to learn to read words, and of adults whose difficulties are not caused by brain injury but are persistent from childhood) were published in medical journals in the 1890s. It is probably to this twin heritage (reports of brain-injured adults, children's word reading difficulties first reported by doctors in medical journals) that we owe the medical terminology still permeating much of the discussion of developmental dyslexia (e.g. 'diagnosis', 'treatment').

Word reading difficulties (developmental dyslexia) in the context of the Simple View of Reading

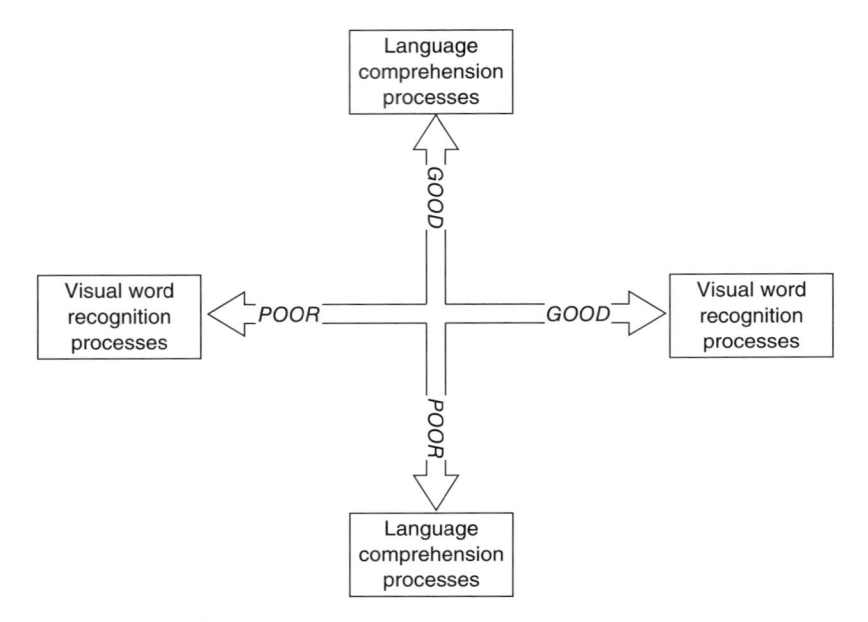

Figure 9.1 The Simple View of Reading

In the Simple View of Reading, visual word recognition processes (word reading skills) exist along a continuum from poor to good. All children in the two left-hand quadrants have average to low word reading skills for their age. Thus, any attempt to consider dyslexia as a distinct category of poor word reading must impose an arbitrary cut-off point somewhere along this side of the continuum. Only children whose word reading skills fall below this arbitrary cut-off would be included in the category of children with dyslexia. Such a category might be useful (and used) in at least two ways. On the positive side, there is evidence that children with word reading difficulties and their families are reassured when the label 'dyslexia' is given them. Despite the fact that the label explains nothing, it does help alleviate feelings of inadequacy, shame and guilt, and helps children feel more positive about themselves. On the negative side, it has the power to limit access to resources, which is clearly inequitable: children whose word reading skills fall just above any arbitrary cut-off require additional provision to overcome their difficulties just as much as children whose word reading skills fall just below, yet only the latter group would be eligible for provision. Traditionally, one way of setting the criterion for the 'dyslexic' label was to accord a diagnosis of dyslexia to children whose word reading achievements were discrepant with (significantly below) their IQ. However, studies have shown that IQ is a poor predictor of reading achievement, and IQ discrepant and non-IQ discrepant poor readers share the same characteristics, rendering unsound this method of categorization (e.g. Gresham & Vellutino, 2010; Hatcher, 2000; Siegel, 1989; Vellutino, Scanlon & Lyon, 2000).

The job of schools is to teach *all* children in their care, to the best of their ability, whether or not children come with a label attached. Thus, when we have children in our classes whose word reading skills lag behind those of their peers, affecting their access to the curriculum, it is *our* responsibility to provide the best teaching we can to enable those children to catch up.

Identifying children with poor word reading skills

First, we need to identify children who are falling behind. In Chapter 8, we suggested using a standardized group reading test annually to identify children whose attainments are poor for their age. Comparison of children's individual standard scores from one year to the next can also identify children who have not made expected progress over the course of the year – standard score remains stable over time if children are making expected progress.

Most group tests do not separately assess word reading skills: these need to be assessed in children identified as a cause for concern, to see whether low levels of word reading skill are responsible for the child's poor-for-age reading. The Diagnostic Test of Word Reading Processes (DTWRP), presented in Chapter 8, gives an overall standard score for word reading skills. It is currently the only standardized test with UK norms that separately assesses phonological recoding processes and lexical processes, by asking children to read sets of well-matched items. It is based on the Dual-Route Cascaded (DRC) model of reading, presented in Chapter 3. As well as the overall standard score for word reading, it gives separate stanine scores for nonword, regular word and exception word reading. As stated in Chapter 8, comparison of nonword with exception word stanine scores reveals a child's profile of relative strengths and weaknesses in phonological recoding and lexical processes. This profile is the first step towards designing a targeted intervention plan, building on the child's broad strengths and addressing their broad weaknesses.

Heterogeneity in developmental dyslexia

There are three possible profiles: children can have significantly more difficulty with phonological recoding than lexical processes (a 'phonological dyslexic' profile), or significantly more difficulty with lexical than phonological recoding processes (a 'surface dyslexic' profile) or equal difficulty with both sets of processes (a 'mixed dyslexic' profile). Notice that these labels, which include the word 'dyslexic', are simply used to describe different patterns of word reading difficulty. There is evidence of heterogeneity of profiles among children with word reading difficulties (e.g. Castles & Coltheart, 1993; Castles, Datta, Gayan & Olson, 1999; Manis, Seidenberg, Doi, McBride-Chang & Petersen, 1996; Petersen, Pennington & Olson, 2013; Sprenger-Charolles, Colé, Lacert & Serniclaes, 2000; Stanovich, Siegel & Gottardo, 1997), but whether or not this heterogeneity represents different *subtypes* or is just variation along a continuum remains in question. The question is theoretically interesting, but irrelevant for teaching purposes, where what matters is discovering as accurately as possible the specific impairments in word reading processes that are causing word reading difficulty in an individual child, and seeking means to remedy and/or work around these impairments.

McArthur, Kohnen, Larsen, Jones et al. (2013) described the patterns of weaknesses and strengths they found most frequently in groups of children with each of these three dyslexic profiles, when children were compared on a set of nine measures designed to tap different elements and links in each processing route of the DRC. This level of theoretically-motivated detailed investigation is usually found only in single case studies of individual children. Figures 9.2, 9.3 and 9.4 illustrate the location within processing routes of the DRC of the different weaknesses and strengths McArthur et al. (2013) found to be associated with each profile.

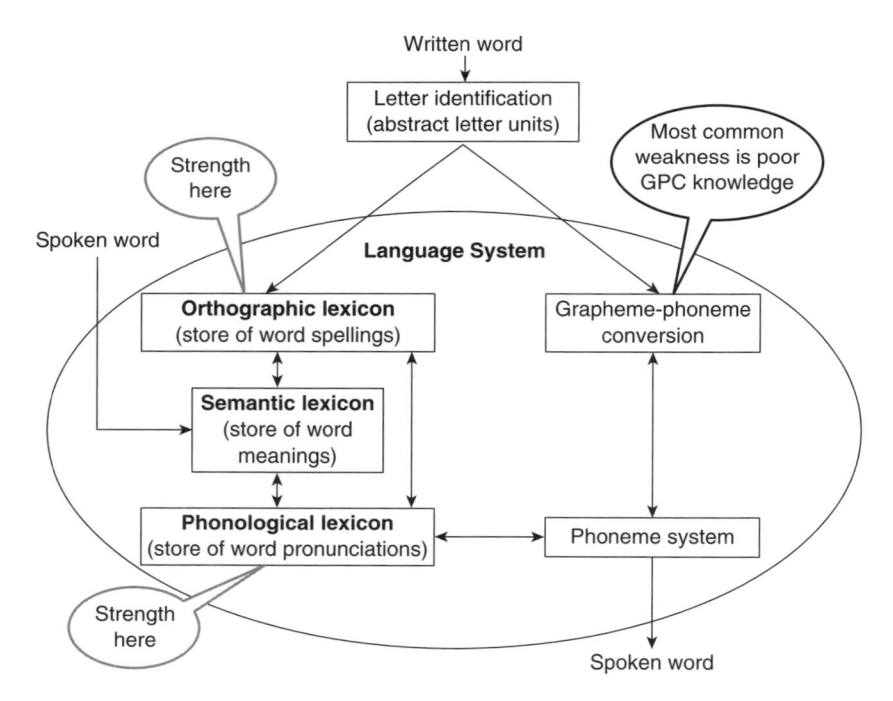

Figure 9.2 Most common weaknesses and strengths in the phonological dyslexic group

Poor grapheme-phoneme correspondence knowledge was the most commonly occurring weakness for children with a phonological dyslexic profile, and was the only measure on which the group performed significantly worse than typically developing children in the age-matched control group. They also showed two areas of strength. They performed significantly better than the control group on a measure designed to tap orthographic representations (an orthographic choice task where they had to decide which word in each word/pseudo-homophone pair shown them (e.g. DOOR DOAR) was the correctly spelled alternative). Performance in this task is assumed to depend on access to the orthographic representations of words – their orthographic representations were significantly better than expected. This finding casts a shadow over Share's (1995) proposal that efficient phonological recoding processes underlie the development of orthographic representations, as this group of phonological dyslexics had apparently acquired better orthographic representations than their age-peers, despite significantly worse phonological recoding ability. They also performed significantly better than the control group on a measure designed to tap phonological representations (an auditory lexical decision task, in which words and nonwords (e.g. RAIN, HANE) were spoken and the child had to say whether each item was a real word), indicating well-specified phonological representations that again were beyond age expectations. This finding casts a shadow over a basic assumption of the phonological deficit theory of developmental dyslexia, which proposes that poorly specified phonological representations are the cause of developmental dyslexics' phonological processing difficulties. But, this is just one study, and replication is needed before we can be sure that either shadow is justified. It would also be useful if future research used a wider variety of measures to tap orthographic and phonological representations, rather than relying on a single measure of each, as in the McArthur et al. (2013) study.

The surface dyslexic group were significantly worse than controls on two measures. They performed badly on the orthographic choice task (described above), indicating a weakness in forming and storing orthographic representations in the orthographic lexicon. They also performed badly on a task designed to tap the link between orthographic and phonological representations of words. In this task, children were asked to look at pairs of written words and say whether the words rhymed. Half of the pairs consisted of two irregular words (e.g. QUEUE, VIEW); regular word pairs also had distinct spelling patterns (e.g. CRANE, PAIN). Thus no rhyme judgements could be made on the basis of spelling pattern alone. The score recorded for this measure was the number of correct rhyme judgements for irregular word rhyming pairs: these judgements could not be made by phonological recoding either, and so must have depended on links from orthographic to phonological representations of words.

No potentially compensating strengths were found in the surface dyslexic group. But the fact that children in this group have age-appropriate GPC knowledge might cast another shadow over the proposal that adequately developed phonological recoding processes are all that is required for children to be able to form and store orthographic representations. We say 'might', because

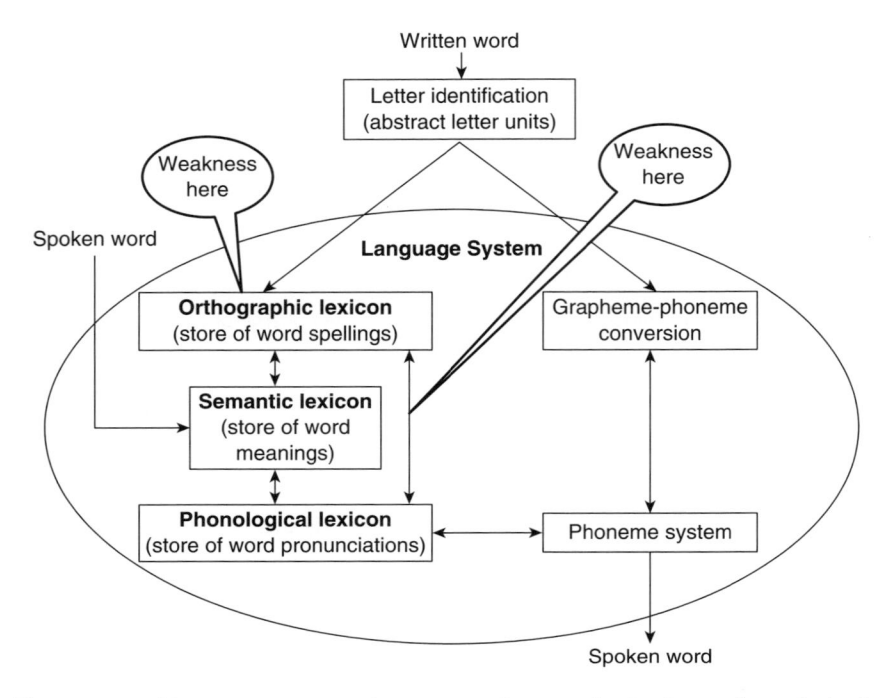

Figure 9.3 Most common weaknesses and strengths in the surface dyslexic group

McArthur et al. (2013) measured children's accuracy rather than speed of response when asked to give the phoneme for each presented grapheme. We argued in Chapter 5 that GPC knowledge needs to be fluent as well as accurate, with fast automatic retrieval of correspondences. Possibly the surface dyslexic group were slower than their age peers in retrieving correspondences between graphemes and phonemes.

Many more weaknesses are evident in the mixed group than either the phonological or surface groups. They have all the weaknesses of both these groups, and a few more besides. Additional weakness in phonological output is indicated by their poor phoneme blending score. Additional weakness in links from orthographic to semantic representations is indicated by their poor performance on a homophone choice task, where the child saw pairs of words (e.g. WEEK, WEAK) and, after the tester read a short sentence defining one word in the pair (e.g. 'The word for seven days'), was asked to circle the word that fitted that definition (WEEK).

Would it ever be feasible to implement this kind of detailed investigation of specific strengths and weaknesses in the school situation?

Probably not. That is why we have suggested limiting investigation to identifying the broad nature of the child's difficulties – do they fit a phonological, a surface or a mixed profile? We will return to this later. The kind of detailed investigation found in single case studies of individuals with developmental dyslexia,

Teaching to overcome word reading difficulties (developmental dyslexia)

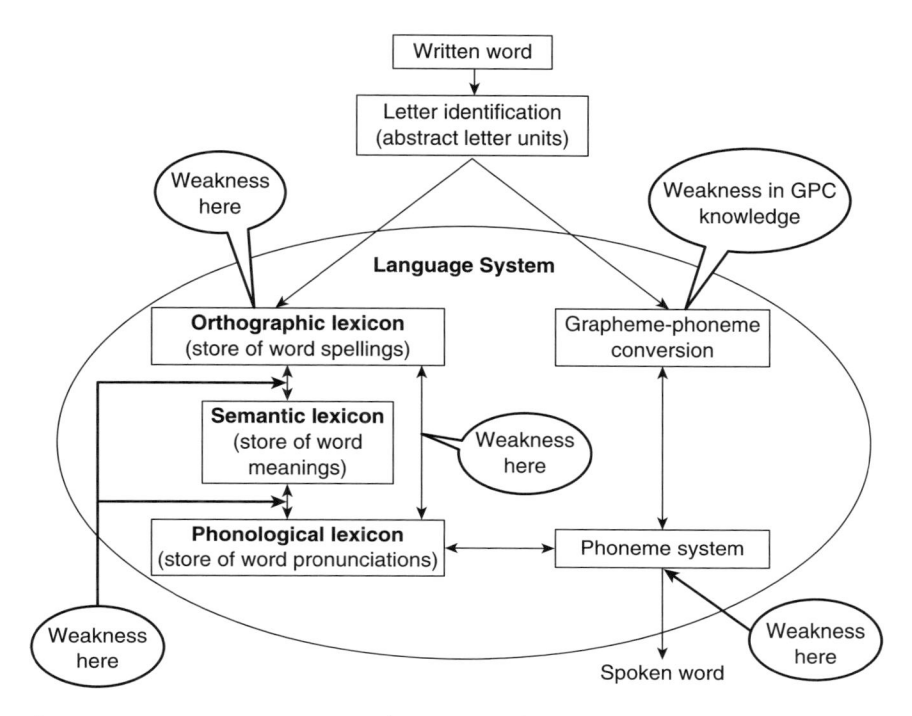

Figure 9.4 Most common weaknesses and strengths in the mixed dyslexic group

and exemplified in the McArthur et al. (2013) group study, does not seem to be the natural territory even of the specialist dyslexia teacher. A survey, reported in Rose (2009: 158–160), of the content of different specialist teacher courses accredited by the British Dyslexia Association (Approved Teacher Status, ATS; Associate Member of the British Dyslexia Association, AMBDA) bears this out. None of the responses from course leaders indicated students were taught in detail and in depth about processing models of word reading, such as the DRC model. There are probably several reasons for this: it is knowledge not widely available beyond psychology journals and university departments of psychology; it is difficult knowledge; and it violates the assumption that in dealing with children's word reading difficulties we need a model of the *development* of word reading rather than a model of skilled performance.

We think schools and teachers do need access to specialists with this kind of knowledge and skill, for those children who do not respond to the kinds of broad and largely phonics-based intervention currently available. Might educational psychologists fulfil this role? At present it seems unlikely their training enables them to do this. But it is a three-year postgraduate doctoral training, and space should be available to ensure educational psychologists have thorough, detailed knowledge of processing models to inform their assessment of word reading and the design of interventions precisely targeting the specific source(s) of an individual's difficulties. Reports of single case intervention studies using this methodology to identify and target highly specific areas of weakness show some impressive improvements (e.g. Broom & Doctor, 1995a, 1995b; Kipp & Mohr, 2008).

In the more general context of schools, the three broad profiles of phonological, surface and mixed dyslexia can provide some guidance towards targeted intervention. Children with phonological and with mixed dyslexia both have weaknesses in GPC knowledge, providing support for the well-documented view that phonological processing deficits are a major cause of word reading difficulties (e.g. Hatcher, Hulme, Miles, Carroll et al., 2006; Share & Stanovich, 1995; Snowling, 1980, 2013; Stanovich & Siegel, 1994; Vellutino, Fletcher, Snowling & Scanlon, 2004; Vellutino & Scanlon, 1987; Wagner & Torgesen, 1987). Thus, many programmes designed to overcome children's word reading difficulties rely largely on structured, cumulative phonics teaching. But, the surface dyslexic group do not share this weakness in GPC knowledge, and therefore phonics teaching likely leaves their difficulty unaddressed.

Teaching to overcome phonological recoding weaknesses

Two major sources of difficulty adversely affect the development and use of phonological recoding processes: inadequate knowledge of grapheme-phoneme correspondence rules (McArthur et al., 2013), and inadequate phoneme segmentation and blending skills[1] (Scammacca, Vaughn, Roberts, Wanzek & Torgesen, 2007; Torgesen, 2005; Wimmer, 1996). Intervention tackling these two sources of difficulty is most likely to be effective in improving word reading skills. This is why early phonics teaching is vitally important, to try to *prevent* word reading difficulties from arising in the first place, or from becoming entrenched. During 'quality first teaching', defined in Rose (2009: 60) as providing 'high quality, systematic phonic work as part of a broad and rich curriculum … to develop their

Table 9.1 Signs of dyslexia at different developmental phases

Developmental phase	Symptoms of dyslexia
Pre-school	Delayed speech
	Poor expressive language
	Poor rhyming skills
	Little interest/difficulty learning letters
Early school years	Poor letter-sound knowledge
	Poor phoneme awareness

[1]Segmentation and blending skills were not measured in the McArthur et al. (2013) study.

Developmental phase	Symptoms of dyslexia
	Poor word attack skills
	Idiosyncratic spelling
	Problems copying
Middle school years	Slow reading
	Poor decoding skills when faced with new words
	Phonetic or non-phonetic spelling
Adolescence and adulthood	Poor reading fluency
	Slow speed of writing
	Poor organization and expression in written work

speaking and listening skills and phonological awareness', we need to pay special attention to children who might be at risk of developing word reading difficulties. Snowling (2008) provides guidance towards recognizing 'at risk' individuals at different phases of development (see Table 9.1).

'At-risk' children require much more practice than typically developing children before their learning is secure. We stated in Chapter 5 that whole-class, small-group and individual teaching are all effective ways of delivering phonics teaching. As with most research findings, this statement depends on studies comparing group differences in mean scores, and therefore does not imply that every child will learn equally well in all three situations. Whether we use Snowling's (2008) guidance, or our own observation and progress monitoring, or a combination of both, to identify 'at risk' children, we need to do something to help these children *as soon as they are noticed*. Intervention is more effective if given earlier rather than later (National Reading Panel Report, NICH & HD, 2000) and there is ample evidence that children who fall behind in reading in first Grade do not catch up. The first few years at school are therefore crucial. The 'quality first' teaching most likely to minimize the occurrence of word reading difficulties involves using a systematic, structured phonics programme in the first few years of school, following the programme faithfully, continually monitoring and recording children's learning, and giving additional opportunities for practice and consolidation to children who need this to keep up.

This inevitably involves supplementing whole-class teaching with small-group teaching and practice. We saw in Chapters 4 and 5 that knowledge of grapheme-phoneme correspondences and their use in reading is essential knowledge: every child in the class needs to learn this essential knowledge. This means not moving children on until their current knowledge is securely established and can be retrieved and applied to reading (and writing) fluently and with ease.

Additional small-group teaching within the classroom for those who need it may not be so difficult to achieve as might first appear. Children progress at sometimes very different rates, so that whole-class teaching becomes no longer the most efficient way of grouping. Grouping in accordance with current states of knowledge may then be preferable. These groupings should be flexible, with children able to move from group to group as their learning needs change, while avoiding the development of perceptions of 'being kept back', with all their negative connotations.

So far, so simple. But what about the children who, despite quality first teaching supplemented with small-group tuition, do not make adequate progress? We might arrange one-to-one teaching for the child. We might make sure these one-to-one sessions are frequent and short (for example, if we are teaching one new GPC, a couple of minutes two or three times during the day would be a good start). We might employ the kinds of instructional practices advocated by Solity and colleagues described in Chapter 5 (e.g. Shapiro & Solity, 2008): making sure when we teach a new GPC, we embed it among several GPCs the child already knows. This serves the dual purpose of motivating the child and consolidating old knowledge. Another useful approach is 'errorless learning', based in the view that errors reinforce wrong learning. For GPC learning, this could mean presenting two graphemes, one a known and one an unknown GPC. Pronounce the known grapheme, and ask the child to select the grapheme that represents that phoneme. Repeat for the unknown grapheme. Gradually increase the set of graphemes shown as the child's knowledge increases. We might employ the practices Hatcher, Hulme and Snowling (2004) found effective with 'at risk' children, of including phoneme awareness training in the teaching they receive. We should ensure children have access to decodable books that require them to put into practice what they have been learning, and give them the chance to feel they *can* read without assistance. We also need constantly to reassure children that they *will* 'get it' eventually – it just takes longer for some of us – and we need to praise them when they try hard as well as when they succeed.

We hope all the references back to Chapter 5 have helped you understand that actually, you do know how to teach young children with word reading difficulties: they are not a different breed; they mostly need more time, more intensity and more practice. Schools must find ways of providing the additional time for consolidation and practice, and for the carefully structured introduction of new material that these children need. Meanwhile, it is important that children slow to develop word reading skills are not disadvantaged by this in other ways. For example, typically developing children will likely be reading more, and their reading will be more challenging, so will serve better to broaden and deepen their vocabulary, and develop their tacit knowledge of linguistic structures. It is important to read to and with the slow developers, to make sure they too have opportunities for language development beyond the confines of their own word reading skills.

What about older children with persisting word reading difficulties? How do we improve their ability to use phonological recoding processes?

Older children with persistent difficulties in phonological recoding processes need to learn the same content as younger children, but it is more difficult to teach to them, because (1) they have experienced years of failure and are likely feeling pretty hopeless; (2) they probably see learning this stuff as babyish and the need to learn it as embarrassing; (3) the teaching materials available (including books they can practise on) are often designed for younger children and are therefore not suitable; and (4) they have probably developed some non-productive strategies for guessing their way through a text, which, being hard won, they cling to.

The teacher's role with these older children is therefore complex. Specialist dyslexia teachers emphasize the importance of developing and maintaining a good rapport with pupils and being sensitive to their emotional needs; planning and delivering lessons so that pupils achieve success; providing regular opportunities for consolidation and reinforcement of teaching points already covered; helping pupils develop their concentration; and teaching them to be aware of their own learning strategies. They also emphasize the importance of teaching a structured and sequential programme of phonics (Rose, 2009).

Slavin, Lake, Davis and Madden (2010) reviewed intervention studies with the aim of identifying 'what works for struggling readers'. Key findings were that one-to-one tutoring works. It is more effective if delivered by teachers rather than teaching assistants. An emphasis on phonics greatly improves tutoring outcomes. Small-group tutoring can also be effective, but typically less so than one-to-one. The effects of one-to-one tutoring in first grade only persist into the upper grades if classroom interventions continue beyond the intervention period. Almost all successful programmes have a strong emphasis on phonics. Slavin et al. (2010) recommend using one-to-one tutoring for pupils having the greatest difficulty.

Brooks (2013) reports that very few of the programmes designed specifically for use with children with word reading difficulties have been evaluated in adequately designed and controlled research studies. However, he lists several programmes that have some support from measured improvement in word reading and spelling from pre- to post-intervention. Systematic, multi-sensory, phonics-based teaching finds support in some studies. Hornsby and Miles (1980) provided this for 20 months to 107 10–11-year-olds: pupils gained on average 1.4 months in reading age for each month of teaching. Thomson (2003), using a similar teaching approach with 252 children aged 10 years at the start of the two- to three-year intervention, found similar ratio gains. Importantly, these two studies show children making somewhat accelerated progress, when without intervention they would have been falling further behind. Brooks (2013: 221 and 222) lists programmes showing sometimes 'remarkable' ratio gains on immediate post-tests, but no long-term follow-up data are available.

Teaching to overcome weaknesses in lexical processing

Lexical processing difficulties are less well understood than difficulties in phonological recoding processes, and there is scarcely any research on interventions for children with these difficulties. That which exists is usually case studies of individual children, and often addresses spelling rather than reading problems. However, where spelling has been taught, the effects are also apparent in improved word reading. Interventions often present whole words on flashcards for children to read.

Judica, de Luca, Spinelli and Zoccolotti (2002) presented words very briefly on computer screens, to force children to extract more information in a single gaze fixation. Children either read the word aloud or typed it into the computer. They found significant improvements in word reading of Italian surface dyslexic children after 35 one-hour individual training sessions.

Broom and Doctor (1995a) report a single case study of DF, an 11-year-old surface dyslexic boy, who was systematically taught a set of 66 exception words over 24 25-minute sessions, delivered three times weekly, plus practice at home. A word was written on a blank page for DF to read, and its meaning was discussed. He wrote the word in cursive handwriting, naming each letter as he wrote it. He checked his copy against the original, and re-read it. This was repeated twice for each word. The word was then covered, and DF wrote it from memory, checked against the original and moved on if it was correct; otherwise, he tried again until it was correct. Then he suggested a sentence illustrating the word meaning, which the teacher dictated for him to write. He was given flashcards of each trained word to practise reading at home. At the start of each lesson, previously trained words were read, defined and written; any word not known was taught again. After 24 sessions, DF was 100% correct. This study illustrates the huge amounts of repetition and practice some children require before learning is secure – but with carefully paced systematic teaching, learning is possible.

Brunsdon, Hannan, Coltheart and Nickels (2002) report a single case study of TJ, a 10-year-old distractible, fidgety, impulsive boy with a mixed dyslexic profile who had received phonics-based remediation throughout his school career. As this had been so unsuccessful (TJ remained unable to read the simplest of nonwords), Brunsdon et al. decided to work on improving his (also very weak) lexical processing. They used flashcards to teach him a set of 60 high frequency regular and exception words at a rate of ten words per week. The ten words were taken home and practised three times each day. After six weeks, TJ read 57/60 words correctly, with 52/60 still correct eight weeks post-training. Then he was taught 100 more high frequency words, at a rate of 14 or 15 per week, with practice at home. After the seven-week training period, he scored 98/100 correct, with 78/100 still correct four weeks post-training.

Dealing with parent/caregiver worries

Parents, quite rightly, worry about their children's progress, and their worries are unlikely to be relieved by bland reassurances that their child will catch up eventually – and, as we have stated, the evidence is that they will not, unless we intervene. We must take parental concerns seriously. First and foremost, this involves listening to and accepting parents' concerns, sharing information, and being open to suggestion. Parents do sometimes have unrealistic expectations of what children of that age can typically achieve, perhaps based on high achievements of other children in the family, or friends' children. We need to be confident that the achievements of our children are at least in line with national achievement levels, as an essential basis for open, non-defensive, discussion. Parents are more reassured when they feel their children's teachers are competent. Discuss the ways in which your teaching might address the concerns shown, and explore the kinds of changes the parent feels might make a difference for their child, and ways in which they might help the child at home. Offer further meeting(s) to share and discuss the child's progress and attainment.

Closing words

There is no magic in teaching children with word reading difficulties (developmental dyslexia) to read: there is hard work and persistence. If we know how to teach children to read in the ways outlined in Chapter 5, with careful attention to detail and close monitoring of progress, we already know how to teach children with word reading difficulties (developmental dyslexia) too. The problem is that it is difficult to find the time to do it, within the school day and in the busy context of a classroom with 30 or so children to attend to. But many of the children we teach would learn to read with minimal instruction from us. Remember, Shapiro and Solity (2008) provided some evidence that knowledge of a small set of GPC rules and high frequency words is all many children need to launch themselves successfully on the self-teaching road to reading. Children with word reading difficulties cannot self-teach. These are the children who most need our teaching, and who need us to continue systematic and structured teaching of word reading skills well beyond the small set of GPC rules and high frequency words that Shapiro and Solity claim is enough. We need knowledge that allows us to identify these children early, at least some of which this book has tried to provide. We also need access to additional resources that will facilitate planning and implementation of small group and individual teaching as and when necessary, and good organizational skills to make sure these additional resources are used effectively.

10
Teaching children with reading comprehension difficulties

Summary

In this chapter, you will learn how children whose reading comprehension is poor despite age-appropriate word reading skills also experience difficulty with language processing, and perform poorly on several factors shown in Chapter 7 to be involved in reading comprehension. You will learn about two effective and evidence-based approaches to teaching children with specific comprehension difficulties: the reciprocal teaching approach first designed by Palincsar and Brown (1984), and the *Reading for Meaning* programme developed by researchers at the University of York (Clarke, Snowling, Truelove & Hulme, 2010). Both programmes can be successfully implemented by sufficiently well-trained classroom teachers and, in the case of *Reading for Meaning*, by similarly well-trained and supported teaching assistants.

Introduction

We begin this final chapter with the figure representing the Simple View of Reading again, but with a minor modification (Figure 10.1).

In this chapter we consider the children who populate the shaded area in the figure, the bottom end of the distribution of language comprehension processes. Their difficulties with language processes may not be immediately obvious in day-to-day conversational interactions, where there are opportunities to identify and repair misunderstandings through ongoing dialogue. Children with poor comprehension may range from those with poor word recognition processes to those with very high levels of ability to read words. After children have been in school for a relatively short time, good teachers are likely to be aware of the children in the bottom left-hand quadrant because they will have the greatest difficulty

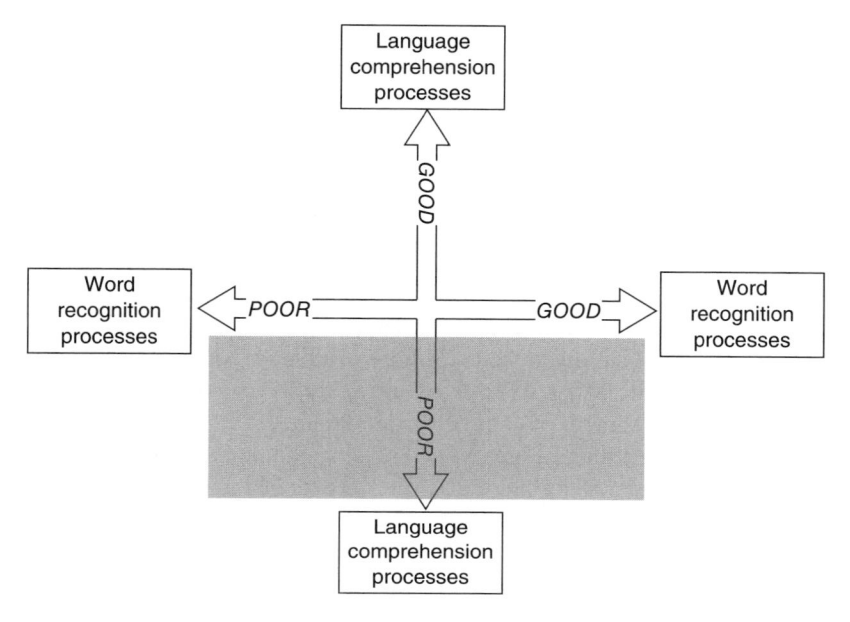

Figure 10.1 Modified Simple View of Reading

starting to read the words in the first place. The children in the bottom right-hand quadrant may well not be recognized as having any particular literacy learning difficulties until later on in the primary years (Leach, Scarborough & Rescorla, 2003). They do not find learning to read words difficult and, because the texts they read in the early stages place fewer requirements on language processes, they seem to be making acceptable progress. However, as the language demands of texts gradually increase throughout the primary years, the mismatch between their word reading skills and their comprehension becomes more apparent and more of an issue. Their poor language comprehension processes begin to compromise their progress. No one would wish poor language processes on anyone. However, we have learned much to support effective teaching of comprehension for *all* children through studying the areas of language that are compromised in children with reading comprehension difficulties.

Yuill and Oakhill (1991) estimated that as many of 10% of 7- to 11-year-old children will show poor ability to comprehend what they are reading. This is a different (though potentially overlapping) population from the children who are identified as dyslexic. As we learn more about this population, we find that the processes which compromise their understanding of written texts also impact on oral language (Cain, Oakhill & Bryant, 2000; Megherbi & Ehrlich, 2005) and ability to produce coherent narratives (Cain, 2003; Cain & Oakhill, 1996).

In the research literature, these children are typically called *poor comprehenders* (Nation, 2005; Nation & Snowling, 1997; Oakhill, 1994), although Oakhill also uses the term *less skilled comprehenders* (Oakhill, 1982, 1984; Oakhill & Yuill, 1986; Oakhill, Yuill & Parkin, 1986). They perform in the normal range for their age on measures of general cognitive processes and word reading, and their phonological awareness is not compromised. Despite this, they do not comprehend what they read at an age appropriate level, with particular difficulty when required to go beyond the literal meaning of the text. In conducting research to identify the sources of this comprehension failure, it is necessary to study children whose word reading is age appropriate and who have no weaknesses in general cognitive ability. If studies simply looked at children with poor comprehension without controlling for word reading skills or cognitive ability, we would not be able to identify the specific sources of comprehension failure.

In real classroom settings, pure cases of reading comprehension failure may be difficult to find. There will be children with a little bit of comprehension difficulty and a little bit of word reading difficulty. The Simple View of Reading provides a framework for identifying the sources of difficulty within the presenting pattern of performance. Teaching programmes can then be planned to address the different processing limitations.

Lower-level and higher-level reading skills

The Simple View of Reading presents reading comprehension as the result of interactions between word reading skills and language comprehension processes. This is not to suggest that there is a hierarchy in terms of importance: as the Simple View of Reading makes clear, each set of processes is necessary and neither is sufficient. Word reading skills, vocabulary knowledge and even syntactic skills are the foundations of comprehension and as such are often described as lower-level text processing skills. The lower-level skills are obviously essential for comprehension but they also *facilitate* comprehension. It is a question of a multiplicative relationship not an additive one. As lower-level skills become automated, processing capacity is freed up for deploying the higher-level skills that support the building of mental models of the text. Once readers are presented with more complex texts to read independently they need to deploy their higher-order processing skills to a greater and greater extent. Higher-level text processing skills include comprehension monitoring, inferencing and working memory capacity (Palincsar & Brown, 1984). This suggests that working memory, inferencing and comprehension monitoring may be candidates for sources of comprehension failure in children who show specific weaknesses in comprehension when reading.

Reading and listening comprehension

There is now ample evidence, including some of the work considered in Chapter 2, that word reading and listening comprehension are independent of each other but together account for between 45% and 85% of the variance in scores on reading comprehension tests (Conners, 2009). The listening comprehension processes are the same as the processes used to comprehend language when reading. However, the relationships between word reading and reading comprehension, and between listening comprehension and reading comprehension, change as readers develop. In the early stages of learning to read the correlation between word reading and reading comprehension is high at around .6, but steadily *decreases* to around .3 by the time children finish school. Conversely, the relationship between listening comprehension and reading comprehension is about .32 at the start but increases to about .69 by the end of schooling (Gough, Hoover & Peterson, 1996). This is not surprising because as word reading becomes skilful and automatic it takes up minimal processing capacity for typical readers and understanding the language and the content become more important. The texts children are presented with become more demanding as they progress through school, with more complex syntax and vocabulary that are less frequent and less likely to be found in everyday discourse. The content itself is challenging because readers are now reading to learn rather than learning to read. Children with poor oral language may begin to fail to make expected levels of progress because they find understanding what they are reading much more challenging. These are the late emerging poor readers.

Working memory as a source of reading comprehension difficulties

In order to build up a mental model of the text as reading progresses we need to be able to remember the content of the sentences we have been reading, relate this to our store of knowledge in our long-term memory and maintain it in consciousness as we actively process the words on the page in the here and now. This all has to be integrated to build up a model that is coherent but flexible so that new information can be incorporated as reading progresses. Working memory is therefore essential to reading comprehension. Working memory is the cognitive process or set of processes that are used as we process transient information concurrently and store it for further use (Baddeley & Hitch, 1974). Baddeley and Hitch conceived of working memory as having a central executive that is responsible for co-ordinating all the cognitive processes that are deployed when more than one task must be done at the same time. On the surface, reading could appear to be one task, but the component subtasks of word reading and comprehension clearly place reading in the category of a very complex multi-process activity. This places considerable demands on the working memory system so one might expect individual differences in working memory capacity to impact on reading comprehension.

Studies investigating working memory deficits as a potential causal source of deficits in poor comprehenders have produced conflicting findings. For example, Stothard and Hulme (1992) investigated listening comprehension and memory functioning in three groups of 7- to 8-year-old children. The first group were all poor comprehenders whose word reading skills were age appropriate but whose reading comprehension was below the age-expected level. The second group was an age-matched control group of children with both word reading skills and comprehension at age-appropriate levels. The final, comprehension-matched control group was composed of younger children whose reading comprehension was the same as that of the poor comprehenders, but who showed no word reading–text comprehension discrepancy. Table 10.1 shows the design of the study.

Table 10.1 Design of the study in Stothard and Hulme (1992)

	Poor comprehenders (PC)	Age-matched control group (AMC)	Comprehension-matched control group (CMC)
Age	8 years	8 years	6–7 years
Word reading	Age appropriate	= PC	< PC
Reading comprehension	Below performance expected for age	> PC	= PC

The complex working memory task they used was designed to require the simultaneous processing and storage of verbal information. The children listened to short one-sentence statements and at the end of each sentence they had to say whether the statement was true or false. This was the processing element. At the same time they had to remember the last word in each sentence, because they had been told they would be asked to recall these words in order once all the sentences had been heard. This was the storage element (e.g. Daneman & Carpenter, 1980).

For example they would listen to sentences like:

- Leaves grow on trees
- Fishes live on land
- Cars drive on the road

They would have to respond: '*yes*', '*no*', '*yes*' to the sentences and then after the last one they would be asked to recall the three last words. In this case: '*trees, land, road*'. The children began by hearing just one sentence and then the number would build up if they were successful until they reached their maximum performance. The cognitive demand required to make a judgement about each sentence was designed to be relatively low. The important element was the requirement to do the simultaneous processing. This is analogous to what is required as we read texts. We have to process the words while at the same time remembering what we have just read so that we can build up a mental model of the meaning of the text.

Stothard and Hulme (1992) did not find any differences between the three groups of children and concluded that individual differences in working memory capacity were not causal in leading to children being poor comprehenders. However, a possibly confound in the study was that all the children taking part found the task very difficult.

Performance levels in all three groups were low, making it less likely that differences between groups would be identified. Certainly there is evidence that working memory capacity continues to increase with age from age 6 years to age 19 years (Siegel, 1994). It is possible that, because of their age, few of the children in this study had sufficient working memory capacity to do the task. A subsequent study by Nation, Adams, Bowyer-Crane and Snowling (1999) used the same task as Stothard and Hulme (1992) but with older 10-year old children, whose working memory capacity might be assumed to have developed to levels where the memory task would be sensitive enough to pick up individual differences. The study also included a visuo-spatial working memory task, to check whether any possible differences between the two groups were due to general working memory problems or confined to the verbal domain.

This new study only included two groups: one group of poor comprehenders and a control group matched for age and non-verbal ability. The poor comprehenders were slightly better at reading nonwords, but the control group children were better at word reading accuracy when reading words in texts. However, all the poor comprehenders had word reading accuracy levels appropriate for age. The main distinction was that the poor comprehenders' reading comprehension was at least one year below that expected for their age.

The poor comprehenders performed worse than the control children on the verbal working memory task, with equal performance of both groups on the visuo-spatial working memory task. These results suggest that poor comprehenders may indeed have working memory deficits that are specific to the verbal domain.

These two studies serve to show that the evidence about a *specific* verbal working memory deficit in poor comprehenders is not clear-cut. The children in Stothard and Hulme's (1992) research were young and therefore the task may have been too demanding. Nation et al. (1999), on the other hand, had established that there was a verbal working memory deficit in late primary age poor comprehenders. However, Nation (2005) suggested that they had not established *causality*. She argued that her finding could be the result of the poor language processes for the poor comprehenders. The processing required in the working memory task was of verbal material which they had to comprehend in order to make a decision about veracity. Rather than verbal working memory compromising language comprehension, it could be that poor language skills may make increased demand on the working memory system in poor comprehenders.

Nevertheless, there is no gainsaying that working memory is involved in reading. Cain, Oakhill and Bryant (2004) reported data from a longitudinal study investigating the relations between working memory capacity and reading comprehension skills in children who were age 8 years at the start of the study and 11 years at the end of their primary schooling by the end of the study. They found that working memory capacity was certainly involved in reading comprehension, but it did not account for everything. Inference-making ability and comprehension monitoring each made a unique contribution to reading comprehension. This means that working memory capacity is a source of reading comprehension difficulties, but not the only source.

Teaching to improve working memory?

There are many computer programs and apps that purport to improve memory capacity. Some of these are free, some very expensive. At present there is no evidence that these are likely to have a positive lasting effect on working memory performance. Melby-Lervåg and Hulme (2013) conducted a meta-analytic review of 23 well-designed studies (randomized control trials or quasi-experiments) investigating working memory training. All studies included at least one group that had received a treatment that included training working memory and one control group that had received an alternative programme or that was an untreated control. The studies included typically developing children, adults, children with learning difficulties, university students with dyslexia, and one study with adult stroke patients. The meta-analysis found that the programs produced improvements in verbal working memory in the immediate term, but these were not sustained. There was also no evidence of transfer from the memory programs to other skills (e.g. word reading, arithmetic). Melby-Lervåg and Hulme concluded that, although there was evidence of memory training programs producing short-term improvements that were specific to the program, these were only short term and did not generalize.

Thus, schools should be wary of using programs claiming to improve memory performance. Children (and adults) might find them entertaining, or even addictive, but there is no evidence that they will improve learning in general or reading comprehension in particular. Instead we need to be conscious of the demands that texts place on working memory. This is especially true for those children identified as being poor comprehenders, but it is also true for all children, particularly English Language Learners, and particularly children in the early years of education. The need for practice in using comprehension strategies was covered in Chapter 7. By giving children practice at these activities we support their memorizing of content and strategies. However, this does not mean that decontextualized working memory activities are called for. It is probably better for teachers to be conscious of the cognitive load of tasks and to seek to reduce this through some of the comprehension strategies discussed in Chapter 7 and those we will cover in the next sections when we present further evidence about the sources of comprehension failure.

Weaknesses in inference making as a source of comprehension difficulties

Oakhill (1982) compared inferencing ability in two groups of children: less-skilled and skilled comprehenders identified from performance on a passage reading test, the Neale Analysis of Reading Ability (NARA) (Neale, 1989). Less-skilled comprehenders showing a mismatch between reading accuracy and reading comprehension were matched for age and reading accuracy with skilled comprehenders whose reading comprehension was in line with their reading accuracy.

As can be seen in Table 10.2, both groups showed high levels of reading accuracy for their age.

Table 10.2 Characteristics of the two groups of participants in Oakhill (1982)

	Chronological age	Reading accuracy age	Reading comprehension age
Less skilled comprehenders	7.7	8.7	7.3
Skilled comprehenders	7.7	8.6	9.2

The children listened to eight 'short stories' composed of three sentences. The structure of each story was the same. The first and final sentences described events and the subject of each sentence was the same. The middle sentence described a state of being (stative) and always began with the noun that had ended the first sentence. The box below shows an example of one of the stories used in Oakhill (1982).

Example of a 'short story' used in Oakhill (1982)

The plane flew over the house. (Event)

The house was in Crawley. (Stative)

The plane landed in a field. (Event)

They then listened to 32 sentences and had to say whether they had heard the sentences before or not. For each story there were four sentences to verify. The next box shows the sentences relating to the 'Crawley' story.

Test statements relating to the Crawley story (Oakhill, 1982)

The plane flew over the house. (Original) Correct answer: YES

The house was in Crawley. (Original) Correct answer: YES

The plane flew over Crawley. (Semantically congruent foil) Correct answer: NO

The house was in a field. (Semantically incongruent foil) Correct answer: NO

For each story there were two sentences that they had heard before and two sentences that were not in the original stories. One of these sentences – the semantically congruent foil – logically could have been in the story. It would have been consistent with a mental model constructed for the story. In the example we have given, since the house was in Crawley and the plane flew over the house, the plane must also have flown over Crawley. The other sentence was composed of words in the original story but did not follow logically from the story. There is nothing in the story which leads us to conclude that the house was in a field.

Oakhill was interested to find out whether there were differences in the error rate to the foil statements. Did the skilled comprehenders make more errors than the less skilled comprehenders to the congruent foils? If they did, this might indicate that they had built up a mental model from which they could draw inferences. Furthermore, if they made fewer errors to the incongruent foils, this would again indicate that they were drawing on their mental models of the stories and not on the vocabulary they had heard.

This was exactly what she found. The skilled comprehenders made more errors judging semantically congruent foils to be 'old' sentences than the less skilled comprehenders, and they made fewer errors when judging the semantically incongruent foils. This early finding would suggest that children who are poorer at comprehending language have greater difficulty in building up mental models of what they hear and therefore have greater difficulty in making inferences. Oakhill (1982) points out that the less skilled comprehenders were not totally wanting in inferencing skills and speculates that they might be helped by training in making summary statements or having discussions about the mental models they build up.

Yuill and Joscelyne (1988) identified less skilled comprehenders using the same criteria as Oakhill and investigated whether they could be helped to improve their comprehension. They created a set of eight what they termed 'abstract' stories for the children to read. The abstractness lay in the fact that the events in the story were not explicit, so inferencing skills were needed to support the construction of mental models. In the first study, each story was given either an integrated title, where the main events were included in the title, or a non-integrated title, where the protagonists were simply listed. The stories included illustrations: either a single integrated picture which drew together the setting and an aspect of the events or a set of non-integrated pictures of a single element interspersed throughout the text. There were four editions of each story:

1. Integrated title – integrated picture
2. Integrated title – non-integrated pictures
3. Non-integrated title – integrated picture
4. Non-integrated title – non-integrated pictures

The children were asked to read each story and told they would be asked questions after each one. It was stressed that they should try to understand the stories rather than remember them verbatim.

An example of one of the stories with titles and questions is shown in the box below.

Titles, a story and the related questions from Yuill and Joscelyne (1988)

Alternative titles: *Billy's sandcastle gets broken by the wave.*

Or

Billy and his mother.

Billy was crying. His whole day was spoilt. All his work had been broken by the wave. His mother came to stop him crying. But she accidentally stepped on the only tower that was left. Billy cried even more. 'Never mind,' said mother, 'We can always build another one tomorrow.' Billy stopped crying and went home to his tea.

Integrated picture: Billy crying, sitting next to broken sandcastle with mother, shrugging, standing on one tower.

Non-integrated pictures: (a) Billy crying, (b) mother shrugging shoulders, and (c) broken sandcastle.

Questions:
1. Where was Billy?
2. Why was Billy crying?
3. What had the wave broken?
4. Why did his mother go to him?
5. What did she do by mistake?

They found that the less skilled comprehenders were able to benefit both from integrated titles and integrated pictures, but these did not have any effect on the performance of the skilled comprehenders. This suggested to them that with graphic support the less skilled comprehenders could improve their inferencing making. They conducted a further study using the same stories with two further groups of less skilled and skilled comprehenders. This time they had two groups who were trained on the components of a story and shown how to search for words that would help them to make inferences and thereby improve comprehension. The results showed that the training had a significant positive effect on the performance of the less skilled comprehenders. There was no improvement in the performance of the skilled comprehenders, from which one might conclude that they used the strategies spontaneously and probably had sufficient comprehension skills to understand these texts without additional support.

These studies suggest that children with poor comprehension when reading *can* make inferences to help them go beyond the literal meaning of the texts. However, they benefit from support to enable them to become aware of the need to do this. They also benefit from being provided with strategies that they can apply when reading. This is in contrast to skilled comprehenders, who seem to have internalized these strategies without specific instruction and so use them spontaneously.

Text cohesion

There is a general consensus that poor inferencing skills and reduced ability to use inferencing spontaneously to support comprehension are a characteristic of poor comprehenders. Not all inferences are the same. Some are necessary to establish the meanings within the text itself: these are called *necessary* or *cohesive inferences*. They are required for combining information across different parts of the text and, when successfully used, they establish a coherent representation of the text. As we saw in Chapter 6, being able to resolve anaphoric reference (understanding the noun to which a pronoun refers) is a necessary skill because it helps to build up local cohesion and thereby create a coherent model of the text. Use of anaphoric reference in both spoken and written language avoids discourse becoming overly long, repetitive and tedious.

Children identified as poor comprehenders are found to have weaknesses in assigning reference to pronouns. Megherbi and Ehrlich (2005) found that poor comprehenders had difficulty with pronouns when listening to short oral passages. This mirrors earlier work on assigning anaphoric reference when reading by Oakhill and Yuill (1986), who studied pronoun resolution in a cloze task where pronouns had to be provided to fill in the gaps. Poor comprehenders found this task more difficult than skilled comprehenders. Yuill and Oakhill (1991) also found that poor comprehenders had greater difficulty in answering questions relating to texts they had just read where the correct answer was dependent on having assigned the correct reference to a pronoun.

Unfortunately, we have found no published research that has established an improvement in comprehension through teaching poor comprehenders about pronouns. However, it is possible to be creative about ways one can discuss with children how they know what or whom pronouns refer to in texts. Substituting pronouns for nouns and nouns for pronouns can also make a playful activity.

It is not just in the domain of resolving these pronominal anaphors that poor comprehenders seem to have difficulties. They also seem to be weak at using and resolving other cohesive devices in language. Understanding the meaning of connectives is essential for building up a mental model of a text by integrating clauses and sentences.

The car skidded *because* of the ice on the road.

Amelia went to her ballet class *after* school *but before* she did her homework.

Yuill and Oakhill (1991) found that poor comprehenders were less likely than good comprehenders to use connectives when retelling a story they had previous listened to.

A further study by Cain (2003) extended this finding. Three groups of children took part: poor comprehenders, younger comprehension-age-matched children, and same-age skilled comprehenders. Children were asked to tell three stories under three different conditions: two conditions where they were given either a simple title such as 'The circus' or a more directive and informative title such as 'How the pirates lost their treasure', and a the third condition where they were given a sequence of six pictures illustrating the story, including a final picture where the denouement was the unintended consequence of a previous picture. The poor comprehenders were weaker than both the other groups in their capacity to produce coherent, cohesive stories. However, they produced more causal connectives when given the support of pictures and a more directed title. This result suggests that providing children with additional scaffolds can improve their use of connectives.

The ability to use and understand interclausal connectives is essential for building up cohesive mental models of texts. In a study of children's ability to select an appropriate connective in a cloze task, Cain, Patson and Andrews (2005) found that 8- and 9-year-old poor comprehenders were less likely to select the target connective, and more likely to select a connective that did not make sense in the context of the surrounding text. However, as part of their study, they also found a mismatch between oral comprehension of connectives and understanding them in written texts. This mismatch was not confined to poor comprehenders. They concluded, therefore, that the poor comprehenders' problems were an indication of delay rather than deviance. When this result is taken together with her 2003 findings, Cain's suggestion that providing support for developing the use of connectives could be a positive approach, not just for poor comprehenders but for younger children who are still developing their comprehension of connectives in written texts.

Comprehension monitoring as a source of comprehension difficulties

Comprehension monitoring was presented as a strategy for teaching comprehension in Chapter 7. When we monitor our comprehension we actively strive for coherence as we attempt to make sense of the information we are processing. It is therefore not surprising that poor comprehenders are poor at monitoring their understanding of what they are reading (Garner & Taylor, 1982). One of the ways this has been studied is to investigate children's ability to detect anomalies in texts. If a reader is building a successful coherent mental model of the text, any anomaly, either at the word or text level, or related to general knowledge, will be noticed because it will lead to a lack of coherence. A study by Oakhill, Hartt and Samols (2005) investigated 9- to 10-year-old children's ability to detect and explain anomalies in texts.

Children were identified as either poor or good comprehenders using the criteria we have already covered, and took part in two experimental conditions. The first condition investigated spontaneous monitoring. Texts were prepared that contained two nonwords substituting for real words (e.g. 'a *bitterly* cold wind' was changed to 'a *ferly* cold wind') and two phrases that had been scrambled so that they no longer made sense (e.g. 'all Joe had to do was sit there' changed to '*all was there sit had to do Joe*'). Children were asked to read the passages aloud and told they would be asked questions at the end. Their reading was recorded to identify instances where pauses and hesitations occurred coincident with anomalies in the text. Such coincidences were taken as indications of spontaneous monitoring. At the end, children were asked if they had noticed anything problematic about the text, and, if so, to indicate where this problem was.

The results showed there were no group differences in behaviours taken to indicate spontaneous monitoring. However, 66.7% of the good comprehenders reported noticing problems in the texts whereas only 17.6% of the poor comprehenders did. The children who reported noticing problems were not actually able to say where they had noticed them, which suggested to Oakhill et al. (2005) that they just had a vague sense of a problem without being able to be exact. However, they also wondered whether children saying there was a problem but they weren't sure where it was might have been a device to avoid having to re-read the passages.

The second condition investigated 'directed' monitoring. Children read texts silently or aloud, as they preferred, but this time they were told they should pay attention to the meaning of the text, that some parts might not make sense, and asked to underline any words or phrases they did not understand. In this underlining task there was no difference between the two groups in detecting word anomalies but good comprehenders were more likely to underline anomalous phrases.

Not surprisingly, the good comprehenders showed superior comprehension of the passages, but both groups made similar numbers of correct answers to comprehension questions in spontaneous as in directed monitoring conditions: there was no evidence that being *directed* to monitor comprehension led to better comprehension. However, in the directed condition (study 2) there was a correlation between the proportion of anomalous phrases detected and performance on the comprehension questions. This is an interesting finding because it suggests that being directed to monitor comprehension can have a positive effect.

In the second study of this research Oakhill et al. (2005) asked the children to return. This time there were told they were going to act as editors to detect if there were any passages containing problematic information. Texts had been prepared that contained contradictory information. An example is given in the box below:

Moles cannot see very well, but their hearing and sense of smell are good.

Moles are easily able to find food for their young because their eyesight is so good.

The children had to read the passages and fill in a form to say whether the passage made sense and didn't need to be changed, or did not make sense and required changing. They had to provide an explanation of the problems and the required changes.

For half the problematic passages the two contradictory sentences were adjacent (adjacent condition) to each other and for half there were three intervening sentences (distant condition).

The good comprehenders were significantly better at detecting and explaining anomalies whether sentences were adjacent or distant. The poor comprehenders were poorer at detecting and explaining the anomalies overall, but they were better when the problematic sentences were adjacent.

This work provided evidence supporting the view that poor comprehenders are less able to monitor their own comprehension and strive for coherence. This is likely to compromise their ability to build mental models of what they are reading. This does not just impact on reading comprehension *per se*, but is likely to have a negative effect on their ability to understand the content of the texts they have to read across the curriculum.

There is thus evidence that children with reading comprehension difficulties have problems with inferencing and comprehension monitoring, which significantly affect their capacity to understand what they read. They do not seem to have the necessary drive for coherence that supports good comprehension. However, these problems seem to be matters of degree, with a lack of insight into the need for coherence rather than an absence of capacity. In a follow-up study (Cain & Oakhill, 2006) of 11-year-old children first assessed at the age of 8 years, they found that poor comprehenders were at risk for generally poor attainment in school. Though all the children showed weaknesses relative to unimpaired children, no single consistent pattern of deficits was evident by the age of 11 years. Cain and Oakhill concluded that profiles of strengths and weaknesses of individual children were necessary to inform approaches to teaching. This would suggest a need for teaching across a range of language and cognitive strategies to compensate for a profile of weaknesses rather than a single deficit.

Reciprocal teaching

Any account of reading comprehension teaching would be empty without reference to 'reciprocal teaching'. Palincsar and Brown (1984) developed this programme to meet the needs of poor comprehenders directly. The approach includes both things to be taught and organizational strategies for teaching: the *what* and the *how* of teaching. In this section we are going to provide a summary of this seminal paper, but it is important to read the original if possible. There are thousands of citations to this research, but people often report they are using the approach in ways that might not be recognized by its original authors (Brown & Campione, 1996).

Reciprocal teaching was designed to improve students' ability to learn from texts; to provide direct support to enhance text comprehension in children with adequate word reading ability. There was an initial pilot study (Brown & Palincar, 1982) where the procedures for reciprocal teaching were developed in one-to-one settings. Teacher and child took turns in leading a dialogue about the text. To begin with, the teacher took the lead role and modelled summarizing, questioning, clarifying and predicting activities for the child. Both members of the pair would read a segment of the text silently and then the teacher would model strategies similar to those we covered in Chapter 7. The idea was that the pair would both take on the role of being 'teacher' and 'student'. This is where the reciprocity took place. The rationale for this procedure was that children observed comprehension strategies being overtly practised and saw how these strategies supported comprehension of the texts.

Initially, the children found taking on the 'teacher' role very challenging and the teacher would have to scaffold for them by providing questions and paraphrases for them to imitate. But after around ten sessions, children began generating genuine questions about the text and producing acceptable summaries. This pilot study produced impressive improvements that were maintained over a six-month period, indicating that the children had internalized the strategies they had been exposed to and had practised during the training.

The development of the reciprocal teaching programme reported in Palincsar and Brown (1984) capitalized on what had been learned from the pilot study and involved two further studies. In the first, children attended the reciprocal teaching intervention in pairs, with a member of the research team as the adult teacher. In the second, four classroom teachers were recruited to deliver the programme, with children taught in groups of between four and six.

The first study included four groups: a group who received the reciprocal teaching intervention (RT group); an alternative intervention group (AT group) who received a programme on locating information in texts. These two interventions lasted for 20 days of 30 minutes a day. There were two control groups. The first control group (group T) was tested every day on their comprehension of a set of texts that were also administered to the intervention groups. The second control group was a no-treatment control (NT group), who were just assessed at the beginning and end of the project.

A set of 13 expository texts on a range of topics across the curriculum was selected as the training passages to be read by both the RT and the AT groups during the intervention. A further 45 passages were selected as assessment passages. A set of ten questions was developed for each of the 45 assessment passages. There were literal questions where the answer was stated explicitly in the text and inference questions. The inference questions required either integration of information across the text, or integration of prior knowledge with the information in the text. The RT, AT and T groups were tested on one of the assessment passages after every intervention session. All groups were assessed at the beginning of the project to establish baseline performance; for five days at the end of the intervention to establish maintenance of the effect of the programme; and eight weeks after the end of maintenance testing to investigate the long-term effects. The daily assessments were integral to the programmes so the children were given daily feedback on their performance and shown graphs of their cumulative weekly record.

Reciprocal teaching programme. The teacher would begin by introducing a passage with a brief discussion designed to activate the children's prior knowledge about the content of the passage. Where the passage was new, the teacher would begin by introducing the title and leading a discussion about the content of the passage that might be predicted from it. If the session involved a passage continued from previous days, there would be some discussion about what had been covered already. The teacher and the children would then silently read a segment of the text, often a paragraph. For every segment one of the children would be assigned the role of 'teacher'. The child taking the teacher role was then asked to lead on four strategies relating to comprehension of the text: questioning, summarizing, clarifying and predicting.

The adult teacher would provide support and modelling to enable the child to generate effective questions. Examples of this, given by Palincsar and Brown (1984) include:

- prompting 'What do you think a teacher might ask?'
- scaffolding the child with questions such as 'What would be a good question that starts with the word "why?"'
- provision of a model question with an invitation for the child to imitate and develop it.

For summarizing, the child would be reminded that a summary includes the main points but not the detail. The adult would support summarizing through asking questions, drawing attention to salient points in the text and, if necessary, providing model summaries that illustrated the need to identify the most important information points in the segment.

Clarifying discussions enabled the children to externalize where they might have difficulty understanding the text or where they may have misinterpreted the author's intention. This provided strategies to support their drive for coherence.

Predicting activities required the children to integrate across the text and to work out where it seemed to be leading them, again supporting coherence.

The child-teachers and the child-pupils took turns and were encouraged to be active participants in the interactions. Though the sessions covered questioning, summarizing, clarifying and predicting activities, these were not formulaic. If a child was finding it difficult to generate a question, he or she might be invited to try summarizing so that the main points might become more obvious; or to externalize where a point in the text needed clarification.

The children were told very explicitly why they were being asked to engage in the activities. They were told these were activities they would find useful in all their reading. They were encouraged to remember to try to use them whenever they were reading and not just overtly in the intervention sessions. Central to the teaching philosophy was that children would receive positive constructive feedback. The adult teacher provided specific praise that was designed to help the children understand why what had been done actually worked but, particularly in the early stage, this would be supported by modelling of how to improve performance.

Locating information alternative programme. This programme involved the children engaging with the same passages as were read by the RT group, but the focus was on answering questions related to the texts. They were taught how to look in the text for where information to answer literal questions might be. They were shown about combining information from different sections of the text to find answers to text-implicit questions and attention was drawn to the fact that they might need to use their prior knowledge to work out the answers to some questions. As in the RT intervention, the adult and the children read the passages silently and then the teacher worked with them on answering questions. Praise was given for immediate correct answers and support was given to guide them to where they might find the information in the text when the answer was incorrect.

The results were highly significant. The children in the RT group improved to the level of average readers following the 20-day intervention. One child in this group did not make the level of progress of the majority of the group, but even this child made significant progress and performed well above the children in the three other groups. The AT intervention group and the two control groups did not make progress. Because all interactions with the children had been taped, it was possible for a qualitative analysis to be made of the children's language in the sessions. There was a gradual shift so that main idea questions and summaries came predominant. These were increasingly well formed and child-generated rather than being inchoate or simply copied from the texts. The improvements in performance were maintained at the long-term follow-up.

The second study extended the range of reciprocal teaching to more natural classroom settings and involved volunteer classroom teachers. The use of small groups was beneficial because the children were able to learn from the example of other children in the group and not just from the adult's modelling. The transcripts of sessions showed that over the 20 sessions, the children were able to take greater and greater control over the dialogues. This suggests they were beginning to become active readers of texts using effective strategies to support their comprehension.

Reciprocal teaching of this type involves specific instruction with modelling of the four strategies of questioning, summarizing, clarifying and predicting. This requires teachers to be aware of the language demands of the texts and to be able to scaffold effectively, gradually letting the children take control of their own learning. A part of the study that is often down played in commentaries of reciprocal teaching is the role of daily assessment with feedback on performance. Not only did the children exercise the comprehension strategies, but they had daily feedback on the positive impact this was having on their performance.

Reciprocal teaching is an excellent example of an approach that covers both the *what* and the *how* of teaching children with reading comprehension difficulties. As we reported in Chapter 7, the National Reading Panel report on *Teaching Children to*

Read (National Institute of Child Health and Human Development, 2000) concluded that multiple strategy teaching was one of the effective approaches to teaching comprehension for mainstream children. Their reading of the evidence led them to believe that multiple strategy teaching is particularly good when used flexibly by teachers so that readers learn to use the strategies appropriately through interactions with teachers and texts. Reciprocal teaching is clearly an example of a programme that includes teaching multiple strategies through flexible teacher–child interactions. It is not possible to isolate whether it is the teaching approach or the strategies taught that has the impact. It is likely that both are instrumental in improvement.

The York Reading for Meaning project

A multiple strategy intervention has recently been developed by the Centre for Reading and Language at the University of York as part of the *Reading for Meaning* project (Clarke, Snowling, Truelove & Hulme, 2010). The project involved conducting a randomized control trial to evaluate three different intervention programmes designed to improve reading comprehension in 9-year-old children (Year 4) identified as have comprehension difficulties.

The three programmes were: a Text Comprehension (TC) programme; an Oral Language (OL) programme; and a programme that combined the two (COM). Each programme was designed to last for 20 weeks in two blocks of ten weeks. Each child received three 30-minute blocks of tuition a week: one session involved one-to-one tuition and two sessions involved the children in pairs.

The oral and the text programmes were designed to mirror one another as far as possible. Thus each programme took a pedagogic approach based on reciprocal teaching with the teacher taking a role in promoting active learning. Work with texts included developing the strategies of question generation, summarizing, clarification and prediction, which were part of Palincsar and Brown's (1984) programme. In the OL programme these strategies related to listening. There was also work on developing narratives, through writing in TC and through story telling in OL. Unique to the TC programme was work on promoting the use of metacognitive strategies through the use of re-reading, think alouds, mental imagery and explanations when working with texts. There was also specific work on developing inferencing skills. The activities unique to the OL programme were developing vocabulary and understanding figurative language such as metaphors and idioms. The COM programme included all parts of both programmes, but it only lasted for the same length of time. The design of the project meant that children were randomly assigned to one of the three programmes and their progress was mapped against that of a waiting list control group.

These programmes were designed to be delivered by teaching assistants. In order to ensure fidelity to the programme so that any effects could be considered to be reliable and valid, the teaching assistants received training in how to teach, and fortnightly tutorials throughout the programme. They were also observed teaching the programme in school.

The results from assessments made immediately after the programme showed that all three programmes worked, with children making significant gains in their reading comprehension relative to the waiting list control group. These gains were sustained when the children were re-assessed 11 months after the end of the programme. An unexpected result was that the children in the OL group made significantly greater progress than the children in the other two groups. Perhaps this result is not that unexpected if we consider that the major source of comprehension problems in poor comprehenders stema from language processing difficulties. Clarke et al. (2010) suggest that a practical implication of their work could be that by identifying children with oral language difficulties early and working on vocabulary and inferencing, it might be possible to avoid quite so many children experiencing reading comprehension difficulties in the future.

Closing words

If there is one message to take from the evidence in this chapter it is that reading and language are inseparable. Reciprocal teaching and *Reading for Meaning* are both text-based approaches and they are both approaches that rely heavily on discussion about language and texts. The logical conclusion is that we need to provide children with as many opportunities as possible to read engaging texts for entertainment and equally engaging texts for learning across the curriculum. Exposure to print is vital. Those children who read more improve more and learn more (Cipielewski & Stanovich, 1992; Stainthorp, 1997), but if they do not have a chance to read and talk, their reading, and therefore their learning, will not improve.

Reciprocal teaching and *Reading for Meaning* are both programmes developed to support those children with reading comprehension difficulties, but their foundations are the strategies that have been found to work for teaching comprehension in general. A good approach to teaching is that all children deserve the best.

Finale

Knowledge is always a work in progress. Some of the ideas we have presented here may ultimately turn out to be incorrect, or to require modification. In writing the book, we have inevitably made choices. In the interests of brevity and clarity, we have omitted both ideas and knowledge that deserved to be included. We hope we have provided enough reliable, evidence-based information to allow you to begin to understand what lies beneath the miracle of reading and its development.

References

Aaron, P. G., Joshi, M., & Williams, K. A. (1999). Not all reading disabilities are alike. *Journal of Learning Disabilities, 32*, 120–137.

Adlof, S. M., Catts, H. W., & Little, T. D. (2006). Should the simple view of reading include a fluency component? *Reading and Writing, 19*, 933–958.

Andre, M. D. A., & Anderson, T. H. (1978–79). The development and evaluation of a self questioning study technique. *Reading Research Quarterly, 14*, 605–623.

Anglin, J. M. (1993). Vocabulary development: A morphological analysis. *Monographs of the Society for Research in Child Development, 58* (Serial no. 238).

Armbruster, B. B., Anderson, T. H., & Meyer, J. L. (1991). Improving content-area reading using instructional graphics. *Reading Research Quarterly, 26*(4), 393–416.

Arrow, A. W. (2007). Potential precursors to the development of phonological awareness in preschool children. Unpublished doctoral thesis, University of Auckland, Auckland, New Zealand.

Babayigit, S., & Stainthorp, R. (2007). Preliterate phonological awareness and early literacy skills in Turkish. *Journal of Research in Reading, 30*, 394–413.

Baddeley, A., & Hitch, G. (1974). Working memory. *Psychology of Learning and Motivation, 8*, 47–89.

Ball, E. W., & Blachman, B. A. (1991). Does phoneme awareness training in kindergarten make a difference in early word recognition and developmental spelling? *Reading Research Quarterly, 26*, 49–66.

Baron, J., & Strawson, C. (1976). Use of orthographic and word-specific knowledge in reading words aloud. *Journal of Experimental Psychology: Human Perception and Performance, 4*, 207–214.

Baumann, J. F. (1984). The effectiveness of an instruction paradigm for teaching main idea comprehension. *Reading Research Quarterly, 20*(1), 93–115.

Baumann, J. F., Seifert-Kessell, N., & Jones, L. A. (1992). Effect of think-aloud instruction on elementary students' comprehension monitoring abilities. *Journal of Reading Behavior, 24*(2), 143–172.

Beck, I., & Hamilton, R. (2000). *Beginning reading module.* Washington, DC: American Federation of Teachers. (Original work published 1996.)

Beck, I., McKeown, M., & Kucan, L. (2002). *Bringing words to life: Robust vocabulary instruction.* New York: Guilford Press.

Bond, G. L., & Dykstra, R. (1967). The cooperative research program in first-grade reading instruction. *Reading Research Quarterly*, *2*, 5–142.

Boulware-Gooden, R., Carreker, S., Thornhill, A., & Joshi, R. M. (2007). The instruction of metacognitive strategies enhances reading comprehension and vocabulary achievement of third-grade students. *Reading Teacher*, *61*(1), 70–77.

Bowey, J. A., & Hansen, J. (1994). The development of orthographic rimes as units of word recognition. *Journal of Experimental Child Psychology*, *58*, 465–488.

Bowey, J. A., & Muller, D. (2005). Phonological recoding and rapid orthographic learning in third-graders' silent reading: A critical test of the self-teaching hypothesis. *Journal of Experimental Child Psychology*, *92*, 203–219.

Bowey, J. A., & Rutherford, J. (2007). Imbalanced word-reading profiles in eighth-graders. *Journal of Experimental Child Psychology*, *96*, 169–196.

Bowey, J. A., & Underwood, N. (1996). Beginning reader's use of orthographic analogies in word reading. *Journal of Experimental Child Psychology*, *63*, 526–562.

Bowey, J. A., Vaughn, L., & Hansen, J. (1998). Beginning readers' use of orthographic analogies in word reading. *Journal of Experimental Child Psychology*, *68*, 108–133.

Bradley, L., & Bryant, P.E. (1983). Categorising sounds and learning to read – a causal connection. *Nature*, 301, 419–421.

Bransford, J. D., Barclay, J. R., & Franks, J. J. (1972). Sentence memory: A constructive vs. interpretive approach. *Cognitive Psychology*, *3*, 193–209.

Bransford, J. D., & Johnson, (1972).Contextual prerequisites for understanding some investigations of comprehension and recall. *Journal of Verbal Learning and Verbal Behavior*, *11*, 717–726.

Brett, A., Rothlein, L., & Hurley, M. (1996). Vocabulary acquisition from listening to stories and explanations of target words. *Elementary School Journal*, *96*(4), 415–422.

Brooks, G. (2013). *What works for children with literacy difficulties: The effectiveness of intervention schemes* (4th Edition). London: The Dyslexia-SpLD Trust. Retrieved from www.interventionsforliteracy.org.uk/widgets_GregBrooks/What_works_for_children_fourth_ed.pdf (accessed 20 March 2015).

Broom, Y. M., & Doctor, E. A. (1995a). Developmental surface dyslexia: A case study of the efficacy of a remediation programme. *Cognitive Neuropsychology*, *12*, 69–110.

Broom, Y. M., & Doctor, E. A. (1995b). Developmental phonological dyslexia: A case study of the efficacy of a remediation programme. *Cognitive Neuropsychology*, *12*, 725–766.

Brown, A. L., & Campione, J. C. (1996). Psychological theory and the design of innovative learning environments: On procedures, principles, and systems. In L. Schauble & R. Glaser (Eds.), *Innovations in learning* (pp. 289–325). Mahwah, NJ: Lawrence Erlbaum Associates.

Brown, A. L., Day, J. D., & Jones, R. S. (1983). The development of plans for summarizing texts. *Child Development*, *48*, 968–979.

Bruck, M., & Treiman, R. (1992). Learning to pronounce words: The limitations of analogies. *Reading Research Quarterly*, *27*, 375–389.

Brunsdon, R. K., Hannan, T. J., Coltheart, M., & Nickels, L. (2002). Treatment of lexical processing in mixed dyslexia: A case study. *Neuropsychological Rehabilitation*, *12*, 385–418.

Bryant, P. E., Bradley, L., MacLean, M., & Crossland, J. (1989). Nursery rhymes, phonological skills and reading. *Journal of Child Language*, *16*, 407–428.

References

Burge, B., Styles, B., Brzyska, B., Cooper, L., Shamsan, Y., Saltini, F., & Twist, L. (2010). *New Group Reading Test*. Chiswick: GL-Assessment

Burgess, S. R., Hecht, S. A., & Lonigan, C. J. (2002). Relations of the Home Literacy Environment (HLE) to the development of reading-related abilities: A one-year longitudinal study. *Reading Research Quarterly, 37*, 408–426.

Burgess, S. R., & Lonigan, C. (1998). Bidirectional relations of phonological sensitivity and pre-reading abilities: Evidence from a preschool sample. *Journal of Experimental Child Psychology, 70*, 117–141.

Burns, M. K. (2004). Empirical analysis of drill ratio research: Refining the instructional level for drill tasks. *Remedial and Special Education, 25*, 167–174.

Bus, A. G., van IJzendoorn, M. H., & Pellegrini, A. D. (1995). Joint book reading makes for success in learning to read: A meta-analysis on intergenerational transmission of literacy. *Review of Educational Research, 65*(1), 1–21.

Byrne, B., & Fielding-Barnsley, R. (1989). Phonemic awareness and letter knowledge in the child's acquisition of the alphabetic principle. *Journal of Educational Psychology, 81*, 805–812.

Cain, K. (2003). Text comprehension and its relation to coherence and cohesion in children's fictional narratives. *British Journal of Developmental Psychology, 21*, 335–51.

Cain, K., & Oakhill, J. (1996). The nature of the relationship between comprehension skill and the ability to tell a story. *British Journal of Developmental Psychology, 14*, 187–201.

Cain, K., & Oakhill, J. (2006). Profiles of children with specific reading comprehension difficulties. *British Journal of Educational Psychology, 73*, 683–696.

Cain, K., Oakhill, J. V., & Bryant, P. E. (2000). Phonological skills and comprehension failure: A test of the phonological processing deficit hypothesis. *Reading and Writing, 13*, 31–56.

Cain, K., Oakhill, J. V., & Bryant, P. E. (2004). Children's reading comprehension ability: Concurrent prediction by working memory, verbal ability, and component skills. *Journal of Educational Psychology, 96*(1), 31–42.

Cain, K., Patson, N., & Andrews, L. (2005). Age- and ability-related differences in young readers' use of conjunctions. *Journal of Child Language, 32*(4), 877–892.

Carney, J. J., Anderson, D., Blackburn, C., & Blessing, D. (1984). Preteaching vocabulary and the comprehension of social studies materials by elementary school children. *Social Education, 48*(3), 195–196.

Carnine, D. W., Kameenui, E. J., & Woolfson, N. (1982). Training of textual dimensions related to text-based inferences. *Journal of Reading Behavior, 14*(3), 335–340.

Castles, A., & Coltheart, M. (1993). Varieties of developmental dyslexia. *Cognition, 47*, 149–180.

Castles, A., Coltheart, M., Wilson, K., Valpied, J., & Wedgwood, J. (2009). The genesis of reading ability: What helps children learn letter–sound correspondences? *Journal of Experimental Child Psychology, 104*, 68–88.

Castles, A., Datta, H., Gayan, J., & Olson, R. K. (1999). Varieties of developmental reading disorder: Genetic and environmental influences. *Journal of Experimental Child Psychology, 72*, 73–94.

Catts, H. W., Adlof, S. M., & Weismer, S. E. (2006). Language deficits in poor comprehenders: A case for the simple view of reading. *Journal of Speech, Language and Hearing Research, 49*, 278–293.

Charniak, E. (1972). *Towards a model of children's story comprehension*. Technical Report TR266, Artificial Intelligence Laboratory, Massachusetts Institute of Technology, Cambridge, MA.

Christensen, C. A., & Bowey, J. A. (2005). The efficacy of orthographic rime, grapheme–phoneme correspondence, and implicit phonics approaches to teaching decoding skills. *Scientific Studies of Reading*, *9*, 327–349.

Cipielewski, J., & Stanovic, K. E. (1992). Predicting growth in reading ability from children's exposure to print. *Journal of Experimental Child Psychology*, *54*, 74–89.

Clark, E. V., & Sengul, C. J. (1978). Strategies in the acquisition of deixis. *Journal of Child Language*, *5*, 457–475.

Clarke, P. J., Snowling, M. J., Truelove, E., & Hulme, C. (2010). Ameliorating children's reading comprehension difficulties: A randomised controlled trial. *Psychological Science*, *21*, 1106–1116.

Coltheart, M. (1984). Writing systems and reading disorders. In L. Henderson (Ed.), *Orthographies and reading: Perspectives from cognitive psychology, neuropsychology, and linguistics* (pp. 67–80). Mahwah, NJ, and London: Lawrence Erlbaum Associates.

Coltheart, M. (2006). Dual route and connectionist models of reading: An overview. *London Review of Education*, *4*(1), 5–17.

Coltheart, M., Rastle, K., Perry, C., Langdon, R., & Ziegler, J. (2001). DRC: A dual-route cascaded model of visual word recognition and reading aloud. *Psychological Review*, *108*, 204–256.

Conners, F. A. (2009). Attentional control and the simple view of reading. *Reading and Writing*, *22*, 591–613.

Cortese, M. J., & Simpson, G. B. (2000). Regularity effects in word naming: What are they? *Memory and Cognition*, *28*, 1269–1276.

Crawford, C., Dearden, L., & Meghir, C. (2010). 'When you are born matters: the impact of date of birth on educational outcomes in England', Institute for Fiscal Studies (IFS), Working Paper no. 10/06. Retrieved from www.ifs.org.uk/publications/4866 (accessed 20 March 2015).

Cunningham, A. (1990). Explicit versus implicit instruction in phonemic awareness. *Journal of Experimental Child Psychology*, *50*, 429–444.

Cunningham, A. E. (2006). Accounting for children's orthographic learning while reading text: Do children self-teach? *Journal of Experimental Child Psychology*, *95*, 56–77.

Cunningham, A. E., Perry, K. E., Stanovich, K. E., & Share, D. L. (2002). Orthographic learning during reading: Examining the role of self-teaching. *Journal of Experimental Child Psychology*, *82*, 185–199.

Cunningham, A. J., & Carroll, J. M. (2011). The development of early literacy in Steiner- and standard-educated children. *British Journal of Educational Psychology*, *81*, 475–490.

Cutting, L. E., & Scarborough, H. S. (2006). Prediction of reading comprehension: Relative contributions of word recognition, language proficiency, and other cognitive skills can depend on how comprehension is measured. *Scientific Studies of Reading*, *10*, 277–299.

Daneman, M., & Carpenter, P. A. (1980). Individual differences in working memory and reading. *Journal of Verbal Learning and Verbal Behavior*, *19*, 450–466.

Davis, F. B. (1942). Two new measures of reading ability. *Journal of Educational Psychology*, *33*, 365–372.

de Jong, P. F., Bitter, D. J. L., van Setten, M., & Marinus, E. (2009). Does phonological recoding occur during silent reading, and is it necessary for orthographic learning? *Journal of Experimental Child Psychology*, *104*, 267–282.

de Jong, P. F., & Share, D. L. (2007). Orthographic learning during oral and silent reading. *Scientific Studies of Reading*, *11*, 55–71.

References

Department for Children, Schools and Families (DCSF). (2007). *Letters and Sounds: Principles and Practice of High Quality Phonics*. Primary National Strategy. Retrieved from www.gov.uk/government/uploads/system/uploads/attachment_data/file/190599/Letters_and_Sounds_-_DFES-00281-2007.pdf (accessed 10 January 2015).

Department for Education. (2014). National Curriculum in England: Programme of Study for English. London: Department of Education. Retrieved from www.gov.uk/government/publications/national-curriculum-in-england-english-programmes-of-study/(accessed 30 March 2015).

Dhillon, R. (2010). *Examining the 'Noun Bias': A Structural Approach*. University of Pennsylvania Working Papers in Linguistics 16.

Dickinson, D. K., & Smith, M. W. (1994). Long-term effects of preschool teachers' book readings on low-income children's vocabulary and story comprehension. *Reading Research Quarterly*, *29*, 104–122.

Dixon, M., Stuart, M., & Masterson, J. (2002). The role of phonological awareness and the development of orthographic representations. *Reading and Writing: An Interdisciplinary Journal*, *15*, 295–316.

Dockrell, J., Stuart, M., & King, D. (2011). Supporting early oral language skills for English language learners in inner city preschool provision. *British Journal of Educational Psychology*, *80*, 497–516.

Downing, J. (1967). *Research report on the British experiment with i.t.a.*. In National Foundation for Educational Research, *The i.t.a. symposium*. Slough, Buckinghamshire: National Foundation for Educational Research in England and Wales.

Duff, F. J., & Hulme, C. (2012). The role of children's phonological and semantic knowledge in learning to read. *Scientific Studies of Reading*, *16*, 504–525.

Duncan, L. G., Castro, S. L., Defior, S., Seymour, P. H. K., Baillie, S., Leybaert, J., Mousty, P., et al. (2013). Phonological development in relation to native language and literacy: Variations on a theme in six alphabetic orthographies. *Cognition*, *127*, 398–419.

Duncan, L. G., Seymour, P. H. K., & Hill, S. (1997). How important are rhyme and analogy in beginning reading? *Cognition*, *63*, 171–208.

Duncan, L. G., Seymour, P. H. K. & Hill, S. (2000). A small-to-large unit progression in metaphonological awareness and reading? *Quarterly Journal of Experimental Psychology. A, Human Experimental Psychology*, *53*, (4), 1081–1103.

Dunn, L. M., Dunn, L. M., Styles, B., & Sewell, J. (2009). *British Picture Vocabulary Scale* (3rd Edition) (BPVS-III). London: GL Assessment.

Dunn, L. M., Dunn, L. M., Whetton, C., & Burley, J. (1997). *The British Picture Vocabulary Scale* (2nd Edition). Windsor, UK: NFER-Nelson.

Durkin, D. (1993). *Teaching them to read* (6th Edition). Boston, MA: Allyn & Bacon.

Early Years Foundation Stage Profile Handbook (2014). Retrieved from www.education.gov.uk/assessment (accessed 6 February 2015).

Ehri, L. C. (1999). Phases of development in learning to read words. In J. Oakhill & R. Beard (Eds), *Reading development and the teaching of reading: A psychological perspective* (Chapter 5). Oxford: Blackwell Science.

Ehri, L. C. (2005). Learning to read words: Theory, findings and issues. *Scientific Studies of Reading*, *9*, 167–188.

Ehri, L. C. (2014). Orthographic mapping in the acquisition of sight word reading, spelling memory and vocabulary learning. *Scientific Studies of Reading*, *18*, 5–21.

Ehri, L. C., & Roberts, T. (2006). The roots of learning to read and write: Acquisition of letters and phonemic awareness. In D. K. Dickinson & S. B. Neuman (Eds.), *Handbook of early literacy research* (Vol. 2). New York: Guilford Press.

Ellefson, M. R., Treiman, R., & Kessler, B. (2009). Learning to label letters by sounds or names: A comparison of England and the United States. *Journal of Experimental Child Psychology*, *102*, 323–341.

Elley, W. B. (1989).Vocabulary acquisition from listening to stories. *Reading Research Quarterly*, *24*, 174–187.

Elliott, C. D., Murray, D. J., & Pearson, L. S. (1983). *British ability scales.* Windsor, UK: NFER-Nelson.

Elliot-Faust, D. J., & Pressley, M. (1986). How to teach comparison processing to increase children's short- and long-term listening comprehension monitoring. *Journal of Educational Psychology*, *78*, 27–33.

Evans, M. A., Bell, M., Shaw, D., Moretti, S., & Page, J. (2006). Letter names, letter sounds and phonological awareness: An examination of kindergarten children across letters and letters across children. *Reading and Writing*, *19*, 959–989.

Foorman, B. R., Francis, D. J., Fletcher, J. M., Schatshneider, C., & Mehta, P. (1998). The role of instruction in learning to read: Preventing reading failure in at-risk children. *Journal of Educational Psychology*, *90*, 37–55.

Forum for Research in Literacy and Language (2012). *Diagnostic test of word reading processes*. London: GL-Assessment.

Foy, J. G., & Mann, V. (2006). Changes in letter-sound knowledge are associated with development of phonological awareness in pre-school children. *Journal of Research in Reading*, *29*, 143–161.

Fries, C. (1963). *Linguistics and reading.* New York: Holt, Rhinehart & Winston.

Garner, R., & Taylor, N. (1982). Monitoring of understanding: An investigation of attentional assistance needs at different grade and reading proficiency levels. *Reading Psychology*, *3*, 1–6.

Gates, A. (1949). Character and purposes of the year book. In N. Henry (Ed.), *The forty-eighth year book of the National Society for the Study of Education: Part II. Reading in the elementary school* (pp. 1–9). Chicago, IL: University of Chicago Press.

Gelb, I. J. (1963). *A study of writing* (2nd Edition). Chicago, IL: University of Chicago Press.

Gibbs, S., & Bodman, S. (2014). *Phonological Assessment Battery 2* (2nd Edition). Chiswick: GL-Assessment.

Goff, D. A., Pratt, C., & Ong, B. (2005). The relations between children's reading comprehension, working memory, language skills, and components of reading decoding in a normal sample. *Reading and Writing*, *18*, 583–616.

Goswami, U. (1986). Children's use of analogy in learning to read: A developmental study. *Journal of Experimental Child Psychology*, *42*, 73–83.

Gough, P. B., Hoover, W. A., & Peterson, C. (1996). Some observations on the simple view of reading. In C. Cornoldi & J. Oakhill (Eds.), *Reading comprehension difficulties* (pp. 1–13). Hillsdale, NJ: Lawrence Erlbaum Associates.

Gough, P. B., Juel, C., & Griffith, P. L. (1992). Reading, spelling and the orthographic cipher. In P. B. Gough, L. C. Ehri & R. Treiman (Eds.), *Reading acquisition* (pp. 35–48). Hillsdale, NJ: Lawrence Erlbaum Associates.

Gough, P. B., & Tunmer, W. E. (1986). Decoding, reading, and reading disability. *RASE: Remedial and Special Education*, *7*(1), 6–10.

Gresham, F., & Vellutino, F. (2010). What is the role of intelligence in the identification of specific learning disabilities? Issues and clarifications. *Learning Disabilities Research and Practice*, *25*, 194–206.

References

Hargrave, A. C., & Sénéchal, M. A. (2000). Book reading intervention with preschool children who have limited vocabularies: The benefits of regular reading and dialogic reading. *Early Childhood Research Quarterly*, *15*(1), 75–90.

Harris, T. L., & Hodges, R. E. (Eds.) (1995). *The literacy dictionary: The vocabulary of reading and writing*. Newark, DE: International Reading Association.

Hatcher, P. J. (2000). Sound links in reading and spelling with discrepancy-defined dyslexics and children with moderate learning difficulties. *Reading and Writing*, *13*, 257–272.

Hatcher, P. J., Hulme, C., & Ellis, A. W. (1994). Ameliorating early reading failure by integrating the teaching of reading and phonological skills: The phonological linkage hypothesis. *Child Development*, *65*, 41–57.

Hatcher, P. J., Hulme, C., Miles, J. N. V., Carroll, J. M., Hatcher, J., Gibbs, S., Smith, G., Bowyer-Crane, C., & Snowling, M. J. (2006). Efficacy of small group reading intervention for beginning readers with reading-delay: A randomised controlled trial. *Journal of Child Psychology and Psychiatry*, *47*, 820–827.

Hatcher, P. J., Hulme, C., & Snowling, M. J. (2004). Explicit phoneme training combined with phonic reading instruction helps young children at risk of reading failure. *Journal of Child Psychology and Psychiatry*, *45*, 338–358.

Hawking, S. (1988). *A Brief History of Time*. London: Random House.

Henderson, L. (1984). *Orthographies and reading: Perspectives from cognitive psychology, neuropsychology, and linguistics*. Mahwah, NJ, and London: Lawrence Erlbaum Associates.

Hoien, T., Lundberg, I., Stanovich, K. E., & Bjaalid, I.-K. (1995). Components of phonological awareness. *Reading and Writing*, *7*, 171–188.

Hoover, W. A., & Gough, P. B. (1990). The simple view of reading. *Reading and Writing*, *2*(2), 127–160.

Hornsby, B., & Miles, T. R. (1980). The effects of a dyslexia-centred teaching programme. *British Journal of Educational Psychology*, *50*, 236–242.

Huang, F. L., Tortorelli, L. S., & Invernizzi, M. A. (2014). An investigation of factors associated with letter-sound knowledge at kindergarten entry. *Early Childhood Research Quarterly*, *29*, 182–192.

Hulme, C., Hatcher, P. J., Nation, K., Brown, A., Adams, J., & Stuart, G. (2002). Phoneme awareness is a better predictor of early reading skill than onset-rime awareness. *Journal of Experimental Child Psychology*, *82*, 2–28.

Hulme, C., Stothard, S. E., Clarke, P., Bowyer-Crane, Harrington, A., Truelove, E., & Snowling, M. J. (2009). *York Assessment of Reading for Comprehension*. Chiswick: GL-Assessment.

Iverson, S., & Tunmer, W. E. (1993). Phonological processing skills and the reading recovery programme. *Journal of Educational Psychology*, *85*, 112–126.

Jackson, N. E., & Coltheart, M. (2001). *Routes to reading success and failure: Toward an integrated cognitive psychology of atypical reading*. New York: Psychology Press.

Jared, D. (1997). Spelling-sound consistency affects the naming of high frequency words. *Journal of Memory and Language*, *36*, 505–529.

Jared, D. (2002). Spelling-sound consistency and regularity effects in word naming. *Journal of Memory and Language*, *46*, 723–750.

Jared, D., McRae, K., & Seidenberg, M.S. (1990). The basis of consistency effects in word naming. *Journal of Memory and Language*, *29*, 687–715.

Jenkins, J. R., Bausell, R. B., & Jenkins, L. M. (1972). Comparison of letter name and letter sound training as transfer variables. *American Educational Research Journal*, *9*, 75–86.

Jenkins, J. R., Peyton, J. A., Sanders, E. A., & Vadasy, P. F. (2004). Effects of reading decodable texts in supplemental first-grade tutoring. *Scientific Studies of Reading*, *8*, 53–85.

Johnson-Laird, P. N. (1983). *Mental models: Towards a cognitive science of language, inference and consciousness*. Cambridge, MA: Harvard University Press.

Johnston, R. S., McGeown, S., & Watson, J. (2012). Long-term effects of synthetic versus analytic phonics teaching on the reading and spelling ability of 10 year old boys and girls. *Reading and Writing*, *25*(6), 1365–1384.

Johnston, R. S., & Watson, J. (2005). The effects of synthetic phonics teaching on reading and spelling attainment: A seven-year longitudinal study. Edinburgh, Scotland: Scottish Executive Education Department. Retrieved from www.scotland.gov.uk/library5/education/sptrs-00.asp (accessed 18 January 2015).

Johnston, T. C., & Kirby, J. R. (2006). The contribution of naming speed to the simple view of reading. *Reading and Writing*, *19*, 339–361.

Judica, M., de Luca, M., Spinelli, D., & Zoccolotti, P. (2002). Training of developmental surface dyslexia improves reading performance and shortens eye fixation. *Neuropsychological Rehabilitation*, *12* (3), 177–197

Juel, C., & Roper-Schneider, D. (1985). The influence of basal readers on first grade reading. *Reading Research Quarterly*, *20*, 134–152.

Just, M. A., & Carpenter, P. A. (1987). *The psychology of reading and language comprehension*. Boston, MA: Allyn & Bacon.

Justice, L. M., Pence, K., Bowles, R. B., & Wiggins, A. (2006). An investigation of four hypotheses concerning the order by which 4-year-old children learn the alphabet letters. *Early Childhood Research Quarterly*, *21*, 374–389.

Kameenui, E., Carnine, D., & Freschi, R. (1982). Effects of text construction and instructional procedures for teaching word meanings on comprehension and recall. *Reading Research Quarterly*, *17*(3), 367–388.

Kendeou, P., Savage, R., & van den Broek, P. (2009). Revisiting the simple view of reading. *British Journal of Educational Psychology*, *79*, 353–370.

Kim, Y., Petscher, Y., Foorman, B. R., & Zhou, C. (2010). The contributions of phonological awareness and letter-name knowledge to letter-sound acquisition: A cross-classified multilevel model approach. *Journal of Educational Psychology*, *102*, 313–326.

Kintsch, W. (1998). *Comprehension: A paradigm for cognition*. Cambridge: Cambridge University Press.

Kintsch, W., & Rawson, K. (2005). Comprehension. In M. J. Snowling & C. Hulme (Eds.), *The science of reading: A handbook* (pp. 209–226). Oxford: Blackwell.

Kipp, K. H., & Mohr, G. (2008). Remediation of developmental dyslexia: Tackling a basic memory deficit. *Cognitive Neuropsychology*, *25*, 38–55.

Kirby, J. R., & Savage, R. S. (2008). Can the simple view deal with the complexities of reading? *Literacy*, *42*, 75–82.

Kirtley, C., Bryant, P., MacLean, M., & Bradley, L. (1989). Rhyme, rime and the onset of reading. *Journal of Experimental Child Psychology*, *48*, 224–245.

Kyte, C. S., & Johnson, C. J. (2006). The role of phonological recoding in orthographic learning. *Journal of Experimental Child Psychology*, *93*, 166–185.

Landi, N., Perfetti, C. A., Bolger, D. J., Dunlap, S., & Foorman, B. R. (2006). The role of discourse context in developing word form representations: A paradoxical relation between reading and learning. *Journal of Experimental Child Psychology*, *94*, 114–133.

Laxon, V., Masterson, J., & Moran, R. (1994). Are children's representations of words distributed? Effects of orthographic neighbourhood size, consistency, and regularity of naming. *Language and Cognitive Processes*, *9*, 1–27.

Leach, J. M., Scarborough, H. S., & Rescorla, L. (2003). Late-emerging reading disabilities. *Journal of Educational Psychology*, *95*(2), 211–224.

Lee, J. (2011). Size matters: Early vocabulary as a predictor of language and literacy competence. *Applied Psycholinguistics*, *32*(1), 69–92.

Leung, C. B. (1992). Effects of word-related variables on vocabulary growth through repeated read-aloud events. In C. K. Kinzer & D. J. Leu (Eds.), *Literacy research, theory, and practice: Views from many perspectives. Forty-first Yearbook of the National Reading Conference* (pp. 491–498). Chicago, IL: The National Reading Conference.

Levy, B. A., & Lysynchuk, L. (1997). Beginning word recognition: Benefits of training by segmentation and whole word methods. *Scientific Studies of Reading*, *1*, 359–387.

Liberman, I. Y., Shankweiler, D., Fischer, F. W., & Carter, B. (1974). Explicit syllable and phoneme segmentation in the young child. *Journal of Experimental Child Psychology*, *18*, 201–212.

Maclean, M., Bryant, P., & Bradley, L. (1987). Rhymes, nursery rhymes and reading in early childhood. *Merrill-Palmer Quarterly*, *33*, 255–281.

Manis, F., Seidenberg, M., Doi, L., McBride-Chang, C., & Petersen, A. (1996). On the bases of two subtypes of developmental dyslexia. *Cognition*, *58*, 57–195.

Markman, E. M. (1979). Realizing that you don't understand: Elementary school children's awareness of inconsistencies. *Child Development*, *50*, 643–655.

Martin, M. E., & Byrne, B. (2002). Teaching children to recognize rhyme does not directly promote phonemic awareness. *British Journal of Educational Psychology*, *72*, 561–572.

Mason, J. (1980). When do children begin to read? An exploration of four-year-old children's letter and word reading competencies. *Reading Research Quarterly*, *2*, 203–227.

Masonheimer, P., Drum, P., & Ehri, L. C. (1984). Does environmental print identification lead children into word reading? *Journal of Reading Behavior*, *16*, 257–272.

Masterson, J., Stuart, M., Dixon, M., & Lovejoy, S. (2010). Children's printed word database: Continuities and changes over time in children's early reading vocabulary. *British Journal of Psychology*, *101*, 221–242.

McArthur, G., Kohnen, S., Larsen, L., Jones, K., Anandakumar, T., Banales, E., & Castles, A. (2013). Getting to grips with the heterogeneity of developmental dyslexia. *Cognitive Neuropsychology*, *30*, 1–24.

McBride-Chang, C. (1999). The ABCs of the ABCs: The development of letter-name and letter-sound knowledge. *Merrill-Palmer Quarterly*, *45*, 285–308.

McCandliss, B., Beck, I. L., Sandak, R., & Perfetti, C. (2003). Focusing attention on decoding for children with poor reading skills: Design and preliminary tests of the word building intervention. *Scientific Studies of Reading*, *7*, 75–104.

McGinty, A., Fan, X., Breit Smith, A., Justice, L. M., & Kaderavek, J. (2011). Does intensity matter? Preschoolers' print knowledge within a classroom-based intervention. *Early Childhood Research Quarterly*, *26*, 255–267.

McGuiness, D. (2004). *Early reading instruction: What science really tells us about how to teach reading*. Cambridge, MA: The MIT Press.

McKague, M., Pratt, C., & Johnston, M. B. (2001). The effect of oral vocabulary on reading visually-novel words: A comparison of the dual-route cascaded and triangle frameworks. *Cognition*, *80*, 231–262.

Megherbi, H., & Ehrlich, M. F. (2005). Language impairment in less skilled comprehenders: The on-line processing of anaphoric pronouns in a listening situation. *Reading and Writing*, 18, 715–753.

Melby-Lervåg, M., & Hulme, C. (2013). Is working memory training effective? A meta-analytic review. *Developmental Psychology*, 49(2), 270–291.

Moats, L. C. (1994). The missing foundation in teacher education: Knowledge of the structure of spoken and written language. *The Annals of Dyslexia*, 44, 81–102.

Mullis, I. V. S., Martin, M. O., Foy, P., & Drucker, K. T. (2012). *PIRLS 2011 international results in reading*. Chestnut Hill, MA: TIMSS & PIRLS International Study Center, Boston College.

Mullis, I. V. S., Martin, M. O., Gonzalez, E. J., & Kennedy, A. M. (2003). *PIRLS 2001 international report: IEA's study of reading literacy achievement in primary schools*. Chestnut Hill, MA: TIMSS & PIRLS International Study Center, Boston College.

Mullis, I. V. S., Martin, M. O., Kennedy, A. M., & Foy, P. (2007). *IEA's progress in international reading literacy study in primary school in 40 countries*. Chestnut Hill, MA: TIMSS & PIRLS International Study Center, Boston College.

Muter, V., Hulme, C., Snowling, M. J., & Stevenson, J. (2004). Phonemes, rimes, vocabulary and grammatical skills as foundations of early reading development: Evidence from a longitudinal study. *Developmental Psychology*, 40, 665–681.

Muter, V., Hulme, C., Snowling, M. J., & Taylor, S. (1998). Segmentation, not rhyming, predicts early progress in learning to read. *Journal of Experimental Child Psychology*, 71, 3–27.

Muter V., Snowling, M. & Taylor, S. (1994). Orthographic analogies and phonological awareness: Their role and significance in early reading development. *Journal of Child Psychology and Psychiatry*, 35, 293–310.

Nag, S., & Snowling, M. J. (2012). Reading in an alphasyllabary: Implications for a language universal theory of learning to read. *Scientific Studies of Reading*, 16, 404–423.

Nagy, W. E., & Scott, J. A. (1990). Word schemas: Expectations about the form and meaning of new words. *Cognition and Instruction*, 7, 105–127.

Nagy, W. E., & Scott, J. A. (2000). Vocabulary processes. In M. Kamil, P. B. Mosenthal, P. D. Pearson & R. Barr (Eds.), *Handbook of reading research* (Vol. 3, pp. 269–284). Hillsdale, NJ: Lawrence Erlbaum Associates.

Nation, K. (2005). Children's reading comprehension difficulties. In M. J. Snowling & C. Hulme (Eds.), *The science of reading: A handbook* (pp. 248–265). Oxford: Blackwell.

Nation, K., Adams, J. A., Bowyer-Crane, C. A., & Snowling, M. J. (1999). Working memory deficits in poor comprehenders reflect underlying language impairments. *Journal of Experimental Child Psychology*, 73, 139–158.

Nation, K., Allen, R., & Hulme, C. (2001). The limitations of orthographic analogy in early reading development: Performance on the clue-word task depends on phonological priming and elementary decoding skill, not the use of orthographic analogy. *Journal of Experimental Child Psychology*, 80, 75–94.

Nation, K., Angell, P., & Castles, A. (2007). Orthographic learning via self-teaching in children learning to read English: Effects of exposure, durability, and context. *Journal of Experimental Child Psychology*, 96, 71–84.

Nation, K., Clarke, P., Marshall, C. M., & Durand, M. (2004). Hidden language impairments in children: Parallels between poor reading comprehension and specific language impairment? *Journal of Speech, Language, and Hearing Research*, 47, 199–211.

Nation, K., & Cocksey, J. (2009). The relationship between knowing a word and reading it aloud in children's word reading development. *Journal of Experimental Child Psychology*, *103*, 296–308.

Nation, K., & Snowling, M. J. (1997). Assessing reading difficulties: The validity and utility of current measures of reading skill. *British Journal of Educational Psychology*, *67*, 359–370.

Nation, K., & Snowling, M. J. (2004). Beyond phonological skills: Broader language skills contribute to the development of reading. *Journal of Research in Reading*, *27*, 342–356.

National Early Literacy Panel (NELP). (2008). *Developing early literacy: Report of the National Early Literacy Panel.* Washington, DC: National Institute for Literacy. Retrieved from http://lincs.ed.gov/publications/pdf/NELPReport09.pdf (accessed 14 July 2015).

National Institute of Child Health and Human Development. (2000). *Teaching children to read: An evidence-based assessment of the scientific research literature on reading and its implications for reading instruction.* National Reading Panel Report. Washington, DC: US Government Printing Office. Retrieved from www.nichd.nih.gov/publications/nrp/documents/reports.pdf (accessed 14 July 2015).

Neale, M. D. (1989). *The Neale analysis of reading ability* (Revised British Edition). Windsor, UK: NFER-Nelson.

Nicholson, T., & Whyte, B. (1992). Matthew effects in learning new words while listening to stories. In C. K. Kinzer & D. J. Leu (Eds.), *Literacy research, theory, and practice: Views from many perspectives: Forty-first Yearbook of the National Reading Conference* (pp. 499–503). Chicago, IL: The National Reading Conference.

Oakhill, J. (1982). Constructive processes in skilled and less-skilled comprehenders' memory for sentences. *British Journal of Psychology*, *73*, 13–20.

Oakhill, J. (1984). Inferential and memory skills in children's comprehension of stories. *British Journal of Educational Psychology, 54*, 31–39.

Oakhill, J. (1994). Individual differences in children's text comprehension. In M. A. Gernsbacher (Ed.), *Handbook of psycholinguistics.* San Diego, CA: Academic Press.

Oakhill, J., Cain, K., & Bryant, P. E. (2003). The dissociation of word reading and text comprehension: Evidence from component skills. *Language and Cognitive Processes*, *18*, 443–468.

Oakhill, J., Hartt, J., & Samols, D. (2005). Levels of comprehension monitoring and working memory in good and poor comprehenders. *Reading and Writing*, *18*, 657–686.

Oakhill, J., & Yuill, N. (1986). Pronoun resolution in skilled and less-skilled comprehenders: Effects of memory load and inferential complexity. *Language and Speech*, *29*(1), 25–37.

Oakhill, J., Yuill, N., & Parkin, A. J. (1986). On the nature of the difference between skilled and less-skilled comprehenders. *Journal of Research in Reading*, *9*(2), 80–91.

Ouellette, G. P. (2006). What's meaning got to do with it: The role of vocabulary in word reading and reading comprehension. *Journal of Educational Psychology*, *98*, 554–566.

Ouellette, G. P., & Beers, A. (2010). A not-so-simple view of reading: How oral vocabulary and visual-word recognition complicate the story. *Reading and Writing*, *23*, 189–208.

Ouellette, G. P., & Fraser, J. R. (2009). What exactly is a *yait* anyway? The role of semantics in orthographic learning. *Journal of Experimental Child Psychology*, *104*, 239–251.

Ouellette, G. P., & Tims, T. (2014). The write way to spell: Printing vs. typing effects on orthographic learning. *Frontiers in Psychology*, *5*, Article 117.

Palincsar, A. S., & Brown, A. L. (1984). Reciprocal teaching of comprehension – fostering and comprehension-monitoring activities. *Cognition and Instruction*, *2*, 117–175.

Paris, S. G. (2005). Re-interpreting the development of reading skills. *Reading Research Quarterly*, *40*(2), 184–202.

Parish, H. (2004) *Calling Doctor Amelia Bedelia*. New York: Harper Collins.

Pelli, D. G., Farell, B., & Moore, D. C. (2003). The remarkable inefficiency of word recognition. *Nature*, *423*, 752–756.

Perfetti, C. A. (1999). Comprehending written language: A blueprint of the reader. In P. Hagoort & C. Brown (Eds.), *Neurocognition of language processing* (pp. 167–208). Oxford: Oxford University Press.

Perfetti, C. A., Landi, N., & Oakhill, J. (2005). The acquisition of reading comprehension skill. In M. J. Snowling & C. Hulme (Eds.), *The science of reading: A handbook* (pp. 227–247). Oxford: Blackwell.

Peterson, R., Pennington, B., & Olson, R. (2013). Subtypes of developmental dyslexia: Testing predictions of the dual-route and connectionist frameworks. *Cognition*, *126*, 20–38.

Phillips, B. M., Piasta, S. B., Anthony, J. L., Lonigan, J. C., & Francis, D. J. (2012). IRTs of the ABCs: Children's letter name acquisition. *Journal of School Psychology*, *50*, 461–481.

Phillips, L. M., Norris, S. P., & Anderson, J. (2008). Unlocking the door: Is parents' reading to children the key to early literacy development? *Canadian Psychology*, *49*(2), 82–88.

Piasta, S. B., Purpura, D. J., & Wagner, R. K. (2010). Fostering alphabet knowledge development: A comparison of two instructional approaches. *Reading and Writing*, *23*, 607–626.

Piasta, S. B., & Wagner, R. K. (2010). Learning letter names and sounds: Effects of instruction, letter type, and phonological processing skill. *Journal of Experimental Child Psychology*, *105*, 324–344.

Polk, T. A., Lacey, H. P., Nelson, J. K., Demiralp, E., Newman, L. I., Krauss, D. A., Raheja, A., & Farah, M. J. (2009). The development of abstract letter representations for reading: Evidence for the role of context. *Cognitive Neuropsychology*, *26*, 70–90.

Popp, H. M. (1964). Visual discrimination of alphabet letters. *The Reading Teacher*, *17*, 221–226.

Pressley, M., Almasi, J., Schuder, T., Bergman, J., & Kurita, J. A. (1994). Transactional instruction of comprehension strategies: The Montgomery County, Maryland, SAIL program. *Reading & Writing Quarterly: Overcoming Learning Difficulties*, *10*(1), 5–19.

Pressley, M., Duke, N. K., Gaskins, I. W., et al. (2008). Working with struggling readers: Why we must get beyond the simple view of reading and visions of how it might be done. In T. B. Gutkin & C. R. Reynolds (Eds.), *The handbook of school psychology* (4th Edition) (Chapter 25). New York: Wiley.

Protopapas, A., Simos, P. G., Sideris, G. D., & Mouzaki, A. (2012). The components of the simple view of reading: A confirmatory factor analysis. *Reading Psychology*, *33*, 217–240.

Rau, A. K., Moeller, K., & Landerl, K. (2014). The transition from sublexical to lexical processing in a consistent orthography: An eye-tracking study. *Scientific Studies of Reading*, *18*, 224–233.

Ricketts, J., Bishop, D. V. M., Pimperton, H., & Nation, K. (2011). The role of self-teaching in learning orthographic and semantic aspects of new words. *Scientific Studies of Reading*, *15*, 47–80.

Ricketts, J., Nation, K., & Bishop, D. V. M. (2007). Vocabulary is important for some, but not all reading skills. *Scientific Studies of Reading*, *11*, 235–257.

Robbins, C., & Ehri, L. C. (1994). Reading storybooks to kindergartners helps them learn new vocabulary words. *Journal of Educational Psychology*, *86*(1), 54–64.

Robins, S., Treiman, R., & Rosales, N. (2014). Letter knowledge in parent–child conversations. *Reading and Writing: An Interdisciplinary Journal, 27*, 407–429.

Rose, J. (2006). *Independent review of the teaching of early reading*. Nottingham: DfES Publications.

Rose, J. (2009). *Identifying and teaching children and young people with dyslexia and literacy difficulties*. Nottingham: DCSF Publications.

Rosenshine, B., Meister, C., & Chapman, S. (1996). Teaching students to generate questions: A review of the intervention studies. *Review of Educational Research*, *66*(2), 181–221.

Savage, R. (1997). Do children need concurrent prompts in order to use lexical analogies in reading? *Journal of Child Psychology and Psychiatry and Allied Disciplines*, *38*, 235–246.

Savage, R., & Carless, S. (2004). Predicting growth of nonword reading and letter-sound knowledge following rime- and phoneme-based teaching. *Journal of Research in Reading*, *27*, 195–211.

Savage, R., & Carless, S. (2005). Learning support assistants can deliver effective reading interventions for 'at-risk' children. *Educational Research*, *47*, 45–61.

Savage, R., & Stuart, M. (1998). Sublexical inferences in beginning reading: Medial vowel digraphs as functional units of transfer. *Journal of Experimental Child Psychology*, *69*, 85–108.

Savage, R., & Stuart, M. (2006). A developmental model of reading acquisition based upon early scaffolding errors and subsequent vowel inferences. *Educational Psychology*, *26*, 33–53.

Savage, R., Stuart, M., & Hill, V. (2001). The role of scaffolding errors in reading development: Evidence from a longitudinal and a correlational study. *British Journal of Educational Psychology*, *71*, 1–13.

Savage, R. S., & Wolforth, J. (2007). An additive simple view of reading describes the performance of good and poor readers in higher education. *Exceptionality Education Canada*, *17*, 243–268.

Scammacca, N., Vaughn, S., Roberts, G., Wanzek, J., & Torgesen, J. K. (2007). *Extensive reading interventions in Grade K-3: From research to practice*. Portsmouth, NH: RMC Research Corporation, Center on Instruction.

Scanlon, D. M., Anderson, K. L., & Sweeney, J. M. (2010). *Early intervention for reading difficulties: The interactive strategies approach*. New York: Guilford Press.

Scarborough, H. S., Dobrich, W., & Hager, M. (1991). Literacy experience and reading disability: Reading habits and abilities of parents and young children. *Journal of Learning Disabilities*, *24*, 508–511.

Schmalz, X., Marinus, E., & Castles, A. (2013). Phonological decoding or direct access? Regularity effects in lexical decision in Grade 3 and 4 children. *Quarterly Journal of Experimental Psychology, 66*, 338–346.

Seabrook, R., Brown, G. D. A., & Solity, J. E. (2005). Distributed and massed practice: From laboratory to classroom. *Applied Cognitive Psychology*, *19*, 107–122.

Seidenberg, M. S., & McClelland, J. L. (1989). A distributed developmental model of word recognition. *Psychological Review*, *96*, 523–568.

Seidenberg, M. S., Waters, G. S., Barnes, M. A., & Tanenhaus, M. K. (1984). When does irregular spelling or pronunciation influence word recognition? *Journal of Verbal Learning and Verbal Behaviour*, *23*, 383–404.

Seligman, M. E. P. (1975). *Helplessness: On depression, development, and death*. San Francisco, CA: W. H. Freeman.

Sénéchal, M. (1997). The differential effect of storybook reading on preschoolers' acquisition of expressive and receptive vocabulary. *Journal of Child Language*, *24*(1), 123–138.

Sénéchal, M., & Cornell, E. H. (1993). Vocabulary acquisition through shared reading experiences. *Reading Research Quarterly*, *28*(4), 360–374.

Sénéchal, M., Cornell, E. H., & Broda, L. S. (1995). Age-related changes in the organization of parent–infant interactions during picture-book reading. *Early Childhood Research Quarterly, 10*, 317–337.

Seymour, P. H. K., Aro, M., & Erskine, J. M. (2003). Foundation literacy acquisition in European orthographies. *British Journal of Psychology*, *94,* 143–174.

Shahar-Yames, D., & Share, D. L. (2008). Spelling as a self-teaching mechanism in orthographic learning. *Journal of Research in Reading*, *31*, 22–39.

Shapiro, L. R., & Solity, J. (2008). Delivering phonological and phonics training within whole-class teaching. *British Journal of Educational Psychology*, *78*, 597–620.

Share, D. L. (1995). Phonological recoding and self-teaching: *sine qua non* of reading acquisition. *Cognition*, *55*, 151–218.

Share, D. L. (1999). Phonological recoding and orthographic learning: A direct test of the self-teaching hypothesis. *Journal of Experimental Child Psychology*, *72*, 95–129.

Share, D. L. (2004a). Orthographic learning at a glance: On the time course and developmental onset of self-teaching. *Journal of Experimental Child Psychology*, *87*, 267–298.

Share, D. L. (2004b). Knowing letter names and learning letter sounds: A causal connection. *Journal of Experimental Child Psychology*, *88*, 213–233.

Share, D. L., Jorm, A. F., Maclean, R., & Matthews, R. (1984). Sources of individual differences in reading acquisition. *Journal of Educational Psychology*, *76*, 1309–1324.

Share, D. L., Jorm, A. F., Maclean, R., Matthews, R., & Waterman, B. (1983). Early reading achievement, oral language ability, and a child's home background. *Australian Psychologist*, *18*, 75–89.

Share, D. L., & Stanovich, K. E. (1995). Cognitive processes in early reading development: Accommodating individual differences into a model of acquisition. *Issues in Education: Contributions from Educational Psychology*, *1*, 1–57.

Siegel, L. (1989). IQ is irrelevant to the definition of learning disabilities. *Journal of Learning Disabilities*, *22*, 469–478.

Siegel, L. S. (1994). Working memory and reading: A life-span perspective. *International Journal of Behavioral Development*, *17*(1), 109–124.

Silberberg, N. E., Silberberg, M. C., & Iverson, I. A. (1972). The effects of kindergarten instruction in alphabet and numbers on first grade reading. *Journal of Learning Disabilities*, *5*, 54–261.

Slavin, R. E., Lake, C., Davis, S., & Madden, N. A. (2010). Educator's guide: Identifying what works for struggling readers. *Best Evidence Encyclopedia*. Retrieved from www.bestevidence.org (accessed 16 July 2015).

Snowling, M. J. (1980). The development of grapheme–phoneme correspondence in normal and dyslexic readers. *Journal of Experimental Child Psychology*, *29*, 294–305.

Snowling, M. J. (2008). *State of science review SR-D2: Dyslexia*. Foresight Mental Capital and Wellbeing project. Available at: http://webarchive.nationalarchives.gov.uk/20140108144555/http://www.bis.gov.uk/assets/foresight/docs/mental-capital/sr-d2_mcw_v2.pdf (accessed 12 January 2015).

References

Snowling, M. J. (2013). Early identification and interventions for dyslexia: A contemporary view. *Journal of Research in Special Educational Needs, 13*, 7–14.

Solity, J., & Vousden, J. (2009). Real books vs. reading schemes: A new perspective from instructional psychology. *Educational Psychology, 29*, 469–511.

Spooner, A. L. R., Baddeley, A. D., & Gathercole, S. E. (2004). Can reading and comprehension be separated in the Neale analysis of reading ability? *British Journal of Educational Psychology, 74*, 187–204.

Sprenger-Charolles, L., Colé, P., Lacert, P., & Serniclaes, W. (2000). On subtypes of developmental dyslexia: Evidence from processing time and accuracy scores. *Canadian Journal of Experimental Psychology, 54*, 88–104.

Stainthorp, R. (1997). A children's author recognition test: A useful tool in reading research. *Journal of Research in Reading, 20*, 148–158.

Stainthorp, R. (2004). W(h)ither phonological awareness? Literate trainee teachers' lack of stable knowledge about the sound structure of words. *Educational Psychology, 24*, 753–766.

Stanovich, K. E. (1986). Matthew effects in reading: Some consequences of individual differences in the acquisition of literacy. *Reading Research Quarterly, 22*, 360–407.

Stanovich, K. E., Cunningham, A. E., & Cramer, B. B. (1984). Assessing phonological awareness in kindergarten children: Issues of task comparability. *Journal of Experimental Child Psychology, 38*, 175–190.

Stanovich, K. E., & Siegel, L. S. (1994). Phenotypic performance profile of children with reading disabilities: A regression-based test of the phonological-core variable-difference model. *Journal of Educational Psychology, 86*, 24–53.

Stanovich, K. E., Siegel, L. S., & Gottardo, A. (1997). Converging evidence for phonological and surface subtypes of reading disability. *Journal of Educational Psychology, 89*, 114–127.

Storch, S. A., & Whitehurst, G. J. (2002). Oral language and code-related precursors to reading: Evidence from a longitudinal structural model. *Developmental Psychology, 38*(6), 934–47.

Stothard, S. E., & Hulme, C. (1992). Reading comprehension difficulties in children: The role of language comprehension and working memory skills. *Reading and Writing, 4*, 245–256.

Stuart, K.M. (1986). Phonological awareness, letter-sound knowledge and learning to read. Unpublished PhD Thesis, University of London.

Stuart, M. (1990). Factors influencing printed word recognition in pre-reading children. *British Journal of Psychology, 81*, 135–146.

Stuart, M. (1999). Getting ready for reading: Early phoneme awareness and phonics teaching improves reading and spelling in inner-city second language learners. *British Journal of Educational Psychology, 69*, 587–605.

Stuart, M. (2004). Getting ready for reading: A follow-up study of inner city second language learners at the end of Key Stage 1. *British Journal of Educational Psychology, 74*, 15–36.

Stuart, M., & Coltheart, M. (1988). Does reading develop in a sequence of stages? *Cognition, 30*, 139–181.

Stuart, M., Dixon, M., Masterson, J., & Gray, B. (2003). Children's early reading vocabulary: Description and word frequency lists. *British Journal of Educational Psychology, 73*, 585–598.

Stuart, M., & Masterson, J. (1991). Phonological awareness at four, reading and spelling at ten: What's the connection? *Mind and Language, 6*, 156–160.

Stuart, M., Masterson, J., & Dixon, M. (2000). Spongelike acquisition of sight vocabulary in beginning readers? *Journal of Research in Reading*, *23*, 12–27.

Stuart, M., Masterson, J., Dixon, M., & Quinlan, P. (1999). Inferring sublexical correspondences from sight vocabulary: Evidence from 6- and 7-year-olds. *Quarterly Journal of Experimental Psychology*, *52A*, 353–366.

Tannenbaum, K.R., Torgesen, J. K., & Wagner, R. K. (2006). Relationships between word knowledge and reading comprehension in third grade children. *Scientific Studies of Reading, 10*, 381–398.

Taylor, B. M. (1982). Text structure and children's comprehension and memory for expository material. *Journal of Educational Psychology*, *74*(3), 323–340.

Thompson, G. B., & Johnston, R. (2007). Visual and orthographic information in learning to read and the influence of phonics instruction. *Reading and Writing*, *20*, 859–884.

Thomson, M. (2003). Monitoring dyslexics' intelligence and attainments: A follow-up study. *Dyslexia, 9*, 3–17.

Tilstra, J., McMaster, K., Van den Broek, P., Kendeou, P., & Rapp, D. (2009). Simple but complex: Components of the simple view of reading across grade levels. *Journal of Research in Reading*, *32*, 383–401.

Torgesen, J. K. (2005). Recent discoveries from research on remedial intervention for children with dyslexia. In M. J. Snowling & C. Hulme (Eds.), *The science of reading: A handbook*. Oxford: Blackwell.

Treiman, R., & Broderick, V. (1998). What's in a name: Children's knowledge about the letters in their own names. *Journal of Experimental Child Psychology*, *70*, 97–116.

Treiman, R., & Kessler, B. (2003). The role of letter names in the acquisition of literacy. In R. V. Kail (Ed.), *Advances in child development and behavior* (Vol. 31). San Diego, CA: Academic Press.

Treiman, R., Kessler, B., & Pollo, T. C. (2006). Learning about the letter name subset of the vocabulary: Evidence from US and Brazilian preschoolers. *Applied Psycholinguistics*, *27*, 211–227.

Treiman, R., Mullennix, J., Bijeljac-Babic, R., & Richmond-Welty, E. D. (1995). The special role of rimes in the description, use, and acquisition of English orthography. *Journal of Experimental Psychology: General*, *124*, 107–136.

Treiman, R., & Rodriguez, K. (1999) Young children use letter names in learning to read words. *Psychological Science*, *10*, 334–338.

Treiman, R., Tincoff, R., & Richmond-Welty, E. D. (1996). Letter names help children to connect print and speech. *Developmental Psychology*, *32*, 505–514.

Treiman, R., Tincoff, R., Rodriguez, K, Mouzaki, A., & Francis, D. J. (1998). The foundations of literacy: Learning the sounds of letters. *Child Development, 69,* 1524–1540.

Twist, L., Sainsbury, M., Woodthorpe, A., & Whetton, C. (2003). Reading all over the world: Progress in international reading literacy study (PIRLS). National Report for England. Slough: NFER.

Twist, L., Schagen, I., & Hodgson, C. (2007). *Readers and reading: The national report for England 2006*. PIRLS: Progress in International Reading Literacy Study. Slough: NFER.

Twist, L., Sizmur, J., Bartlett, S., & Lynn, L. (2012). *PIRLS 2011: Reading achievement in England*. Slough: NFER.

Vadasy, P. F., & Sanders, E. A. (2012). Two-year follow-up of a kindergarten phonics intervention for English learners and native English speakers: Contextualizing treatment impacts by classroom literacy instruction. *Journal of Educational Psychology*, *104*, 987–1005.

Vadasy, P. F., & Sanders, E. A. (2013). Two-year follow-up of a code oriented intervention for lower-skilled first-graders: The influence of language status and word reading skills on third grade literacy outcomes. *Reading and Writing, 26*, 821–843.

van den Boer, M., de Jong, P. F., & Haentjens-van Meeteren, M. M. (2013). Modeling the length effect: Specifying the relation with visual and phonological correlates of reading. *Scientific Studies of Reading, 17*, 243–256.

Vellutino, F. R., Fletcher, J. M., Snowling, M. J., & Scanlon, D. M. (2004). Specific reading disability (dyslexia): What have we learned in the past four decades? *Journal of Child Psychology and Psychiatry, 45*, 2–40.

Vellutino, F. R., & Scanlon, D. M. (1987). Phonological coding, phonological awareness, and reading ability: Evidence from a longitudinal and experimental study. *Merrill-Palmer Quarterly, 33*, 321–363.

Vellutino, F. R., Scanlon, D. M., & Lyon, G. R. (2000). Differentiating between difficult-to-remediate and readily remediated poor readers: More evidence against the IQ–achievement discrepancy definition of reading disability. *Journal of Learning Disabilities, 33*, 223–238.

Venezky, R. (1975). The curious role of letter names in reading instruction. *Visible Language, 9*, 7–23.

Vousden, J. I., Ellefson, M. R., Solity, J., & Chater, N. (2011). Simplifying reading: Applying the simplicity principle to reading. *Cognitive Science, 35*, 34–78.

Wagner, R. K., & Torgesen, J. K. (1987). The nature of phonological processing and its causal role in the acquisition of reading skills. *Psychological Bulletin, 101*, 192–212.

Walsh, D. J., Price, G. G., & Gillingham, M. G. (1988). The critical but transitory importance of letter naming. *Reading Research Quarterly, 23*, 108–122.

Wang, H.-C., Castles, A., Nickels, L., & Nation, K. (2011). Context effects on orthographic learning of regular and irregular words. *Journal of Experimental Child Psychology, 109*, 39–57.

Wang, H.-C., Nickels, L., Nation, K., & Castles, A. (2013). Predictors of orthographic learning of regular and irregular words. *Scientific Studies of Reading, 17*, 369–384.

Wasik, B. A. (2001). Teaching the alphabet to young children. *Young Children*, January, 34–39.

Waters, G. S., & Seidenberg, M. S. (1985). Spelling-sound effects in reading: Time course and decision criteria. *Memory and Cognition, 13*, 557–572.

Whipple, G. (Ed.). (1925). *The twenty-fourth yearbook of the National Society for the Study of Education: Report of the National Committee on Reading*. Bloomington, IL: Public School Publishing Company.

Whitehurst, G. J., Falco, F. L., Lonigan, C. J., Fischel, J. E., DeBaryshe, B. D., Valdez-Menchaca, M. C., & Caufield, M. (1988). Accelerating language development through picture book reading. *Developmental Psychology, 24*, 552–559.

Whitehurst, G. J., & Lonigan, C. J. (2001). Emergent literacy: Development from prereaders to readers. In S. B. Neuman & D. K. Dickinson (Eds.), *Handbook of early literacy research* (pp. 11–29). New York: Guilford Press.

Wimmer, H. (1996). The early manifestation of developmental dyslexia: Evidence from German children. *Reading and Writing, 8*, 171–188.

Wise, B. W., Olson, R. K., & Treiman, R. (1990). Subsyllabic units as aids in beginning readers word learning: Onset-rime versus post-vowel segmentation. *Journal of Experimental Child Psychology, 49*, 1–19.

Worden, P. E., & Boettcher, W. (1990). Young children's acquisition of alphabet knowledge. *Journal of Reading Behavior, 22*, 277–295.

Wyse, D., & Goswami, U. (2008). Synthetic phonics and the teaching of reading. *British Educational Research Journal, 34*, 691–710.

Yuill, N., & Joscelyne, T. (1988). Effects of organizational cues and strategies on good and poor comprehenders' story understanding. *Journal of Educational Psychology, 80*, 152–158.

Yuill, N., & Oakhill, J. (1986). Understanding of anaphoric relations in skilled and less skilled comprehenders. *British Journal of Psychology, 79*, 173–186.

Yuill, N., & Oakhill, J. (1991). *Children's problems in text comprehension: An experimental investigation.* Cambridge: Cambridge University Press.

Ziegler, J.C., & Goswami, U. (2005). Reading acquisition, developmental dyslexia, and skilled reading across languages: A psycholinguistic grain size theory. *Psychological Bulletin, 131*, 3–29.

Author Index

Aaron, P.G., 28, 29
Adams, J., 57
Adams, J.A., 185
Adlof, S.M., 28–9
Allen, R., 59
Almasi, J., 138
Armbruster, B.B., 140
Anderson, D., 133, 143
Anderson, K.L., 72
Anderson, T.H., 142, 140
Andre, M.D.A., 142
Andrews, L., 191
Angell, P., 61, 63, 65
Anthony, J.L., 73
Arrow, A.W., 46

Babayigit, S., 14
Baddeley, A., 28, 183
Ball, E.W., 56
Barclay, J.R., 120
Baron, J., 40
Bartlett, S., 152
Baumann, J.F., 139, 140, 142
Bausell, R.B., 46
Beck, I., 131
Beck, I.L., 92
Beers, A., 29
Bell, M., 46, 72
Bergman, J., 138
Bijeljac-Babic, R., 58
Bishop, D.V.M., 61, 62, 65, 131
Bitter, D.J.L., 51
Bjaalid, I.-K., 57
Blachman, B.A., 56
Blackburn, C., 133
Blessing, D., 133
Bodman, S., 163
Boettcher, W., 46, 49, 76
Bolger, D.J., 53
Bond, G.L., 46

Boulware-Gooden, R., 140
Bowey, J.A., 58, 59, 61, 62, 65, 84–5
Bowles, R.B., 72, 77
Bowyer-Crane, C.A., 185
Bradley, L., 47, 56, 78
Bransford, J.D., 120–2
Breit Smith, A., 81
Brett, A., 133
Broda, L.S., 136
Broderick, V., 72
Brooks, G., 177
Broom, Y.M., 174, 178
Brown, A., 57
Brown, A.L., 138, 142, 182, 193–7
Brown, G.D.A., 85
Bruck, M., 59
Brunsdon, R.K., 178
Bryant, P.E., 28, 47, 56, 78, 126, 181, 185
Burge, B., 162
Burgess, S.R., 47, 76
Burley, J., 91
Burns, M.K., 86
Bus, A.G., 142
Byrne, B., 56, 78

Cain, K., 28, 126, 181, 185, 191, 193
Campione, J.C., 193
Carless, S., 88
Carter, B., 56
Carney, J.J., 133
Carnine, D.W., 133–4, 142
Carpenter, P.A., 131, 184
Carreker, S., 140
Carroll, J.M., 83, 88, 174
Castles, A., 61, 63, 65, 73, 94–5, 170
Castro, S.L., 71
Catts, H.W., 28–9
Chapman, S., 138
Charniak, E., 123–4
Chater, N., 59

Author Index

Christensen, C.A., 84–5
Cipielewski, J., 126, 198
Clark, E.V., 117
Clarke, P., 28
Clarke, P.J., 180, 197, 198
Cocksey, J., 65
Colé, P., 170
Coltheart, M., 13, 25–6, 35, 41, 48, 50–2, 63, 73, 170, 178
Conners, F.A., 28, 183
Cornell, E.H., 132, 136
Cortese, M.J., 41
Cramer, B.B., 47
Crawford, C., 154
Crossland, J., 47
Cunningham, A.E., 47, 56, 61, 63–6
Cunningham, A.J., 83
Cutting, L.E., 29, 30

Daneman, M., 184
Datta, H., 170
Davis, F.B., 131
Davis, S., 177
Day, J.D., 142
de Jong, P.F., 61, 62, 94, 95
de Luca, M., 178
Dearden, L., 154
Defior, S., 71
Dickinson, D.K., 132
Dixon, M., 53–4, 59, 63, 85
Dockrell, J., 80, 91
Doctor, E.A., 174, 178
Dobrich, W., 143
Downing, J., 15
Drucker, K.T., 148
Drum, P., 49
Duff, F.J., 66
Duncan, L.G., 57, 71
Dunn, L.M., 91, 104
Durand, M., 28
Durkin, D., 130
Dykstra, R., 46

Ehri, L.C., 49, 52, 75, 132, 143
Ehrlich, M.F., 181, 190
Ellefson, M.R., 46, 59
Elley, W.B., 143
Elliot, C.D., 51
Elliot-Faust, D.J., 140
Ellis, A.W., 56
Evans, M.A., 46, 49, 72

Fan, X., 81
Farell, B., 46
Fielding-Barnsley, R., 56
Fischer, F.W., 56
Fletcher, J.M., 84, 174
Foorman, B.R., 72, 84

Foy, J.G., 72
Foy, P., 148
Francis, D.J., 48, 73, 84
Franks, J.J., 120
Fraser, J.R., 61, 64, 66
Freschi, R., 133–4
Fries, C., 23

Gates, A., 23
Garner, R., 191
Gathercole, S.E., 28
Gayan, J., 170
Gelb, I.J., 12
Gibbs, S., 163
Gillingham, M.G., 46
Goff, D.A., 65
Gonzalez, E.J., 148
Gottardo, A., 170
Goswami, U., 58–9, 83
Gough, P.B., 24–6, 49, 183
Gray, B., 59, 85
Gresham, F., 169
Griffith, P.L., 49

Haentjens van Meeteren, M.M., 94
Hager, M., 143
Hamilton, R., 92
Hannan, T.J., 178
Hansen, J., 58, 59
Hargrave, A.C., 142, 143
Harris, T.L., 129
Hartt, J., 191
Hatcher, P.J., 56, 57, 84–5, 88, 169, 174, 176
Hawking, Stephen, 138
Hecht, S.A., 47
Henderson, L., 3
Hill, S., 59
Hill, V., 63
Hitch, G., 183
Hodges, R.E., 129
Hodgson, C., 152
Hoien, I., 57
Hoover, W.A., 25–6, 183
Hornsby, B., 177
Huang, F.L., 71–2
Hulme, C., 27–8, 56, 57, 66, 84–5, 88, 164, 174, 176, 180, 183–6, 197
Hurley, M., 133

Invernizzi, M.A., 71–2
Iverson, S., 46, 56

Jackson, N.E., 48
Jared, D., 41
Jenkins, J.R., 46, 89
Jenkins, L.M., 46
Johnson, C.J., 61, 62
Johnson-Laird, P.N., 120

Author Index

Johnston, R., 48, 66
Johnston, T.C., 28
Jones, K., 170
Jones, L.A., 13
Jones, R.S., 139, 142
Jorm, A.F., 46, 47
Joscelyne, T., 188–9
Joshi, M., 28, 29, 140
Judica, M., 178
Juel, C., 49, 89
Just, M.A., 131
Justice, L.M., 72, 77, 81

Kaderavek, J., 81
Kameenui, E., 133–4, 142
Kendeou, P., 27
Kennedy, A.M., 148
Kessler, B., 46, 72
Kim, Y., 72
King, D., 80, 91
Kintsch, W., 120
Kipp, K.H., 174
Kirby, J.R., 28
Kirtley, C., 56
Kohnen, S., 170
Kyte, C.S., 61, 62
Kucan, L., 131
Kurita, J.A., 138

Lacert, P., 170
Lacey, H.P., 49
Lake, C., 177
Landerl, K., 94
Landi, N., 53, 131
Langdon, R., 35
Larsen, L., 170
Laxon, V., 58
Leach, J.M., 181
Lee, J., 131
Leung, C.B., 132
Levy, B.A., 59
Liberman, I.Y., 56
Little, T.D., 28, 29
Lonigan, J.C., 47, 73, 76, 131
Lovejoy, S., 59
Lundberg, I., 57
Lynn, L., 152
Lyon, G.R., 169
Lysynchuk, L., 59

MacLean, M., 46, 47, 56, 78
Madden, N.A., 177
Manis, F., 170
Mann, V., 72
Marinus, E., 94–5
Markman, E.M., 126–7, 139
Marshall, C.M., 28

Martin, M.E., 78
Martin, M.O., 148, 150
Mason, J., 46
Masonheimer, P., 49
Masterson, J., 51, 53–4, 58–9, 63, 85
Matthews, R., 46, 47
McArthur, G., 170–3, 174
McBride-Chang, C., 46, 72, 170
McCandliss, B., 92
McClelland, J.L., 41
McGinty, A., 81
McGuiness, D., 76
McKague, M., 66
McKeown, M., 131
McRae, K., 41
Megherbi, H., 181, 190
Meghir, C., 154
Mehta, P., 84
Melby-Lervåg, M., 186
Meyer, J.L., 140
Miles, J.N.V., 57, 88, 174
Miles, T.R., 177
Moats, L.C., 6
Mohr, G., 174
Moeller, K., 94
Moore, D.C., 46
Moran, R., 58
Moretti, S., 46, 72
Mouzaki, A., 27, 48
Mullennix, J., 58
Muller, D., 61, 62
Mullis, I.V.S, 148, 150
Murray, D.J., 51
Muter, V., 27–8, 57, 58, 123

Nag, S., 14
Nagy, W.E., 126, 137
Nation, K., 27–8, 57, 59, 61, 62, 63, 64, 65, 131, 182, 185
Neale, M.D., 186
Nelson, J.K., 49
Nicholson, T., 132
Nickels, L., 61, 63
Norris, S.P, 143

Oakhill, J., 28, 123, 126–7, 131, 181, 182, 185–8, 190–3
Olson, R.K., 59, 170
Ong, B., 65
Ouellette, G.P., 29, 61, 62, 64, 66, 104

Page, J., 46, 72
Palincsar, A.S., 138, 142, 179, 182, 193–7
Paris, S.G., 101
Parish, Herman, 118
Parkin, A.J., 182
Patson, N., 191

Pearson, L.S., 51
Pellegrini, A.D., 143
Pelli, D.G., 46
Pence, K., 72, 77
Pennington, B., 170
Perfetti, C.A., 53, 92, 129, 131
Perry, C., 35
Perry, K.E., 61, 63–6
Petersen, R., 170, 183
Petscher, Y., 72
Peyton, J.A., 89
Phillips, B.M., 73
Phillips, L.M., 143
Piasta, S.B., 72, 73, 76
Pimperton, H., 61, 65
Polk, T.A., 49
Pollo, T.C., 72
Popp, H.M., 75
Pratt, C., 65, 66
Pressley, M., 29–30, 138, 140
Price, G.G., 46
Protopapas, A., 27
Purpura, D.J., 76

Quinlan, P., 63

Rastle, K., 35
Rau, A.K., 94
Rawson, K., 120
Rescorla, L., 181
Ricketts, J., 61, 64, 65, 131
Richmond-Welty, E.D., 46, 57
Robbins, C., 132, 142
Roberts, G., 174
Roberts, T., 75
Robins, S., 71
Rodriguez, K., 46, 48
Roper-Schneider, D., 89
Rosales, N., 71
Rose, J., 27, 68, 83, 129, 166, 167, 173–4
Rothlein, L., 133
Rutherford, J., 65

Samols, D., 191
Sainsbury, M., 152
Sandak, R., 92
Sanders, E.A., 89–91
Savage, R., 27–8, 58, 59, 63, 88
Scammacca, N., 174
Scanlon, D.N., 72, 169, 174
Scarborough, H.S., 29, 30, 143, 181
Schagen, I., 152
Schatschneider, C., 84
Schmalz, X., 94–5
Schuder, T., 138
Scott, J.A., 126, 137
Seabrook, R., 85

Seidenberg, M.S., 40, 41, 170
Seifert-Kessell, N., 139
Seligman, M.E., 138
Sénéchal, M., 132, 135–6, 142, 143
Sengul, C.J., 117
Serniclaes, W., 170
Sewell, J., 104
Seymour, P.H.K., 57, 59
Shahar-Yames, D., 61, 62
Shankweiler, D., 56
Shapiro, L.R., 60, 85–7, 176, 179
Share, D.L., 46, 47, 60–6, 72, 95, 171, 174
Shaw, D., 46, 72
Sideris, G.D., 27
Siegel, L., 169, 170, 174, 185
Silberberg, M.C., 46
Silberberg, N.E., 46
Simos, P.G., 27
Simpson, G.B., 41
Sizmur, J., 152
Slavin, R.E., 177
Smith, M.W., 132
Snowling, M.J., 14, 27–8, 57, 58, 64, 84–5, 174, 175–6, 180, 182, 185, 197
Solity, J., 59–60, 85–7, 90, 176, 179
Spinelli, D., 178
Spooner, A.L.R., 28
Stanovich, K.E., 47, 57, 63–6, 126, 132, 170, 174, 198
Stainthorp, R., 6, 14, 126, 198
Stevenson, J., 27–8
Storch, S.A., 131
Stothard, S.E., 183–5
Strawson, C., 40
Stuart, G., 57
Stuart, M. 46, 47, 48–9, 50–54, 59, 63, 80, 85, 90, 91
Styles, B., 104
Sweeney, J.M., 72

Tanenhaus, M.K., 40
Tannenbaum, K.R., 104
Taylor, B.M., 142
Taylor, N., 191
Taylor, S., 57, 58
Thompson, G.B., 48
Thomson, M., 177
Thornhill, A., 140
Tilstra, J., 28, 29
Tims, T., 62
Tincoff, R., 46, 48
Torgesen, J.K., 104, 174
Tortorelli, L.S., 71–2
Treiman, R., 46, 48, 58, 59, 71, 72
Truelove, E., 180, 107
Tunmer, W.E., 24–5, 56
Twist, L., 152

Author Index

Underwood, N., 59

Vadasy, P.F., 89–91
Vaughn, L., 59
Vaughn, S., 174
Valpied, J., 73, 78
van den Boer, M., 94
van den Broek, P., 27
van IJzendoorn, M.H., 143
Vellutino, F., 169, 174
Venezky, R., 47
Vousden, J., 59–60, 90

Wagner, R.K., 72, 76, 104, 174
Walsh, D.J., 46
Wang, H.-C., 61, 62, 63
Wanzek, J., 174
Waterman, B., 47
Waters, G.S., 40
Wasik, B.A., 47
Wedgwood, J., 73, 78, 41
Weismer, S.E., 28

Whetton, C., 91, 152
Whipple, G., 130
Whitehurst, G.J., 131, 136
Whyte, B., 132
Wiggins, A., 72, 77
Williams, K.A., 28, 29
Wilson, K., 73
Wimmer, H., 174
Wise, B.W., 59
Wolforth, J., 28
Woodthorpe, A., 152
Woolfson, N., 142
Worden, P.E., 46, 49, 79
Wren, Sebastian, 75
Wyse, D., 83

Yuill, N., 181, 182, 188–91

Zhou, C., 72
Ziegler, J., 35, 59
Zoccolotti, P., 178

Subject Index

abstract letter units (ALUs), *36–7,* 48–9, 73, 75
adjectives, 115
adverbs, 115
affixes, 107–8
alphabet knowledge, 80; *see also* letter identification; letter knowledge; letter names; letter sounds
alphabetic principle, 70, 78, 86–7
alphabetic writing systems, 12, 14–16, 56
alphasyllabaries, 12, 14
   Kannada script, 14
anaphoric reference and *anaphoric resolution*, 124, 190
anomalies in texts, 191–3
Arabic language, 14
assessment of reading, 147–8, 165
   alternate forms of tests, 162
   English children's reading scores, 148, 151–2
   girls' and boys' relative performance in reading, 152–3
   group tests, 161–2, 169
   norm-based tests, 158–61
   see also Diagnostic Test of Word Reading Processes (DTWRP); Phonics Screening Check; Phonological Assessment Battery (PhAB); Progress in Reading Literacy Studies (PIRLS); Standard Assessment Tasks (SATs); standardised tests; York Assessment of Reading Comprehension (YARC)
'at-risk' children, 175

background knowledge, 29–30
body patterns, 11, 21–2, 58
boundary letters and phonemes, 52, 55, 63–4; *see also* initial and final letters
British Picture Vocabulary Scales (BPVS), 91, 104

Children's Printed Word Database, 49, 85
clauses, 110
closed class words, 102–3

clue words, 58–59, 63
coda patterns, 10
coherence, need for, 193
cohesive devices in language, 190–1
'common letter names' hypothesis, 48–9
comprehension
   monitoring, 119, 126–7, 138–40, 182, 185, 191–3
   monitoring and comprehension difficulties, 191–3
   processes involved in, 128–9
   strategies for, 137–8, 142
   of texts, 66, 120, 127, 164
   see also language comprehension; listening comprehension; 'poor comprehenders'; reading comprehension
conjugation, 114
conjunctions, 116
connectives, 190–1
'consistent' and 'inconsistent' words, 37, 41
consonant letters, 8, 20
consonant phonemes, 4–8, 12, 14
   definition of, 7
consonants, reading of, 19–20
content words, 102–3
count nouns, 111
curriculum-specific words and meanings, 104–5

decodable texts, 89–90, 176
decoding, definition of, 25–6
deixis, 117
determiners, 116–17
Diagnostic Test of Word Reading Processes (DTWRP), 162–3, 169
digraphs, 17–18, 20
diphthong vowels, 5–6
Dual-Route Cascaded (DRC) model of reading, 35, 41–2, 169–70, 173
dyslexia, 166–79
   definition of, 166–7
   developmental, 167–74
   etymology of the term, 169
   heterogeneity in, 169–74

Subject Index

dyslexia *cont.*
   phonological, *surface* and *mixed* profiles, 169–74, 178
   phonological deficit theory of, 171, 174
   signs seen at different developmental stages, 174–5
   teachers specialising in, 177

early start on learning to read, 83, 148
Early Years Foundation Stage (EYFS), 68–70
Early Years Learning Goal for Reading, 68–70
English language learners, 90–1, 156, 186
'errorless learning', 176
'exception' words, 35–42, 60, 64–6, 162–3, 169, 178
   regularisation of, 39
   see also 'irregular' words

fidelity to the teaching programme, 88–9
flashcards, use of, 53–4, 93, 178
fluency in handling of language, 29, 94, 104, 119, 129

geminates, 19
grapheme-phoneme correspondences (GPCs), 20, 40–2, 57–60, 63, 69–70, 82–7, 90, 95, 154, 163, 171, 174–5, 179
grapheme-to-phoneme conversion, 44
graphemes, 16–20, 56, 58
   definition of, 16
   in German and in English, 20
graphic organizers, 140–2

Hebrew language, 14
hieroglyphic system, 13
homophones, 37–8, 41, 172; *see also* pseudo-homophones

ideographic writing systems, 12, 13, 14
   Chinese language, 13
   Japanese language, 13
   Kanji, 13
   see also logographic orthography
inconsistencies in text, 126–7
inferences, *necessary* or *cohesive*, 190
inferencing, 123–6, 186–90
inferential learning from reading experience, 60
infinitive form of a verb, 113
initial and final letters, 52–5
internalisation of comprehension strategies, 137–8
International Association for the Evaluation of Educational Achievement (IEA), 148
International Phonetic Alphabet (IPA), 4–7
international studies of reading, 148–52
intonation, 119
'irregular' words, 35, 63, 68–70, 87, 89, 95, 171

language comprehension, 23–9, 91
   children's difficulties with, 180–2
   as a dimension of the Simple View of Reading, 99–100
   see also listening comprehension; reading comprehension

language systems, 100–1
languages, number of, 100
late-emerging poor readers, 183
league tables of school performance, 153
learned helplessness, 138
learning support assistants, 88; *see also* teaching assistants
letter identification, 46, 49
letter knowledge, 71–2, 75–6
letter-length effects in reading, 94
letter names, 46–7, 76–7
letter shapes, 46
letter-sound correspondences, 63, 73
letter sounds, 47–8, 51–3, 76–7
letters
   discrimination between, 75
   distinguished from numbers, 46, 73–4
   occurring in children's names, 77–8
   upper case and *lower case*, 74–5
'Letters and Sounds' phonics programme, 69–70, 90
lexical decision tasks, 40–1, 94–5
lexical processing, 36–9, 42–5, 52, 64, 94–5, 163
   weaknesses in, 177–8
lexicon
   orthographic, 36, 44–5, 48–52, 63–5, 170–3
   phonological, 36–7, 43–5, 52, 55, 61, 64, 170–3
   semantic, 36–7, 43–5, 52, 55, 64, 170–3
   see also semantic representations
listening comprehension, 182–3; *see also* language comprehension; reading comprehension
literacy, 100, 130; *see also* reading literacy
logographic orthography, 12–13; *see also* ideographic writing systems

mass nouns, 111–12
'Matthew effects' in reading, 132
memory capacity, 186; *see also* working memory
mental models, 120–7, 129–32, 137–8, 142, 188, 191, 193
metaphor, 101–2
mispronunciation, 37–8
modal auxiliary verbs, 114
modelling by teachers, 86, 138–143, 195–6
   directed, 192
monophthong vowels, 5, 18
mora in Japanese, 13
morphemes
   bound, 9, 22, 107-8
   definition of, 8
   free, 9
morphology, 106–8
   derivational and *inflectional*, 107
   of verbs, 113
multiple forms of texts, 130
multiple strategy teaching, 196–7

National Curriculum, 9, 83, 130, 132, 152, 161
National Early Literacy Panel (NELP), US, 70–1

National Foundation for Educational Research (NFER), 152, 162
National Institute of Child Health and Human Development (NICH & HD), US, 80, 84, 131
National Reading Panel (NRP), US, 80, 84, 92, 134–6, 143, 196–7
neologisms, 18
nonwords, 34–5, 40–1, 61, 63, 65–6, 70, 89–90, 92, 95, 154–6, 162–3, 169, 171, 178, 185, 192; see also pseudo-homophones
normal distribution, 149–50, 159
norming populations, 158
nouns, 111–12

one-to-one tutoring, 177
onset, 10
onset and rime, 47, 58, 60, 82, 84–5
opaque graphemes, 17
open class words, 102–3
oral language, 43–6, 130–1; see also language comprehension *and* vocabulary
orthographic learning, 61–5
orthographic representations, 35–6, 44, 52–7, 60–6, 70, 163, 171–2
  helping children with development of, 93–5
  influences of oral vocabulary on, 64–6
  and phonological recoding processes, 60–4
  see also lexicon
orthography, 3–4, 10–12, 16, 20–2
  definition of, 3
'overlearning', 59

parental worries, 178–9
'partial alphabetic' reading, 52
parts of speech, 111–17
Phoenician script, 14
phoneme awareness, 6–9, 47–8, 51–7, 70–1, 78–80, 84, 89, 163, 176
  and word reading, 56–7
phoneme blending and phoneme segmentation, 57, 78–9, 82, 174
phonemes, 4–9, 16
  definition of, 6
  words as sequences of, 8
  see also grapheme-phoneme correspondences
phonic rules, 25, 36, 42
Phonics Screening Check, 154–7, 163
phonics teaching, 46, 50, 57–60, 68–71, 79–84, 89–92, 95, 156, 174–7
  delivery by teaching assistants, 88
  long-lasting effects of, 91–2
  for older struggling readers, 92
  synthetic approach to, 83–4, 91
  types of, 57–60, 82, 84
Phonological Assessment Battery (PhAB2), 163
phonological awareness, 50, 56–7, 70–2, 78, 80, 84, 163–4, 175

phonological recoding processes, 36–45, 52, 55–7, 60–5, 68, 81, 90, 92, 94–5, 155, 162–3, 171
  contribution to orthographic representations, 60–4
  development of, 56
  weaknesses in, 174–7
phonological representations, 35, 39, 65, 171; see also lexicon
phonology, 4
  units of, 8–9
phrases, 110
'poor comprehenders', 182–93
pragmatics, 117–18
'pre-alphabetic' children, 49
predicates, 109
prepositions, 115
print vocabulary, 53–4
professional judgement, use of, 88–90
Programme of Study for English, 83; see also National Curriculum
Progress in Reading Literacy Studies (PIRLS), 148–53
'progressive minimal contrasts', 92–3
pronouns, 112–13
  resolution of, 190
pronunciation, 58, 61; see also mispronunciation
pseudo-homophones, 41, 61, 171
punctuation, 119

'quality first' teaching, 174–5
questioning as a comprehension strategy, 141

reading
  active engagement in, 30
  definition of, 23
  dual-route models of; see Dual-Route Cascaded (DRC) model
reading ages, 160
reading aloud tasks, 40–1
reading comprehension, 26–9, 91, 110, 118–19, 131–2, 164–5, 183, 185, 196–8
  definitions of, 129
  tests of, 165
  and weaknesses in inference-making, 186–90, 193
  and working memory, 183–5
reading delay, 57
reading literacy, definition of, 148
reading skills, 3–4, 21
  lower-level and *higher-level*, 182
  nature of, 33–5, 39–42, 48, 50
  oral language basis of, 43–6
reading speed, 40–1, 95
reciprocal teaching, 142, 193–8
'regular' words, 16, 37, 40, 68–9, 156
representations, 35; see also orthographic representations; phonological representations; semantic representations
rhyme, 11, 21, 47, 78

Subject Index

rime *and* rime patterns, 10–11, 21, 41, 47, 56–60, 84–5, 163
roots of words, 106, 108
Rose Review into the Teaching of Early Reading (2006), 27, 83, 156, 166–7

'scaffolding errors', 63
self-monitoring by children, 138
self-teaching, 60–2, 87, 90
semantic knowledge, 65
semantic representations, 35; *see also* lexicon
sentences
    definition of, 109
    structure of, 109–11
sight vocabulary, 25, 35, 39–43
Simple View of Reading (SVoR), 23–30, 66, 95, 129, 161–5, 168, 180–2
    as a complete description, 28–30
    language comprehension dimension of, 99–100
    validity as a conceptual framework, 27–8
small-group teaching, 80–1, 84, 175
'spaced sessions' technique, 85–6
spelling, 8, 10, 35, 49–50, 83, 108
    reform of, 15
stanines, 159–62, 169
standard assessment tasks (SATs), 52–3, 156, 161
    attainment levels, 147; *see also* assessment of reading
standardised tests, 158–62, 169; *see also* assessment of reading
Standards and Testing Agency, 154
story structure, 125–6, 143–4
structural words, 103
subject of a sentence, 109
subject-verb-object sentences, 109
subsyllabic units, 10–11, 47; *see also* body onset, phoneme, rime
summarisation by children, 142–3
'summer-born' children, 154
syllabaries, 12
syllabic writing systems, 13
syllables
    definition of, 9
    structure of, 10, 22
syntax, 108–11

tacit knowledge, 24
teaching assistants, use of, 88, 197; *see also* learning support assistants
tenses, 113–14

testing, 147–8, 152–62, 165
    for purposes of research, 148
text cohesion, 190–1
transparent words, 16
Turkish writing system, 14–16

unfamiliar words, 35, 39, 58–61, 133
unpredictability of language, 20–2

'value added', 154
verbs, 113–15
    categories of meaning expressed in, 113
visual word recognition processes, 23–9, 35, 94, 168
    development of, 51–7, 60–5, 93–5
    two sets of, 40–1; *see also* lexical processing *and* phonological recoding processes
vocabulary, 100–6, 130–2
    breadth and *depth* of, 104, 106, 108
    oral, 29, 43, 64
    pre-teaching of, 136–7
    receptive and *expressive*, 100–1, 136
    size of, 103–4, 108
    subject-specific, 137
    see also print vocabulary; sight vocabulary
vocabulary teaching, 132–7
    explicit, *implicit* and *combined*, 133–6
vowel digraphs, 63–4
vowel letters, 8
vowel phonemes, 5–8, 16–20, 48
    definition of, 7
vowel pronunciation, 58
vowels
    long, 17–18
    reading of, 16–17

whole-class teaching, 85–6, 175
'Word Building' programme, 92
word families, 20–1
word order, 108–11
word reading processes, 162–3
    categories of error in, 51–2
word recognition, 46, 48, 66, 95; *see also* visual word recognition processes
working memory, 183–6
    improvement of, 186
writing systems, 12–16

<Y> as a peculiar case, 19
York Assessment of Reading for Comprehension (YARC), 164
York Reading for Meaning Project, 197–8